Principles
in Practice

The Principles in Practice imprint offers teachers concrete illustrations of effective classroom practices based in NCTE research briefs and policy statements. Each book discusses the research on a specific topic, links the research to an NCTE brief or policy statement, and then demonstrates how those principles come alive in practice: by showcasing actual classroom practices that demonstrate the policies in action; by talking about research in practical, teacher-friendly language; and by offering teachers possibilities for rethinking their own practices in light of the ideas presented in the books. Books within the imprint are grouped in strands, each strand focused on a significant topic of interest.

Adolescent Literacy Strand

Adolescent Literacy at Risk? The Impact of Standards (2009) Rebecca Bowers Sipe

Adolescents and Digital Literacies: Learning Alongside Our Students (2010) Sara Kajder

Adolescent Literacy and the Teaching of Reading: Lessons for Teachers of Literature (2010) Deborah Appleman

Rethinking the "Adolescent" in Adolescent Literacy (2017) Sophia Tatiana Sarigianides, Robert Petrone, and Mark A. Lewis

Restorative Justice in the English Language Arts Classroom (2019) Maisha T. Winn, Hannah Graham, and Rita Renjitham Alfred

Writing in Today's Classrooms Strand

Writing in the Dialogical Classroom: Students and Teachers Responding to the Texts of Their Lives (2011) Bob Fecho

Becoming Writers in the Elementary Classroom: Visions and Decisions (2011) Katie Van Sluys

Writing Instruction in the Culturally Relevant Classroom (2011) Maisha T. Winn and Latrise P. Johnson

Writing Can Change Everything: Middle Level Kids Writing Themselves into the World (2020) Shelbie Witte, editor

Growing Writers: Principles for High School Writers and Their Teachers (2021) Anne Elrod Whitney

Literacy Assessment Strand

Our Better Judgment: Teacher Leadership for Writing Assessment (2012) Chris W. Gallagher and Eric D. Turley

Beyond Standardized Truth: Improving Teaching and Learning through Inquiry-Based Reading Assessment (2012) Scott Filkins

Reading Assessment: Artful Teachers, Successful Students (2013) Diane Stephens, editor

Going Public with Assessment: A Community Practice Approach (2018) Kathryn Mitchell Pierce and Rosario Ordoñez-Jasis

Literacies of the Disciplines Strand

Entering the Conversations: Practicing Literacy in the Disciplines (2014) Patricia Lambert Stock, Trace Schillinger, and Andrew Stock

Real-World Literacies: Disciplinary Teaching in the High School Classroom (2014) Heather Lattimer

Doing and Making Authentic Literacies (2014) Linda Denstaedt, Laura Jane Roop, and Stephen Best

Reading in Today's Classrooms Strand

Connected Reading: Teaching Adolescent Readers in a Digital World (2015) Kristen Hawley Turner and Troy Hicks

Digital Reading: What's Essential in Grades 3–8 (2015) William L. Bass II and Franki Sibberson

Teaching Reading with YA Literature: Complex Texts, Complex Lives (2016) Jennifer Buehler

Teaching English Language Learners Strand

Beyond "Teaching to the Test": Rethinking Accountability and Assessment for English Language Learners (2017) Betsy Gilliland and Shannon Pella

Community Literacies en Confianza: Learning from Bilingual After-School Programs (2017) Steven Alvarez

Understanding Language: Supporting ELL Students in Responsive ELA Classrooms (2017) Melinda J. McBee Orzulak

Writing across Culture and Language: Inclusive Strategies for Working with ELL Writers in the ELA Classroom (2017) Christina Ortmeier-Hooper

Students' Rights to Read and Write Strand

Adventurous Thinking: Fostering Students' Rights to Read and Write in Secondary ELA Classrooms (2019) Mollie V. Blackburn, editor

In the Pursuit of Justice: Students' Rights to Read and Write in Elementary School (2020) Mariana Souto-Manning, editor

Already Readers and Writers: Honoring Students' Rights to Read and Write in the Middle Grade Classroom (2020) Jennifer Ochoa, editor

Children's and YA Literature Strand

Challenging Traditional Classroom Spaces with YA Literature: Students in Community as Course Co-Designers (2022) Ricki Ginsberg

Technology in the Classroom Strand

Reimagining Literacies in the Digital Age: Multimodal Strategies to Teach with Technology (2022) Pauline S. Schmidt and Matthew J. Kruger-Ross

Literacies Before Technologies: Making Digital Tools Matter for Middle Grades Learners (2023) Troy Hicks and Jill Runstrom

Literacies Before Technologies

Making Digital Tools Matter
for Middle Grades Learners

Troy Hicks
Central Michigan University

Jill Runstrom
Ann Arbor Public Schools

National Council of
Teachers of English

340 N. Neil St., Suite #104, Champaign, Illinois 61820
www.ncte.org

Staff Editor: Cynthia Gomez
Imprint Editor: Cathy Fleischer
Interior Design: Victoria Pohlmann
Cover Design: Pat Mayer
Cover Image: istock.com/MachineHeadz

ISBN 978-0-8141-0081-3 (paperback); 978-0-8141-0082-0 (epub)

Library of Congress Control Number: 2022952251

Dear Reader,

As a former high school teacher, I remember the frustration I felt when the gap between Research (and that is how I always thought of it: Research with a capital R) and my own practice seemed too wide to ever cross. So many research studies were easy to ignore, in part because they were so distant from my practice and in part because I had no one to help me see how that research would make sense in my everyday practice.

That gap informs the thinking behind this book imprint. Designed for busy teachers, Principles in Practice publishes books that look carefully at NCTE's research reports and policy statements and puts those policies to the test in actual classrooms. The goal: to familiarize teachers with important teaching issues, the research behind those issues, and potential resources, and—most of all—make the research and policies come alive for teacher-readers.

This book is part of a strand that focuses on Technology in the Classroom. Each book in the strand highlights a different aspect of this important topic and is organized in a similar way: immersing you first in the research principles surrounding technology use (as laid out in NCTE's *Beliefs for Integrating Technology into the English Language Arts Classroom)* and then taking you into actual classrooms, teacher discussions, and student work to see how the principles play out. Each book closes with a teacher-friendly annotated bibliography to offer you even more resources.

Good teaching is connected to strong research. We hope these books help you continue the good teaching that you're doing, think hard about ways to adapt and adjust your practice, and grow even stronger and more confident in the vital work you do with kids every day.

Best of luck,

Cathy Fleischer
Imprint Editor

Contents

Acknowledgments ix

*Beliefs for Integrating Technology into the English
Language Arts Classroom* xi

Chapter 1 . . . . A Year Unlike Any Other 1

Chapter 2 . . . . Unpacking the Position Statement 14

Chapter 3 . . . . Close Reading 34

Chapter 4 . . . . Research, Inform, Explain 54

Chapter 5 . . . . Reading Literary Texts in Substantive Ways 81

Chapter 6 . . . . Arguing and Persuading across Media 107

Chapter 7 . . . . Toward Hybridity 134

Voices from the Middle Reprint: The Next Decade of
Digital Writing 159

Annotated Bibliography 167

References 177

Index 183

Authors 189

Acknowledgments

First, we acknowledge all educators who have persevered during the past few years of pandemic pedagogy and those who we have lost due to both COVID-19 and the continuing gun violence that has manifested itself across the country and here in our home state of Michigan. To the students, teachers, and families of Michigan State University, Oxford—and all communities—we write with hope that some of the lesson ideas in this book lead to further dialogue, compassion, and empathy that may preclude the repetition of such tragedies.

Second, we thank the contributors to this book, whose teaching inspires both their students as well as fellow educators: Tricia Clancy, Alex Corbitt, Towanda Harris, Megan Kowalski, Joseph Pizzo, Detra Price-Dennis, Kathleen Rowley, Jenny Sanford, Blaine Smith, and Justin Stygles. Your voices—as well as your students'—remind us that we can put literacies before technologies, and that our classrooms can center the practices of inquiry, discovery, and creativity, all habits of mind that can be cultivated beyond school.

Third, we offer our appreciation to the entire editorial team and book production staff at NCTE, including Principles in Practice Editor Cathy Fleischer, Senior Books Editor Kurt Austin, Senior Editor for Digital Publishing Cynthia Gomez, and everyone else who helped to bring this book to life. Moreover, we thank the three anonymous reviewers whose insights and critiques—as well as their complimentary words—encouraged us in the final stages of revision.

From Jill, much love and gratitude to my Skyline ninth-grade teacher learning network (TLN): Alaina, Serena, and Amanda. Our assignment to teach freshmen English brought us together, but our love of learning and sharing ideas made us a formidable team and fast friends. Thanks for making our year together the best professional development a teacher could have.

From Troy, a thank-you to all the coauthors of the *Beliefs for Integrating Technology into the English Language Arts Classroom* statement is in order, as this book represents the end of an arc of inquiry that began in earnest in 2017 at the then-Conference on English Education (CEE)—now called the English Language Arts Teacher Educators (ELATE)—summer meeting at The Ohio State University. The colleagues who met in Columbus that summer began with the idea that we would revise a statement, but ultimately produced multiple pieces of scholarship over the past few years, bringing the ideas from that statement to life in NCTE publications and beyond. Cochair of that group Tom Liam Lynch, deserves special thanks for his perseverance and insights on how best to work with the group and produce the statement. Also, a special thanks to Lauren Zucker for her willingness to collaborate on multiple articles with Troy and provide extensive feedback on his related work.

And, finally, we thank our families. As has been said in many ways by many other authors, the writing of a book is a labor of love and certainly takes away time from our spouses, children, and extended families. From Jill, thank you to Eric, Charlie, and Katie for your laughter, support, and love—always. And Troy shares his love for his "Brady Bunch" blended family, which keeps growing year by year: Sara, Ty, Liz, McKenna, Lexi, Beau, Shane, and Cooper.

Beliefs for Integrating Technology into the English Language Arts Classroom

This statement, formerly known as **Beliefs about Technology and the Preparation of English Teachers,** *was updated in October 2018 with the new title,* **Beliefs for Integrating Technology into the English Language Arts Classroom.**
Originally developed in July 2005; revised by the ELATE Commission on Digital Literacy in Teacher Education (D-LITE), October 2018

Preamble

*W*hat it means to communicate, create, and participate in society seems to change constantly as we increasingly rely on computers, smartphones, and the web to do so. Despite this change, the challenge that renews itself—for teachers, teacher educators, and researchers—is to be responsive to such changes in meaningful ways without abandoning the kinds of practices and principles that we as English educators have come to value and know to work.

That's why we created this document—a complete update and overhaul of a 2005 document published on behalf of the Conference on English Education, "Beliefs about Technology and the Preparation of English Teachers: Beginning the Conversation," published in *Contemporary Issues in Technology and Teacher Education.*

With some members of that original working group, as well as with many colleagues who have emerged in our field since that time, we offer a layered framework to support colleagues in their efforts to confidently and creatively explore networked, ubiquitous technologies in a way that deepens and expands the core principles of practice that have emerged over the last century in English and literacy education.

We begin by articulating four belief statements, crafted by this working group, composed of teachers as well as teacher educators and researchers. Then, we unpack each of the four belief statements in the form of an accessible summary paragraph followed by specific suggestions for K–12 teachers, teacher educators, and researchers. We conclude each section with a sampling of related scholarship.

As you read, you will notice that the beliefs are interwoven and echo each other necessarily; they are recursive but not redundant. We anticipate that as you read, you will see ways that they complement (or even conflict with) each other in theory or practice. Our field is complex, as is human experience. Our goal is to offer the field something well researched, usable, and empowering. If any of those words occur to you while reading, we will have considered our task complete, for now.

All contributors have offered their time, talent, and energy. Without the people noted at this document's conclusion, this simply would not have happened. Moreover, we thank our four external reviewers whose feedback was thorough and thoughtful, and contributed with expertise, collegiality, and aplomb.

Tom Liam Lynch, Pace University   Troy Hicks, Central Michigan University

Beliefs for Integrating Technology into the English Language Arts Classroom

1. **Literacy means *literacies*.** Literacy is more than reading, writing, speaking, listening, and viewing as traditionally defined. It is more useful to think of *literacies*, which are social practices that transcend individual modes of communication.
2. **Consider literacies before technologies.** New technologies should be considered only when it is clear how they can enhance, expand, and/or deepen engaging and sound practices related to literacies instruction.
3. **Technologies provide new ways to consume and produce texts.** What it means to consume and produce texts is changing as digital technologies offer new opportunities to read, write, listen, view, record, compose, and interact with both the texts themselves and with other people.
4. **Technologies and their associated literacies are not neutral.** While access to technology and the internet has the potential to lessen issues of inequity, they can also perpetuate and even accelerate discrimination based on gender, race, socioeconomic status, and other factors.

The Beliefs Expanded

Belief 1: Literacy means *literacies*.

Literacy is more than reading, writing, speaking, listening, and viewing as traditionally defined. It is more useful to think of literacies, *which are social practices that transcend individual modes of communication.*

In today's world, it is insufficient to define literacy as only skills-based reading, writing, speaking, listening, and viewing. Even though common standards documents, textbook series, and views on instruction may maintain the traditional definition of literacy as print-based, researchers are clear that it is more accurate to approach literacy as *literacies* or *literacy practices*. (We'll use the former here.)

There are multiple ways people communicate in a variety of social contexts. What's more, the way people communicate increasingly necessitates networked, technological mediation. To that end, relying exclusively on traditional definitions of literacy unnecessarily limits the ways students can communicate and the ways educators can imagine curriculum and pedagogy.

Understanding the complexities of literacies, we believe:

1. K–12 English teachers, with their students, should
    *   engage literacies as social practices by sponsoring students in digital writing and connected reading to collaboratively construct knowledge, participate in immersive learning experiences, and reach out to their own community and a global audience.
    *   encourage multimodal digital communication while modeling how to effectively compose images, presentations, graphics, or other media productions by combining video clips, images, sound, music, voice-overs, and other media.
    *   promote digital citizenship by modeling and mentoring students' use of devices, tools, social media, and apps to create media and interact with others.
    *   develop information literacies to determine the validity and relevance of media for academic argument including varied sources (e.g., blogs, *Wikipedia*, online databases, YouTube, mainstream news sites, niche news sites).

- foster critical media literacies by engaging students in analysis of both commercial media corporations and social media by examining information-reporting strategies, advertising of products or experiences, and portrayals of individuals in terms of gender, race, socioeconomic status, physical and cognitive ability, and other factors.

2. English teacher educators, with preservice and inservice teachers, should
   - critically evaluate a variety of texts (across genres and media) using a variety of theoretical perspectives (e.g., social semiotics, connectivism, constructivism, posthumanism).
   - consider the influence of digital technologies/networks in English language arts (ELA) methods courses to help preservice and inservice teachers foster use of digital/multimodal/critical literacies to support their students' learning.
   - model classroom use of literacy practices for creating and critiquing texts as well as for engaging with digital and networked technologies.
   - design assignments, activities, and assessments that encourage interdisciplinary thinking, community and civic engagement, and technological integration informed by theories relevant to ELA.

3. English and literacy researchers should
   - study *literacies* as more than general reading and writing abilities and move toward an understanding of teaching and learning within expanded frames of literacies and literacy practices (e.g., new literacies, multiliteracies, and socially situated literacies).
   - question how technologies shape and mediate literacy practices in different scenes and spaces for activating user agency and making change.
   - examine to what degree access to and support of digital tools/technologies and instruction in schools reflects and/or perpetuates inequality.
   - explore how students and/or teachers negotiate the use of various literacies for various purposes.
   - make explicit the ways technologies and literacies intersect with various user identities and understandings about and across different disciplines.
   - articulate how policies and financial support at various levels (local, state, and national) inform both the infrastructure and the capacities for intellectual freedom to engage with literacies in personally and socially transformative ways.

Some Related Scholarship

Bartels, J. (2017). Snapchat and the sophistication of multimodal composition. *English Journal*, *106*(5), 90–92.

Beach, R., Campano, G., Edmiston, B., & Borgmann, M. (2010). *Literacy tools in the classroom: Teaching through critical inquiry, grades 5–12*. New York, NY: Teachers College Press.

Coiro, J., Knobel, M., Lankshear, C., & Leu, D. J. (Eds.). (2014). *Handbook of research on new literacies*. New York, NY: Routledge.

Gee, J. P. (2015). *Social linguistics and literacies: Ideology in discourses* (5th ed.). New York, NY: Routledge.

Hicks, T., Young, C. A., Kajder, S. B., & Hunt, B. (2012). Same as it ever was: Enacting the promise of teaching, writing, and new media. *English Journal*, *101*(3), 68–74.

Kist, W. (2000). Beginning to create the new literacy classroom: What does the new literacy look like? *Journal of Adolescent & Adult Literacy, 43*(8), 710–718.

Kucer, S. B. (2014). *Dimensions of literacy: A conceptual base for teaching reading and writing in school settings* (4th ed.). New York, NY: Routledge.

Leander, K. (2009). Composing with old and new media: Toward a parallel pedagogy. In V. Carrington & M. Robinson (Eds.), *Digital literacies: Social learning and classroom practices* (pp. 147–163). London, England: SAGE.

Lynch, T. L. (2015). *The hidden role of software in educational research: Policy to practice.* New York: Routledge.

Piotrowski, A., & Witte. S. (2016). Flipped learning and TPACK construction in English education. *International Journal of Technology in Teaching and Learning, 12*(1), 33–46.

Rheingold, H. (2012). *Net smart: How to thrive online.* Cambridge, MA: The MIT Press.

Rish, R. M., & Pytash, K. E. (2015). Kindling the pedagogic imagination: Preservice teachers writing with social media. *Voices from the Middle, 23*(2), 37–42.

Rodesiler, L., & Pace, B. (2015). English teachers' online participation as professional development: A narrative study. *English Education, 47*(4), 347–378.

Turner, K. H., & Hicks, T. (2015). *Connected reading: Teaching adolescent readers in a digital world.* National Council of Teachers of English.

Belief 2: Consider literacies before technologies.

New technologies should be considered only when it is clear how they can enhance, expand, and/or deepen engaging and sound practices related to literacies instruction.

In news releases and on school websites, it is not uncommon for educators to promote new technologies that appear to be more engaging for students or efficient for teachers. Engagement and efficiency are worthwhile pursuits, but it is also necessary to ensure that any use of a new technology serves intentional and sound instructional practices. Further, educators must be mindful to experiment with new technologies before using them with students, and at scale, in order to avoid overshadowing sound instruction with technical troubleshooting.

Finally, many new technologies can be used both inside and outside school, so educators should gain a good understanding of both the instructional potential (e.g., accessing class materials from home) and problems (e.g., issues of data privacy or cyber-bullying) of any potential technology use. Technological decisions must be guided by our theoretical and practical understanding of literacies as social practices.

Understanding this need to focus on instructional strategies that promote mindful literacy practices when using technologies, we believe:

1. K–12 English teachers, with their students, should
   - identify the unique purposes, audiences, and contexts related to online/e-book reading as well as digital writing, moving beyond historical conceptions of literature and composition in more narrowly defined, text-centric ways.
   - explore an expanded definition of "text" in a digital world which includes alphabetic text as well as multimodal texts such as images, charts, videos, maps, and hypertexts.
   - discuss issues of intellectual property and licensing in the context of multimodal reading and writing, including concepts related to copyright, fair use, Creative Commons, and the public domain.

2. English teacher educators, with preservice and inservice teachers, should
    - recognize the role of out-of-school literacies and consider the place of students' own language uses in mediated spaces, including the use of abbreviations, acronyms, emojis, and other forms of "digitalk."
    - model instructional practices and engage in new literacies that teachers themselves will employ with their own K–12 students such as composing, publishing, and reflecting on a video documentary or digital story.
    - focus on affordances and constraints of technologies that can be used for varied purposes (e.g., the use of a collaborative word processor for individual writing with peer feedback, for group brainstorming, or for whole-class content curation) over fixed uses of limited tools such as online quiz systems, basic reading comprehension tests, or grammar games.

3. English and literacy researchers should
    - consider how existing paradigms such as New Literacy Studies, New Literacies, and the Pedagogy of Multiliteracies can help to understand how students themselves experience technology, as well as how to use technology to enhance student learning.
    - develop research agendas that examine best practices in K–12 classrooms where teachers leverage the power of literacies and technologies to help foster student voice and activism.
    - build on a rich ethnographic tradition in our field to discover how literacy practices—for teachers and for students—change across time, space, and location.
    - focus on inquiry that balances the novelty of digital tools with the overarching importance of teaching and learning for deep meaning-making, substantive conversation, and critical thinking.

Some Related Scholarship

Garcia, A., Seglem, R., & Share, J. (2013). Transforming teaching and learning through critical media literacy pedagogy. *Learning Landscapes, 6*(2),109–124.

Hammer, R., & Kellner, D. (Eds.). (2009). *Media/cultural studies: Critical approaches.* New York, NY: Peter Lang.

Hicks, T. (2009). *The digital writing workshop.* Portsmouth, NH: Heinemann.

Jones, R. H., & Hafner, C. A. (2012). *Understanding digital literacies: A practical introduction.* Milton Park, Abingdon, Oxon; New York: Routledge.

Kolb, L. (2017). *Learning first, technology second: The educator's guide to designing authentic lessons.* Portland, OR: International Society for Technology in Education.

Kress, G. (2010). *Multimodality: A social semiotic approach to contemporary communication.* London, England: Routledge.

Lankshear, C., & Knobel, M. (2011). *New literacies: Everyday practices and social learning* (3rd Ed.). Berkshire, England ; New York, NY: Open University Press.

Merkley, D. J., Schmidt, D. A., & Allen, G. (2001). Addressing the English language arts technology standard in a secondary reading methodology course. *Journal of Adolescent & Adult Literacy, 45*(3), 220–231.

Mills, K. A. (2010). A review of the "digital turn" in the new literacy studies. *Review of Educational Research, 80*(2), 246–271.

Belief 3: Technologies provide new ways to consume and produce texts.

What it means to consume and produce texts is changing as digital technologies offer new opportunities to read, write, listen, view, record, compose, and interact with both the texts themselves and with other people.

As digital technologies have become more ubiquitous, so too has the ability to consume and produce texts in exciting new ways. To be clear, some academic tasks do not change. Whether a text is a paper-based book or a film clip, what it means to create a strong thesis statement or to ask a critical question about the text remains consistent. Further, some principles of consumption and production transfer across different types of texts, like the idea that an author (or a filmmaker, or a website designer) intentionally composed their text using specific techniques.

However, some things *do* change. For example, students can collaborate virtually on their reading (e.g., annotating a shared text even when not in the same physical space) and their writing (e.g., using collaborative document applications to work remotely on a text at the same time). Educators should be always aware of the above dynamics and plan instruction accordingly.

Understanding that there are dynamic literacy practices at work in the consumption and production of texts, we believe:

1. K–12 English teachers, with their students, should
    - teach students the principles of design and composition, as well as theories connected to issues of power and representation in visual imagery, music, and sound.
    - introduce students to the idea of audience through authentic assignments that have shared purpose and reach beyond the classroom to other youth as well as across generations.
    - ask students to repurpose a variety of digital media (e.g., images, video, music, text) to create a multimodal mashup or explore other emerging media genres (e.g., digital storytelling, infographics, annotated visuals, screencasts) that reflect concepts in literature such as theme, character, and setting.
    - direct students to use a note-taking tool to post text and images connected to a piece of literature they are reading in the form of a character's diary or a reader response journal.
    - immerse students in the world of transmedia storytelling by having them trace the origin and evolution of a character, storyline, issue, or event across multiple online platforms including a photo essay, a timeline, and an interactive game.
    - invite students to investigate their stance on social issues through the multimodal inquiry methods involved in digital storytelling, documentary video, or podcasting.

2. English teacher educators, with preservice and inservice teachers, should
    - harness online platforms for collaborative writing to invite teacher candidates to examine the composing practices of students and create peer feedback partnerships.
    - read, annotate, and discuss both alphabetic and visual texts, leading to substantive discussion about issues of plot, theme, and character development.
    - explore how practicing teachers are facilitating multimodal composition and sharing student writing with audiences beyond the classroom.
    - encourage teacher candidates to design instruction that integrates digital composing and multimodalities with canonical literature.

3. English and literacy researchers should
    *   examine the affordances and constraints of multimodal composition, points of tension with traditional academic literacies, and the role that teachers of writing play in assessment and evaluation of multimodal compositions.
    *   describe and articulate ideas related to authentic writing experiences beyond the classroom, including a better account of audiences for whom students are writing and purposes other than academic argument.
    *   explore what constitutes critical literacy—paying attention to the construction of individual and cultural identities—when composing multimodally with visuals, music, and sound.

Some Related Scholarship

Alpers, M., & Herr-Stephenson, R. (2013). Transmedia play: Literacy across America. *Journal of Media Literacy Education, 5*(2), 366–369.

Bishop, P., Falk-Ross, F., Andrews, G., Cronenberg, S., Moran, C. M., & Weiler, C. (2017). Digital technologies in the middle grades. In S. B. Mertens, & M. M. Caskey (Eds.), *Handbook of resources in middle level education.* Charlotte, NC: Information Age Publishing.

Brandt, D. (2015). *The rise of writing: Redefining mass literacy.* Cambridge, England: Cambridge University Press.

Brownell, C., & Wargo, J. (2017). (Re)educating the senses to multicultural communities: Prospective teachers using digital media and sonic cartography to listen for culture. *Multicultural Education Review, 9*(3), 201–214.

Connors, S. P. (2016). Designing meaning: A multimodal perspective on comics reading. In C. Hill (Ed.), *Teaching comics through multiple lenses: Critical perspectives* (pp. 13–29). London, England: Routledge.

Doerr-Stevens, C. (2017). Embracing the messiness of research: Documentary video composition as embodied, critical media literacy. *English Journal, 106*(3), 56–62.

Garcia, A. (Ed.). (2014). *Teaching in the connected learning classroom.* Irvine, CA: Digital Media and Learning Research Hub.

Hicks, T. (2013). *Crafting digital writing: Composing texts across media and genres.* Portsmouth, NH: Heinemann.

Hobbs, R. (2011). *Digital and media literacy: Connecting culture and classroom.* Thousand Oaks, CA: Corwin.

Ito, M., Gutiérrez, K., Livingstone, S., Penuel, B., Rhodes, J., Salen, K., Schor, J., Sefton-Green, J., & Watkins, S. (2013). *Connected learning: An agenda for research and design.* Digital Media and Learning Research Hub.

Kajder, S. (2010). *Adolescents and digital literacies: Learning alongside our students.* Urbana, IL: NCTE.

Krutka, D. G., & Damico, N. (2017). Tweeting with intention: Developing a social media pedagogy for teacher education. In Society for Information Technology & Teacher Education International Conference (pp. 1674–1678). Association for the Advancement of Computing in Education (AACE).

Moran, C. M. (2016). Telling our story: Using digital scrapbooks to celebrate cultural capital. *International Journal of Designs for Learning, 7*(3), 88–94.

Rodesiler, L., & Kelley, B. (2017). Toward a readership of "real" people: A case for authentic writing opportunities. *English Journal, 106*(6), 22–28.

Rybakova, K. (2016, March). Using Screencasting as a Feedback Tool in Teacher Education. In *Society for Information Technology & Teacher Education International Conference* (pp. 1355-1358). Association for the Advancement of Computing in Education (AACE).

Smith, A., West-Puckett, S., Cantrill, C., & Zamora, M. (2016). Remix as professional learning: Educators' iterative literacy practice in CLMOOC. *Educational Sciences, 6*(12).

Sullivan, S. R., & Clarke, T. (2017). Teachers first: Hands-on PD with digital writing. *English Journal, 106*(3), 69–74.

Yancey, K. B. (2009). 2008 NCTE Presidential address: The impulse to compose and the age of composition. *Research in the Teaching of English, 43*(3), 316–338.

Young, C. A., & Moran, C. M. (2017). *Applying the flipped classroom model to English language arts education.* Hershey, PA: IGI Global.

Belief 4: Technologies and their associated literacies are not neutral.

While access to technology and the internet has the potential to lessen issues of inequity, they can also perpetuate and even accelerate discrimination based on gender, race, socioeconomic status, and other factors.

It is common to hear digital technologies discussed in positive, progressive, and expansive terms; those who speak with enthusiasm may be doing so without an awareness that technology can also deepen societal inequities. Students who have access to technology at home, for example, might appear to understand a subject presented with a digital device faster than those who do not have access to similar devices outside of school.

As another example, some technologies that enable systems like "credit recovery courses" and remedial literacy software—which are frequently used more heavily in "struggling" schools that serve students who are poor and/or of color—can often reduce pedagogy to the mere coverage of shallow content and completion of basic assessments, rather than providing robust innovation for students to creatively represent their learning.

Understanding the complexity of learning how to use technology, and one's own social, political, and personal relationship to issues of gender, race, socioeconomic status, and other factors, we believe:

1. K–12 English teachers, with their students, should
   - promote and demonstrate critical thinking through discussion and identification of the rhetoric of written and digital materials (e.g., political propaganda and groupthink through social media posts and commentary).
   - introduce research skills that complicate and expand upon the trends of online authorship and identity (e.g., censorship, fair use, privacy, and legalities).
   - explore and measure the impact of a digital footprint on readers by analyzing different online identities (e.g., fanfiction, social media, professional websites).
   - choose technology products and services with an intentional awareness toward equity, including the affordances and constraints evident in free/open source, freemium, and subscription-based offerings.

2. English teacher educators, with preservice and inservice teachers, should
   - demonstrate how inequality affects access to technology throughout communities (e.g. policies, funding, stereotyping).
   - advocate for technology in marginalized communities through, for example, grant writing, community outreach programs, and family-oriented workshops.

- model research-driven practices and methods that integrate technology into the English language arts in ways that underscore the learning of conceptual, procedural, and attitudinal and/or value-based knowledge (e.g., lesson and curriculum planning).
- define and provide exemplars of technology use for educational equity that expand beyond gender, race, and socioeconomic status to include mental health, ableism, immigration status, exceptionality, and (dis)ability.

3. English and literacy researchers should

- design research studies that problematize popular assumptions about the nature of societal inequity, as well as issues of power and authority in knowledge production.
- introduce, examine, and question theoretical frameworks that provide principles and concepts which attempt to acknowledge and name inequality in society.
- build methodological frameworks that account for hidden issues of power and stance in research questions, methods, the role of researcher(s), and identification of findings.
- advocate for equitable solutions that employ technology in culturally responsive ways, drawing on students' and teachers' existing funds of knowledge related to literacy, learning, and using digital devices/networks.

Some Related Scholarship

Drucker, M. J. (2006). Commentary: Crossing the digital divide: How race, class, and culture matter. *Contemporary Issues in Technology and Teacher Education, 6*(1), 43–45.

Hicks, T. (2015). (Digital) literacy advocacy: A rationale for creating shifts in policy, infrastructure, and instruction. In E. Morrell & L. Scherff (Eds.), *New directions in teaching English: Reimagining teaching, teacher education, and research* (pp. 143–156). Lanham, MD: Rowman & Littlefield.

Levitov, D. (2017). Using the Women's March to examine freedom of speech, social justice, and social action through information literacy. *Teacher Librarian, 44*(4), 12–15.

Lewis, C., & Causey, L. (2015). Critical engagement through digital media production: A nexus of practice. In E. Morrell & L. Scherff (Eds.), *New directions in teaching English: Reimagining teaching, teacher education, and research* (pp. 123–142). Lanham, MD: Rowman & Littlefield.

McGrail, E. (2006). "It's a double-edged sword, this technology business": Secondary English teachers' perspectives on a schoolwide laptop technology initiative. *Teachers College Record, 108*(6), 1055–1079.

Morrell, E. (2008). *Critical literacy and urban youth: Pedagogies of access, dissent, and liberation.* New York, NY: Routledge.

Norris, P. (2001). *Digital divide: Civic engagement, information poverty, and the Internet worldwide.* Cambridge, England: Cambridge University Press.

Pasternak, D. L., Hallman, H. L., Caughlan, S., Renzi, L., Rush, L. S., & Meineke, H. (2016). Learning and teaching technology in English teacher education: Findings from a national study. *Contemporary Issues in Technology & Teacher Education, 16*(4).

Price-Dennis, D. (2016). Developing curriculum to support black girls' literacies in digital spaces. *English Education, 48*(4), 337–361.

Rice, M., & Rice, B. (2015). Conceptualising teachers' advocacy as comedic trickster behaviour: Implications for teacher education. *The European Journal of Humour Research, 3*(4), 9–23.

Thompson, S. (2004). An imitation of life: Deconstructing racial stereotypes in popular culture. In K. D. McBride (Ed.), *Visual media and the humanities: A pedagogy of representation* (1st ed.). Knoxville, TN: University of Tennessee Press.

Wargo, J. M., & De Costa, P. (2017). Tracing academic literacies across contemporary literacy sponsorscapes: Mobilities, ideologies, identities, and technologies. *London Review of Education, 15*(1), 101–114.

Warschauer, M. (2004). *Technology and social inclusion: Rethinking the digital divide.* Cambridge, MA: MIT Press.

Summary

In offering these four belief statements and numerous examples, the scholars and educators involved in writing this document recognize that we, too, are both informed—and limited—by our own experiences, assumptions, and daily literacy practices. It is our sincere hope that this substantially revised document can be a tool for opening up new conversations, opportunities for instruction, and lines of inquiry within the field of English language arts.

Contributors

Working Group Members

Jonathan Bartels, University of Alaska Anchorage

Richard Beach, University of Minnesota (Emeritus)

Sean Connors, University of Arkansas

Nicole Damico, University of Central Florida

Candance Doerr-Stevens, University of Wisconsin-Milwaukee

Troy Hicks, Central Michigan University

Karen Labonte, independent educational consultant

Stephanie Loomis, Georgia State University

Tom Liam Lynch, Pace University

Ewa McGrail, Georgia State University

Clarice Moran, Kennesaw State University

Donna Pasternak, University of Wisconsin-Milwaukee

Amy Piotrowski, Utah State University

Mary Rice, University of Kansas

Ryan Rish, University of Buffalo

Luke Rodesiler, Purdue University Fort Wayne

Katie Rybakova, Thomas University

Sunshine Sullivan, Houghton College

Mark Sulzer, University of Cincinnati

Stephanie Thompson, Purdue University Global

Carl Young, North Carolina State University

Lauren Zucker, Northern Highlands Regional High School (Allendale, NJ)

External Reviewers

Nadia Behizadeh, Georgia State University

Nicole Mirra, Rutgers, The State University of New Jersey

Ian O'Byrne, College of Charleston

Dawn Reed, Okemos High School (MI)

Amy McClure–Ohio Wesleyan University, Delaware, OH

Donalyn Miller–Author and Consultant, Colleyville, TX

A Year Unlike Any Other

*L*ike you, we teach readers and writers and are compelled to continue thinking about the ways that technology has influenced our students' literacies. When we consider all that we appreciate and enjoy about teaching, there is a common thread that ties us back to the influence of digital tools and the ways that we can bring them into our work with students, doing so in critical and creative ways. In short, we believe that literacy and technology are intertwined and that students can produce amazing work when given the chance.

The two of us have had the opportunity to collaborate many times over the past eight years. Through an initial introduction via mutual colleagues in 2014 and our continued work through affiliation with the Chippewa River Writing Project at Central Michigan University, the two of us have had numerous conversations about what it means to teach English language arts through many formal professional development events as well as countless emails, texts, and video chats. When the opportunity to write this Principles in Practice book arose, we looked at it as an opportunity to engage in even more teacher research, guided by Cathy Fleischer's expertise in that field and her steady hand as an editor.

As we write this introduction, pulling together the individual chapters we've written—as well as the thoughtful vignettes from ten colleagues—into a coherent narrative, it is the end of the summer of 2021. As the Bob Dylan lyric goes, the times are still a-changing. The bulk of this book was composed during the 2020–2021 academic

year, then into the 2021–2022 year, a time that brought two significant changes for
Jill's work as a classroom teacher: the move to a new school and the constant threat
of the COVID-19 pandemic. As a way of reflecting on this statement, in action, and
thinking about implications for a "new normal," the collaboration that the two of us
(Troy and Jill) have had during this strange year has been amazing. We are grateful for
the opportunity to share, for the voices of our colleagues in their vignettes, and Cathy's

 continued guidance, and we hope that the book will be taken
in the spirit it is offered: as a guide for other ELA teachers
to articulate their own beliefs for integrating technology into
their instruction. As we mention many tech tools, we have
collected the links on a single page on Troy's website, available
at <hickstro.org/ncte-middle-grades-tech>. Readers can also
access the page with the QR code here.

First, for Jill, the year of 2020 began with a mid-school year move from a
middle level ELA position in a district that she had worked in for 27 years to a new
opportunity to teach ninth graders at Skyline High School in Ann Arbor. These
exciting changes prompted Jill to think about all the ways that she had integrated
technology before and to adapt these ideas to ninth grade (or, in other words, the
transitional year from middle grades to high school), combined with a school-wide
emphasis on mastery learning. Throughout the 2020–2021 academic year, we met on a
regular basis to discuss what was happening in Jill's virtual classroom, to think through
lesson ideas, and to write this manuscript. Thus, with Cathy's encouragement to think
about how we might stretch our examples to meet the needs of all students from grades
5-9, many of her examples are drawn from the "upper" levels of the middle grades,
and—as we will describe in more detail below—we have brought in the voices of other
ELA educators to share their perspectives, too.

Thus, the two of us worked together, meeting once a week via Zoom to talk
through the changes that Jill was experiencing in remote teaching, how students were
adapting to online lessons, and the ways in which she was trying to use technology
critically and creatively. Like the majority of nearly 50 million other K–12 students
in the United States and their teachers, this school year brought many changes and
challenges for Jill and her students, too. Some of our sessions were more talk than
writing, serving as an opportunity to debrief and brainstorm. Other sessions were
more focused on the writing at hand, as we had each worked during the previous week
to bring a draft of new material and then offer a response to one another during our
Zoom calls. These meetings grew a little more sporadic over the summer and picked up
again in the fall of 2021 as we completed the manuscript. Together, we worked to bring
cohesion to the text—and our voice throughout—and to share exceptional samples of

Jill's students' work. As a note to our readers, we will often shift to first person singular in the book, where Jill's voice is foregrounded.. We have done this—as well as added "Notes from Troy" in separate call outs—in order to maintain consistency for you as you read. That said, we were both actively involved in all aspects of writing and revising the main portions of the text.

This change in teaching context in January 2020 was quite a bit for Jill, as it would be for any of us. Still, it paled in comparison to what she—indeed, all of us— would soon experience, a change that requires a little more exploration before digging into the heart of our work. Our contributors, too, were invited to write brief vignettes that recognized the complexities of their own current teaching and learning contexts, and some of them do explicitly reference work during remote teaching in 2020 and 2021. We thank them for their contributions and will introduce them throughout the book.

To provide some additional context for our work together—as well as Jill's work in a new district, with new colleagues—we begin with a brief explanation of her work with other Skyline HS teachers.

Curriculum, Collaboration, and Change: A Glimpse into the Work of Skyline HS's English Department

As noted above, we now move into the first-person singular with Jill's voice reflecting on her students, her teaching, and the changes she has made to more intentionally integrate technology into her instruction over the past year.

January of 2020 was an exciting time for me. After living and teaching in northern Michigan for 27 years, my family and I were ready for a change. While it is a bit unorthodox for someone to uproot herself after teaching many years in one school district, I always wanted to have the experience of teaching in a larger district, with more resources, and a community rich in diversity to tap into when needed. Ann Arbor doesn't disappoint in any of these categories. Ann Arbor, Michigan, is home to the University of Michigan and is located just southwest of Detroit. According to *US News'* ratings of best high schools, Skyline High School is ranked number one among public high schools in Ann Arbor and 18th in Michigan. Skyline's student-teacher ratio is 18:1 and it serves a population of 1451 students from a variety of ethnic backgrounds. The total teaching staff is 84 with an English department of 15 teachers. The school year is divided into three 12-week trimesters where students take five classes each. Finally, Skyline High School is a "mastery learning" school—based on the ideas originally proposed by Benjamin Bloom (Guskey, 2010)—imbued with formative assessments where students are required to meet the curriculum's mastery standards at a level of eighty percent or higher. Students are engaged in project-based learning that gives them choice and voice in their demonstration of the curriculum's mastery standards.

The English curriculum is divided into grade level offerings that require students to take English for two of the three trimesters each year: English A and English B. Both English sections at each grade level have three units apiece:

- English A—Close Reading, Creative and Narrative Writing, Research to Inform and Explain

- English B—Literary Analysis, Argument Writing, Speaking and Listening

These unit topics remain the same for grades 6–12, and the complexity and rigor spirals up recursively as students work through the secondary grades.

English teachers at Skyline typically do not have the same teaching assignment year after year. Teachers are placed in classes according to learning communities within the school. This can result in teaching a new grade level or class each year. For example, I primarily teach ninth grade, but that is not a given. I have also been assigned English 10 and 11, creative writing, and a support class for struggling students called Academic Literacy. Because teachers' assignments can shift, the culture among all teachers at Skyline High School is collaborative. It is common for a teacher to share a whole trimester of course materials with a colleague; this team spirit is simply a part of what we do.

When faced with the long-term assignment of teaching remotely, the district created "teacher learning networks," or TLNs, for all content areas and divided them into grade levels. If a teacher's assignment encompassed more than one grade level, then they would attend the TLN where the most students were affected. This allowed the district to deliver information and new initiatives—for instance, remote teaching support and Schoology course design for all teachers, as well as subject-specific initiatives like literature circles in English—through smaller groups in the context of the subject taught. Skyline's English department also encouraged this same grade level TLN concept within our school, which placed me with three other teachers who primarily taught ninth grade: Alaina Feliks, Serena Kessler, and Amanda McMurray.

As the year progressed, and as readers will see in this book, my team and I discovered that teaching online is very different from face-to-face instruction. Moreover, if students were to have an engaging learning experience, we had to share the workload. We planned units and lessons together and divided the workload by week. Each of us would volunteer to plan a week's lessons and materials, spacing them so we had a breather before the next one. This provided a break of a week or two between building lessons in order to catch up on feedback and grading (and maybe even to make dinner one night instead of ordering takeout!). Prepping and teaching online were both grueling until we fell into the rhythm of the work. We became a tight-knit group—

providing support to each other along the way in whatever form that took: technology help, emotional support, as well as curricular ideas. These women are no longer just my colleagues; they are all my good friends, and I thank them for their collaborative, generous spirits.

This led to another change in our schooling routines: our year was divided into semesters instead of trimesters, and so we had to rethink the timing of units as well as the number of lessons we could feasibly teach within a block schedule. The decision to go to a semester block schedule was made at the district level, so all the high schools in Ann Arbor Public Schools adopted the following schedule:

- School started at 8:30 am each day and students virtually attended 3 classes per day for 105 minutes each, up until the release time of 3:30 pm.

- Students attended class hours 1, 3, and 5 on Monday and Thursday and class hours 2, 4, and 6 on Tuesday and Friday; lessons on these days were synchronous, requiring students to log into Zoom at the assigned class time.

- Wednesday was asynchronous—teachers would plan a lesson that students could complete on their own. Most of the time, my group planned the asynchronous lessons with a Hyperdoc-style template provided by the district. We relied heavily on videos—both our own screencast creations as well as other materials we found on the internet—to help students complete the work assigned.

So many changes in one school year was a test for all of us. There were many new skills I needed, as did my students. I feel like a really important lesson has surfaced: teachers are in partnership with their students, and the process of learning requires teacher-student collaboration instead of a top-down approach. The whole idea of being the guide on the side instead of the sage on the stage was something I always believed, but the 2020–2021 school year made it a requirement.

Just the new technology skills required of teachers and students to manage our daily work alone required a different kind of collaboration. When I couldn't figure something out, I would ask the students what they saw on their computer screens and, many times, I turned over the reins to a tech-savvy student. The student shared their screen with the class to demo the skill or view the screen in a manner that I didn't have as the teacher. This is one small example of how structural changes in schooling pushed us into productive partnership with our students. They felt the freedom to tell me where there were gaps in the lesson or if I placed something in the Schoology course that was difficult to find. We were learning more than just our curriculum in the moments that required it, and students gave me feedback on my online teaching, in real time, and that really helped.

Maybe part of this is my own comfort level with being vulnerable, but I really liked those moments where we were all teaching each other and learning together.

Notes from Troy

Here, and throughout the book, Troy offers some additional ideas in these "Notes from Troy" sidebars.

Knowing that Jill—like tens of thousands of other educators around the world—was continuing to adapt and change throughout 2020–2021 to teaching contexts that seemed unimaginable reminds me that educators are a resilient bunch. That said, I am also mindful that the stresses were greater on some communities and individuals, especially teachers who work with students who are disproportionately affected by childhood trauma, poverty, racism, and a variety of other factors. Yes, we all experience different stresses in different ways, yet working with Jill reminded me that—even in well-resourced communities—the challenges of remote teaching and learning were exceptional.

Whatever "lessons learned" we take from this era that then encourage the use of technology to support ELA learning in the future, we also know that this moment in our history took its toll on our students, families, and communities. For many reasons, we must always remember those family members and friends that we lost, even as we look ahead to new opportunities for teaching with technology in the future.

Staying Home, Staying Safe, and Going Remote

With the closures of spring 2020 and the continued changes as schools began again in the fall, we knew we were writing this book in a moment unlike any other in our educational careers. Thus, throughout the text, you will find threads of pandemic pedagogy sewn within narratives and examples of our teaching. But, as we've learned as schools have returned to the "new normal" in the fall of 2021 (interrupted by numerous synchronous and asynchronous instructional days that were necessitated by viral outbreaks and substitute shortages, among other unexpected occurrences), the ways of teaching we learned during that time will continue to impact our approaches to teaching, in general, and specifically teaching with technology (as we talk about more throughout the book). So, even though many of the examples come from the time of synchronous and asynchronous online teaching, we were striving to make sure that we were writing about technology and teaching in ways that reflect the best practices for ELA instruction at any time, now and in the future.

None of us could have fully imagined the ways that "emergency remote teaching" (Hodges et al., 2020) that began in the spring of 2020 would impact teaching and learning over the long haul. Hodges et al. characterizes this kind of teaching as

> [A] temporary shift of instructional delivery to an alternate delivery mode due to crisis circumstances. It involves the use of fully remote teaching solutions for instruction or education that would otherwise be delivered

face-to-face or as blended or hybrid courses and that will return to that
format once the crisis or emergency has abated. (para. 13)

In contrast to the kinds of online experiences that have been carefully designed and
implemented in a strategic manner—whether in a hybrid or fully online setting, and
whether completely synchronous or with some asynchronous components—"emergency
remote teaching" was only ever meant to be a temporary solution. That said, depending
on the teaching context in which our readers find themselves, we know that many K–12
ELA teachers and teacher educators may still be balancing the challenges of remote
teaching and learning, even if the immediate "emergency" is over and a more nuanced,
clearly defined definition of "remote" is still elusive.

To that end, both of us have been conscious of the varying and complex teaching
contexts that will likely be in place for years to come and how the position statement,
while not designed for this moment in time, can still serve us well in considering the
role of technology in the ELA classroom.

Notes from Troy

Throughout the year, as Jill and I collaborated on (and commiserated about) the many changes and challenges
she was facing, I was also reminded of the dozens of other teachers with whom I was working in graduate
coursework, professional development sessions, and our Chippewa River Writing Project. Now a documented
phenomenon, the kinds of burnout that teachers experienced in the 2020–2021 academic year were a combination
of many factors, and more than I could name here.

Connecting to the note above, I offer one more time that the challenges that emerged with remote teaching
and learning came at great cost: lives lost, harm to mental and physical health, personal finances, and more. We
need teacher leaders who can guide and mentor both their own students as well as their colleagues, especially
those new to the profession.

This book, then, is a response to an era of technology-infused (though often forced) teaching and learning that,
I hope, serves as a roadmap to the work ahead for all ELA teachers and teacher leaders while also recognizing
the sacrifices that many of us have made.

Examining Our Beliefs about the Integration of Technology into ELA Instruction

And, with that, we transition from this preface into a closer look at the position
statement, *Beliefs for Integrating Technology into the English Language Arts Classroom*
(ELATE Commission on Digital Literacy in Teacher Education, 2018) that is the basis
of this book. Troy was one of the co-chairs leading work on revision of the statement, in

partnership with Tom Liam Lynch, who together led nearly two dozen other English educators through a process of writing and revision over two years (Zucker & Hicks, 2019). In doing so, the committee worked diligently to outline a forward-looking agenda, one in which we would more intentionally integrate technology into our literacy instruction.

From there, in Chapter 2, we unpack the BIT-ELA position statement, delving a bit more into the particular context in which we have written it during two years of continued uncertainty yet with an eye toward the future of ELA instruction. In the process of thinking through BIT-ELA, we also explore the way that Jill has shifted toward the use of digital writers' notebooks.

In Chapter 3, "Close Reading," we dig into techniques and tools for looking carefully at texts. Though the debate about what constitutes "close reading" still goes on, ideas in this chapter will explore what happens when students are engaged both on page and on screen, using digital tools to complement and extend their reading experiences. With ideas for exploring both multimodal and alphabetic texts through the lens of close reading, we will consider ways that students are invited to ask questions and annotate texts.

Then, in Chapter 4, we explore expository writing through the "Research, Inform, Explain" unit. The term "fake news" has become fraught with multiple interpretations yet highlights a problem from decades, even centuries, past that has included propaganda and misinformation. As we consider the ways our students must engage in inquiry, and work to create clear, concise summaries of what they have found, the skills for research that require digital literacies remain pertinent. As one example, Jill documents her experience teaching students the process of "lateral reading" (McGrew et al., 2019), leading them ultimately to the production of an infographic as a companion to their research paper.

Next, we return to a cornerstone practice in the teaching of English: literary analysis. Chapter 5 reminds us that literary analysis of both classic and contemporary texts will remain a key part of what happens in our classrooms. Learning how to analyze and critique works of fiction, drama, and poetry helps build additional skills as well as foster an appreciation of the art form. With texts that are "born digital" that warrant interpretation, as well as a full range of digital tools that can be used to discuss literary works, we know that literary analysis remains an important part of ELA. Remote learning required Jill to think differently about teaching the skills of analysis. She had to replace the face-to-face lessons of the classroom with something new, asking students to work through analyzing a series of texts within the structure of a "Hyperdoc" (Highfill et al., 2016), which we explore in more detail.

Chapter 6 outlines another major genre explored in Jill's classroom: argument. In an age where social media dominates our daily literacy practices, we need to help students develop skills for both traditional, academic argumentation, as well as to explore new modes of expression in which they can make their case through images, videos, infographics, maps, and other unique forms of expression. Building on ideas from the NWP's College, Career, and Community Writers Program—or C3WP (National Writing Project, n.d.a.)—this chapter encourages teachers to explore arguments in terms of dialogue, not just a lop-sided debate. Here, Jill outlines two lessons for strengthening students' argument writing skills with a twist on the process using various forms of public service announcements as a summative assessment.

Finally, in Chapter 7, we conclude our journey through one year of Jill's teaching—and the BIT-ELA statements—and consider next steps in hybrid or blended learning by reiterating key themes, including those of communication and collaboration, creation and exploration, inquiry and equity. Also, we speculate a bit, based on one year's worth of experience. If we believe that screens are not the best way to learn for most students, at least not all the time, then what kinds/forms of hybrid school will emerge? In our minds, teachers will shift their thinking of how to deliver their curriculum by adding another layer of nuance that we want to explore in more detail: planning for what Renee Hobbs and Julie Coiro describe as "real time" and "any time" learning (Coiro & Hobbs, 2021).

And, as we've mentioned, readers will find additional ideas from other middle level educators throughout the book through brief vignettes, expanding the reach of this book into other contexts beyond Jill's classroom. With the introduction of this first vignette in the section below, we pause for just a moment to provide the background for their inclusion in the manuscript. In the fall of 2020, Troy sent invitations to several colleagues and encouraged them to contribute reflections on a teaching practice that highlighted an element of the *Beliefs for Integrating Technology into the English Language Arts Classroom*, giving us a glimpse into their classrooms. Ten of our colleagues took up the invitation, and we thank them for their contributions.

And, with that, we welcome the first voice of a colleague, Jenny Sanford, an ELA teacher at Springport Middle School in a rural/suburban region in Michigan's lower peninsula, who offers us insights on the many ways that she kept her students connected, mostly through what she describes as "In-Person/Virtual Collaborative Book Clubs."

From the Classroom: "In-Person/Virtual Collaborative Book Clubs" by Jenny Sanford

Jenny Sanford is a 6th–8th grade ELA teacher at Springport Middle School. She attained a master's degree in Literacy Instruction from Michigan State University, which included the completion of a K–12 Reading Specialist certification. Jenny holds several leadership positions within her district, sitting on both the district and building leadership teams, as well as functioning as the K–12 ELA PLC leader.

Recently, Jenny served on the statewide team that developed the newly revised Michigan Middle School English Language Arts Units. She is also the Adolescent Literacy co-chair on the Michigan Reading Association board and is the president of the South Central Michigan Reading Council.

In my district this past year, our secondary teachers served both in-person and virtual students. Our virtual students completed their studies asynchronously through videos, lessons, assignments, and assessments posted in Google Classroom, aside from Wednesdays when in-person students were virtual and virtual students were synchronous, Zooming with all of their classroom teachers on a schedule. I came to realize that there was exceeding isolation in this situation for my virtual students. It was reflecting on this realization that drew me to looking for a way to bring both groups of students together, to give them the opportunity to form a community of learners. This is how I came to the idea of creating In-Person/Virtual Collaborative Book Clubs.

Book clubs remain a regular staple in my classroom. In our middle school, we teach our book clubs around genres to ensure that all students encounter as many kinds of literature as possible in their three years of middle school. This school year, my seventh graders completed three book clubs around the following genres and topics: legend, WWII (both historical fiction and narrative nonfiction), and mystery. The WWII unit was taught as an interdisciplinary unit with seventh grade social studies.

As the 2020–2021 year necessitated, much of this book club work took place in a digital space. To begin, all students completed a virtual book pass in the form of a Google Slides presentation in which each book received its own slide with a picture of the book, a synopsis of the plot, and a link to a book trailer (please see the "WWII Book Club Virtual Book Pass" links on the book's companion website). At the end of the slide show, students completed a Google Form indicating the books in which they were most interested. I then grouped students in heterogeneous teams of in-person and virtual students. Additionally, I used a read aloud as an anchor text (please see "*The Diary of Anne Frank* Listening Guide" link on the book's companion website). This allowed me to delve into genre elements and reading comprehension concepts the students were working on in their book club texts. For the virtual students, I recorded videos in which I read the anchor text aloud and hyperlinked the videos to a Google Doc laid out as a table with the date of the recording, the chapter/section recorded, and the link to the recording (please see "*The House with a Clock in Its Walls* Read Aloud Links" link on the book's companion website).

I created a Zoom schedule for meetings, and students began their book club conversations. The first few meetings were clumsy, as would be expected. Students needed scaffolding and support to use the tools effectively. Students had to learn, as the first literacy practice in the NCTE *Beliefs* document states, to "engage as social practices . . . collaboratively construct[ing] knowledge, participat[ing] in immersive learning experiences."

Even with practice, learning to interact across Zoom was a challenge. Some virtual students struggled through connectivity issues that resulted in video or audio not working properly. Some virtual students had difficulty feeling included by the in-person students. Both groups required support and instruction on how to engage across a computer screen. Together we needed to "question how technologies shape and mediate literacy practices" and "explore how [we] negotiate the use of … literacies." We had to ask how Zoom was holding us back and how we could use it more effectively.

Most of all, each group of students needed to learn how to be empathetic to the other group of students. It was important for the virtual kids to realize why it was difficult for in-person students to include them in discussion, and the in-person kids needed to learn how isolating it is to sit by yourself on the other side of a screen from a group of people. Once they placed themselves in the other's shoes and received scaffolded support to address these issues, it was much easier for them to work together and the conversations flowed more freely. For instance, one virtual student sent me an email after her first book club meeting stating that her team members were excluding her from the meeting and treating her very rudely. Upon investigation, I learned that the in-person portion of her group felt distant from her because she kept her camera off and rarely talked during meetings. The in-person students needed support in how to include her in the discussion in a way that was inviting, not demanding. The virtual student needed encouragement to take the chance to have her camera on so that her teammates could feel more connected to her during the meetings. Once each side was able to understand the other's perspective, their group was able to function more effectively.

For the unit assessments, Google Forms was the platform I chose to create a pretest and post-test for students to measure the unit objectives. Using Google Forms to test students is very efficient. Grading tests in ELA can be challenging because open-ended responses have to be viewed by the teacher to be graded. Because Forms produces a spreadsheet of responses, I was able to grade from the spreadsheet and even color-code responses (green for correct, yellow for partially correct, and red for incorrect) to use the pre/post data for my own data conference with my principal at the end of the year. Students took the same Form test but in two separate forms, by making a copy of the pretest for the post test, so that I would have two different spreadsheets for comparison.

I was happy to see that, on the end-of-the-year survey, many virtual and in-person students alike indicated that the book clubs were among their favorite units of the year. Some virtual students noted that book clubs made them feel connected to other students in school. As I move into the new school year, virtual book clubs will likely become a thing of the past, yet there were some important lessons that came out of this experience for both the kids and me. Working with other people can be messy but worthwhile. If we are willing to listen to others, there is so much we can learn from them.

Notes from Troy

Sanford's skillful adaptation of book clubs and the ways in which she intentionally connected students in the classroom with those online (or what became affectionately known as "the roomies" and "the Zoomies" for many teachers) shows us a great deal about what she values. The relationships, as much as the texts themselves, are a core part of the experience for Sanford's students.

With that, we know there are countless numbers of resources related to book clubs and literature circles online, so a web search will yield many ideas for setting them up and getting started. The books that we suggest to students certainly matter; as we look for additional sources to find books that will engage our readers, the teams at both #DisruptTexts and The Nerdy Book Club (links available on the companion site) provide numerous reviews and resources that celebrate the diversity of children and young adult literature.

For more on middle grade reading tips, Jennifer Ochoa's Principles in Practice title, *Already Readers and Writers* (2020), offers dozens of other suggestions for finding worthy texts, too. Balancing the books we choose with an intentional effort at relationship building is the heart of Sanford's approach and illustrates key tenets of the BIT-ELA statement.

Final Thoughts on an Unusual Year with the BIT-ELA Principles in Mind

As we close this introduction and begin to think about the position statement in more detail, we are reminded that English teachers have been taking on the task of integrating technology and media in their classroom for decades. While some efforts have been more successful than others, we are also reminded of the idea from NCTE's *Definition of Literacy in a Digital Age* that "[a]s society and technology change, so [too] does literacy" (2019a). Our students may be able to navigate Instagram, Snapchat, and TikTok more efficiently than we ever could, yet this does not mean that they always bring a critical and creative sensibility to their uses of technology and, as the definition's framework calls us to do, we must teach our students how to utilize these tools in meaningful, substantive ways. Our work as ELA educators will continue to evolve, and yet the need for our work is equally as important now as it was over 100 years ago when NCTE members first began this ongoing journey to better prepare our students for literate lives beyond school.

To guide further discussion and exploration, we encourage teachers to think about the following:

- In what ways are you currently using technology to support reading, writing, speaking, listening, viewing, and visually representing in your middle level ELA classroom?

- What teaching practices, especially with technology, have remained relatively constant for you over the years? What has changed? What might you be ready to change considering the BIT-ELA statement and what you have read so far?

- Reflecting on the effects of remote teaching and learning, whether just a few weeks or an entire school year, what teaching practices have been most useful for you? What do you want to carry forward—and enhance—as you think about digital writing, connected reading, and other technology-enabled literacies?

Also, as we head into chapters with samples of student work, a quick note here on style. When we use student work, please know that minor typos that do not affect the overall meaning of their writing have been revised for clarity.

Chapter Two

Unpacking the Position Statement

Reflections from Jill's Classroom

As so many students in my past ELA classes have done, my ninth graders, too, were beginning the year with an exploration of identity. This year, I adapted a prompt from my colleagues and invited students to describe the rituals, relationships, and restrictions—the three Rs—that regulate their lives. After we finished watching a TED talk to prompt their thinking, I asked them to put their fingers to their keyboards and begin sharing ideas that would, in time, turn into additional ideas for us to mine from their writers' notebooks. In many ways, this process unfolded as it had on other September mornings over the past many years in my ELA classroom.

However, as I enjoyed the silence, I was starkly aware of two differences this fall: none of them were using a physical notebook, and I couldn't hear their fingers clicking on the keys. With their microphones on mute and seeing only their names—and not faces—on the Zoom screen, I was keenly aware that creating a reading and writing workshop through remote teaching in the fall of 2020 was going to be something unlike what I had ever experienced before, despite my long-held interest in using technology to support middle grades students.

Context and Connections to the BIT-ELA Statement

Here in Chapter 2 and through subsequent chapters, after introducing a brief vignette from Jill's teaching practice, we (Jill and Troy) take a moment to set the stage for the deeper dive into the lessons that will come later in the chapter, as well as to make a connection to the BIT-ELA statement. Except for this chapter where we speak in the plural "we" of Jill and Troy, later "Context and Connections" section will introduce the ideas from Jill's perspective in her classroom, even though we collaborated in the writing process.

Jill's experience beginning in the fall of 2020, like tens of thousands of other teachers and millions of students, was something that none of us could have ever predicted. And while even now it is presumptuous to say that the moment was one that English language arts educators had been considering for many years, if not decades (because, of course, it really was not conceivable that the vast majority of students would be learning via synchronous video calls), it is appropriate to note that NCTE members have long been considering the ways that technology could be used for innovative approaches to teach (Palmeri & McCorkle, 2021), releasing dozens of position statements and journal articles, not to mention conference presentations, over our 100+ years of existence.

As one example, in October of 2018, NCTE's English Language Arts Teacher Educators (ELATE) Commission on Digital Literacies and Teacher Education (D-LITE) released a revised position statement, the *Beliefs for Integrating Technology into the English Language Arts Classroom* (2018), referred to below as "BIT-ELA." The statement begins with the idea that integrating technology is complex work, and that the beliefs themselves may sometimes "complement (or even conflict with) each other in theory or practice." Troy was fortunate to co-chair the committee that revised that statement and learned a great deal about the work of English educators from around the country in the process of doing so.

One point became clear in the process of writing: just as we welcome a variety of voices and visions into our conversation about how to teach English language arts (ELA), the statement reminded us that there is no single "right" way to integrate technology into our classrooms. The statement itself grew out of a specialty area in our broader field of ELA, the intersection of literacy and technology. This subfield has deep roots, and our efforts in 2018 were informed by both previous ideas as well as new ideas for contemporary classrooms and technologies.

Specifically, building on the work of Swenson et al.'s 2005 *Beliefs about Technology and the Preparation of English Teachers: Beginning the Conversation,*" published in *Contemporary Issues in Technology and Teacher Education* (2005), this revision of the statement brought together 23 scholars over 22 months to collaboratively design a document that was "well researched, usable, and empowering" (Zucker & Hicks, 2019). The four primary beliefs remind us that:

1. Literacy means *literacies.*

2. Consider literacies before technologies.

3. Technologies provide new ways to consume and produce texts.

4. Technologies and their associated literacies are not neutral.

In considering all this, the authors included, for each belief, a list of suggestions for both English educators as well as K–12 teachers who are compelled to integrate these ideas into their teaching. These belief statements are nuanced and textured. For instance, under the broader third belief statement, "Technologies provide new ways to consume and produce texts," K–12 teachers are encouraged to "invite students to investigate their stance on social issues through the multimodal inquiry methods involved in digital storytelling, documentary video, or podcasting." Even in this glimpse of the position statement, we can see that there are many elements to consider in our planning for, teaching, and assessment of such projects including reading and research skills, both print-based writing in the form of script development and digital writing with media and bringing in activities that scaffold students through an inquiry that is meant to specifically examine social issues.

To enact the BIT-ELA, then, requires a layered approach to teaching English language arts, an approach that aligns with other frameworks and positions that NCTE has advocated for. In fact, this *Beliefs* document was created at a time when, in addition, NCTE had recently updated their *Definition of Literacy in a Digital Age* (2019a), framing that statement around "learner agency, access, action, and opportunities." In doing so, the authors of that statement also asked a series of interwoven questions, each of which positioned the learner in the agentive role. These include implicit instructions to guide educators in planning robust learning experiences, with questions such as "Do learners find relevant and reliable sources that meet their needs?" and "Do learners gain new perspectives because of the texts they interact with?"

Taken together, both of these documents—and the countless position statements, research reports, and articles from NCTE's archive of journals—remind us that teachers of English language arts continue to play a pivotal role in preparing their students to use technology. More than just teaching the skills of word processing or internet searching, and even more than trying to provide students with skills to be good digital citizens, the BIT-ELA document reminds teachers of the ideological nature of literacy and how technology shapes and is shaped by those ideologies. Layer in an understanding that technology, too, carries implicit and explicit biases, and it is clear that the English teacher's role—as one who helps students interrogate texts and write their own way into the world—remains an ever-important set of goals, especially as we fully enter the third decade of the twenty-first century.

Before we begin our journey through the BIT-ELA document in this chapter and the rest of the book—and describe the ways that Jill navigated a school year unlike any other—we offer a few comments about the audience, purpose, and context of this book, welcoming our ELA colleagues into a conversation about how we view these beliefs and work to enact them.

Notes from Troy

In our article, "23 Months x 22 Scholars: Collaboration, Negotiation, and the Revision of a Position Statement on Technology in English Language Arts," Lauren Zucker and I invited the many colleagues who collaborated on the statement to reflect on their process and provide updates on their work.

One key feature of the article is an interactive timeline, "Revising Our Beliefs about Technology in English Teacher Education," a multimodal text that I created using a tool from the Northwestern School of Journalism's Knightlab suite of technologies, Timeline JS.

This process of composing a traditional academic article while simultaneously composing an interactive timeline was useful for me as a writer, encouraging me to move recursively across the two media forms (text only and timeline with text, links, and images) in order to make a more compelling argument in each.

For a link to the timeline alone, as well as all other links in the book, please visit this book's companion page on my website mentioned earlier, and accessible from the QR code shared in the introduction in Chapter 1: <hickstro.org/ncte-middle-grades-tech>

A Special Consideration of Audience, Purpose, and Context for This Book, in This Moment

Though a constant mantra in our experiences of writing about teaching—especially in writing about teaching with technology—has been that we should try to aim for the universal, to aim for producing a text that has a "long shelf life," there are at least two reasons why we will bend this rule just a bit in this manuscript. Of course, as any English teacher will tell you, the rhetorical aspects of audience, purpose, and context matter when one is writing. Rhetoricians would call this "kairos," a Greek term relating to the needs of the moment, the exigencies that push people toward action.

So, as much as we want to create something that is going to be timeless (and, indeed, hope that there are aspects of our work that carry forward for many years to come), we have felt two additional, acute factors at work while writing this book.

First, COVID-19.

We pitched this book proposal in the spring of 2020, right as the world changed. Beyond the major societal changes, it is also important to understand how Jill's day-to-day teaching reality changed as well as the ways in which thousands of teachers and millions of students "did school" changed, as noted in Chapter 1. Some of those changes happened in the spring for some students, yet much more changed in the fall of 2020. Thus, this book has been informed with and influenced by these changes, though we will still aim to make the teaching strategies, technology tips, and integration with the BIT-ELA statements to be as timeless as possible.

As just one example of these stark statistics, UNESCO reported at the end of March 2020 that nearly 2.37 billion students were learning from home, approximately 75% of school-aged children around the world (United Nations Education, Scientific, and Cultural Organization, 2020). The United States Department of Education's National Center for Educational Statistics notes that this affected about 50 million K–12 students (Irwin et al., 2021). And while nearly three million students had been fully online prior to the spring of 2020 (Schroeder, 2019), well over 90% of students in our country moved from face-to-face to remote learning in a very short time.

Moreover, we are well aware that the quality of these remote learning experiences varied significantly. For instance, *The New York Times* reported on the disparities between students in public and private schools, noting that "what the pandemic has made clear is that remote education, especially of the youngest students, requires a rare mix of enthusiastic school leadership, teacher expertise and homes equipped with everything children need to learn effectively" (Goldstein, 2020). We recognize that these inequities in educational opportunities are likely, and sadly, going to persist.

The second effect was technology itself.

Again, while there have not been any incredible innovations in the ways that devices have been designed or online content delivered in 2020—though getting used to teaching in a video conference room like Zoom or Google Meet is a significant change—the world has become even more mediated by technology, reflecting the mass stay-at-home orders that were put in place around the globe. Technology took on a role that it had not before in many lives and households, even though most of what we were doing (like using email, video calls, and collaborative docs) had been around for some time. Still, if it was not the case that our students' lives were full of technology to begin the year, the fact that tens of thousands of school-sponsored laptops and Wi-Fi hotspots have been put into the hands of as many students as possible means that there is no going back. Even though there was not much new about the technologies themselves, there was quite a bit different about the ways in which educators began to use them, as we have become as close to ubiquitous access for nearly all students—still with some notable exceptions—as we are likely to get in this decade.

Though we are still wondering exactly what the entirety of the 2021–2022 school year will hold as we finalize the book in the fall of 2021 as Delta, and now Omicron, enter our vocabularies, and even when students return to "in person" learning on a more consistent, less socially distanced basis, they will have become accustomed to learning with and through technology. The shift in device usage in schools—that many of us have waited decades for—is now here. These critiques of remote learning were many and far beyond the scope of what we want to address here. Instead, as we look forward, and as teachers of language and literacy, we need to work to address these concerns of inadequate assignment design, poor turnaround time on feedback, and a general sense that canned, prepackaged curriculum was quickly replacing any kind of critical or creative approach to teaching in a reading and writing workshop, with an orientation toward equity and social justice.

As we began writing this book, the fall of 2020 brought remote learning into Jill's district (and hundreds of others around the nation), and the urgency to make these changes quickly were present in her efforts to integrate technologies and literacies into her course activities, assignments, and assessments. To that end, our journey through the BIT-ELA in this book is, like all books about teaching, contextual and nuanced, in that we are documenting Jill's teaching practices—and inviting the voices of many other NCTE colleagues—to share what was happening in the moment, in their classrooms, both physical and virtual, in a changed world. Writing it has presented a set of circumstances that are different from anything we have encountered in our lifetimes as we adapt educational practices into blended or fully online environments.

Still, we worked to make the examples throughout the book timely, relevant, and useful, connecting them to NCTE's broader stances on teaching ELA at the middle level and, in particular, in alignment with the *Beliefs for Integrating Technology into the English Language Arts Classroom* (which, as noted above, we will now refer to as the "BIT-ELA document," or simply BIT-ELA). To that end, we now offer one example to demonstrate how we will, in subsequent chapters, attempt to share even more activities and to make connections to the BIT-ELA. We began our work with a look at one of Jill's core practices, one that she has held steady across her entire school year: the writer's notebook. Specifically, as we hinted at in the vignette opening this chapter, we will share here how she adapted her practice to make notebook writing during remote learning into a timely and meaningful experience for her students.

It is, indeed, this experience of building community that many teachers feared would be lost entirely when moving to remote learning. To that end, losing a sense of community is a reasonable assumption and concern. For decades, the stereotype of "online learning" largely meant that students were receiving asynchronous lesson materials like videos and quizzes, usually without much interaction amongst peers, and teachers were not really engaging with students in a consistent, synchronous environment, instead only delivering feedback via email or a learning management system. In this sense, online learning (at least some forms of it) has largely been designed as a glorified correspondence course, what we thought was a relic of education's past. Thus, the fear that we would lose out on the relationships we developed with students was a reasonable one.

Yet, many teachers found that they could, indeed, build community. And as we prepare to move into our first example of how Jill brings the BIT-ELA to life in her classroom through the use of digital writers' notebooks, let's pause for a moment to consider one other way that another colleague, Kathleen Riley, creates a welcoming environment maximizing the use of digital tools. She learns her students' names through the use of Flipgrid, renamed simply to Flip in 2022, a freely available tool from Microsoft that students can use on multiple devices, with video cameras or audio alone.

From the Classroom: "Welcoming Voices by Honoring Names with Flipgrid" by Kathleen Riley

Kathleen Rowley is a teacher-consultant with the UCLA Writing Project and is part of NWP's Ahead of the Code inquiry network. She writes about teaching, justice, and equity at katerowley.medium.com.

Like many teachers, I have collected innumerable index cards with student names at the beginning of each school year, and this practice only changed with the times when I figured out that I could buy colorful cards to differentiate classes in the stack. My practice remained steady, year after year, yet it worked, and I didn't see a need to change. On the first day of school, I asked the usual questions:

- What is your name?
- What would you like to be called?
- How do you pronounce that?

I would flip, flip, flip, and try to match faces from my online roster to the names on my cards. Some teachers would take photos, catch students at the door, and even create nameplates for the first few weeks of school. I would do those things, too. It never felt like quite enough.

As my rosters grew and grew, I needed a better way to see students and know them. I also needed to make sure all students were welcome in my class, not just the ones who have common names. Ethan A., Ethan C., Ethan R., and Ethan S. never have their names mispronounced.

Tyrone Howard, UCLA professor of education and director of the UCLA Center for the Transformation of Schools, and other researchers have pointed out that the majority of teachers are White (including myself) and the majority of students in the country will, in the immediate future, be People of Color (e.g., Howard & Banks, 2020). Our students' diversity is often reflected in their names. To know their name—and to say it correctly—is the bare minimum of respect that every student deserves.

Instead of tripping over pronunciation and apologizing for months, I have finally found a technology that supports my goal to learn students' names and learn about them at the same time. In 2014, a free software emerged to support my first-day attempts at equity in my classroom: Flipgrid. Acquired by Microsoft in 2018, Flipgrid is a free video website that integrates with most learning management systems, like Canvas or Google Classroom (Choney, 2018). Students are able to record themselves saying their names, their nicknames, and their pronouns. I fly through the short videos, which now can even be narrated over photos or images of their families. Students can also see others' videos and comment by saying hello.

I will admit, I administer a "faces quiz" several weeks into our school year. I have to pass it, too. Never, in my class, are you allowed to call someone "that boy over there." He has a name and we all must use it. And, as the *Beliefs for Integrating Technology into the English Language Arts Classroom* reminds us, I have chosen a tool with "an intentional awareness toward equity," both because the platform itself is free, though more importantly because it helps me connect students in a humane, personal manner. It creates community and builds capacity. Here, with Flipgrid, tech meets equity and common sense.

Notes from Troy

Riley's point that knowing a student's name is the bare minimum of respect, especially in environments that are largely mediated by technology, reminds us that we can teach remotely without being distant. Adopting a classroom practice that she had previously used to better understand her students' identities, Riley models a particularly effective use of a technology, Flipgrid (or, now, Flip), which she will be able to use in her teaching in the future, regardless of modality (face-to-face, hybrid, or fully online).

Also, before pushing her students into a deep discussion about a literary text or complex topic, she invites them to use Flipgrid in a low-pressure manner, building trust and community. Though she might use index cards again at some point in the future, it is likely that Riley's use of Flipgrid will continue. It is this kind of "both/and" adoption of technologies in the ELA classroom that can make them particularly robust, both for our own use as teachers as well as for students to use in their own projects.

Connecting to the BIT-ELA: Conceptualizing Digital Writers' Notebooks: Jill's Classroom

Like Kate, I also build community at the beginning of the year in my ELA classes. It begins with the daily routine of thinking, writing, and sharing through a writer's notebook. The writer's notebook has been a long-standing staple in my secondary language arts classes, both when I taught seventh grade in the past and in my current role with my ninth grade students. Many proponents of the writing workshop approach have advocated for the use of writing notebooks, far too many to name here. As just one example, Gallagher and Kittle in *180 Days* pointed out that "Freewriting in notebooks—as a regular practice—generates ideas and confidence" (2018, p. 81).

Similarly, Hicks and Schoenborn have asserted that "[C]hoosing low-risk writing invitations helps students become comfortable with the page, their thoughts, and their writing" (2020, p. 12). From the initial insights on writing notebooks offered by Donald Graves, Nancie Atwell, and Lucy Calkins in the 1980s right up to the voices of (tens of) thousands of writing teachers today, the role of writing notebooks has remained consistent in ELA teaching practice.

Even into the late 2010s, as I was teaching seventh graders, I used the good old black-and-white, marble-style composition notebooks as a way to establish a ritual and begin the school year. Students would number the pages, put their names on them, divide the notebooks into sections, and decorate the covers. It was a physical reminder of who they were, that one object would establish a student's identity as a learner—and as a writer—in my classroom.

As a space and place for student expression and experimentation, the writer's notebook always promotes low-stakes, high-interest writing. The students who don't consider themselves "writers" use a notebook space to struggle through the stops and starts of writing as I lead them through different shorter writing activities. My hope, always, was—and is—that students in my class see the value of writing as a process, an expression of identity, and a practice that leads to confidence and insight. The notebook can become an artifact, a time capsule that showcases growth, stamina, and nuance throughout the year.

In addition to building stamina, a notebook also allows student writers to rehearse their writing. I often say in class that we must read like writers—and demonstrate for them how to do that—so they, too, can mimic what good writers do. We dive into our previous notebook entries to find sentences that may need work; we tinker with them through the lens of the craft, inspired by a favorite author. There are many skills at work here. We practice sentence combining, adding figurative language and dialogue. We think about pacing and rhythm. The low-stakes daily writing passages and first drafts elevate to more sophisticated writing.

Not only do notebooks offer a place for writing process, they also provide a place to develop writing stamina. I noticed how my students' writing endurance increased with the ten-minute writing prompts I offered two times a week. My seventh graders thought of it as a game; they worked to see how many words they could write while the timer ticked down. At the end, when I told them to stop, many of them would put their pencils down to shake out their writing hands, having pushed their manual dexterity to its limit. As the year wore on, they would not shake their hands (quite) so much. Both the physical act of writing and the mental gymnastics were allowing them to think more deeply and engage more completely. By the end of the year, students could look at the history of their ten-minute writing prompts and marvel at how much more they could write. Many often commented on how much better their handwriting was, too.

And, though I certainly did not count all of the handwritten words they produced, I can say the length and complexity of their writing increased as well.

In the past students' year-end reflections of their writers' notebooks, despite the struggles they endured, were validating. For instance, to paraphrase, they would say that using the notebook was "quite cool to see" and "not so bad after all." Even though these are not direct quotes, a seasoned educator could feel their sentiments shining through.

This year, of course, the marble notebooks were never even purchased, let alone decorated and brought to school. Since our district started (and stayed) online, I was faced with a dilemma: how might I replace the marble-cover writer's notebook with something digital? What should I use? Would it work as well as my tried-and-true composition notebooks? Should I design a template or have students build one from scratch?

This then raised another set of questions: if we are all digital, what does that mean for us as we consider the kinds of texts we look to as mentors? The kinds of texts that we can create? Like Marchetti and O'Dell who remind us that "[m]entor texts are model pieces of writing—or excerpts of writing—by established authors that can inspire students and teach them how to write" (2015, p. 3), I wanted them to see their own work as mentor texts, open for revision, and to bring in examples of mentor texts from others. In the past, this involved copying and handwriting the original ideas from other authors onto the page or adding notes into the margins of their previous writing.

Notes from Troy

Mentor texts matter. When used with intention and shared consistently as a practice in our ELA classrooms, a critical and creative examination of mentor texts can lead to new insights for our own students as readers and writers. In addition to their books that inspire us to look at mentor texts, Allison Marchetti and Rebekah O'Dell— as well as an additional team of educators—have continued to share ideas about how to find and use mentor texts in their *Moving Writers* blog.

Additionally, they have a "mentor text dropbox" that they share, via Google Drive, as an accessible link. Another great source for mentor texts is *The New York Times* Learning Network's ongoing and curated collection of resources related to mentor texts.

Both links are available on the book's companion page.

At first, I was disappointed that we would lose these tactile opportunities. Yet, the longer I thought it over in the summer of 2020, the more I realized that going digital with the writer's notebook could provide students with ways to write and express themselves that a pen on paper cannot. While I will always love the simplicity of paper—and would still encourage students to do some notebooking away from their computers and smartphones—I began to realize that switching to a digital writer's notebook could inspire students in ways I never realized.

So, what do I mean here, specifically, by a digital writer's notebook? Just as there are many forms of notebooks we could choose from in the print world, there are countless ways to take notes and share them digitally. From Google Docs to One Note, from Evernote to a blog, I gave many platforms a good deal of thought before settling on something that did not immediately come to mind: Google Slides. At one level, this choice was utilitarian, as our district uses Gsuite. Still, even there, I could have defaulted to Google Docs. Yet, I wanted to move to Google Slides for a number of reasons. In particular, Google Slides allows us to easily integrate:

- Graphic design—Google Slides allows for creativity. There is unlimited flexibility to change fonts, colors, and placement of text on the slide, and there are many sites that offer additional free Google Slides templates such as SlidesCarnival and SlidesGo.

- Video—students can create and embed videos on slides, a terrific tool to express oneself that isn't offered in another platform.

- Images—while students can import photos from Google, slides also allow students to upload their own photography. Some of this is available in Google Docs as well, but the formatting and wrapping of text is so much easier on a slide.

- Revision—slides can be reordered, skipped, and duplicated much easier than other platforms.

A number of other teachers made this move to Google Slides as their tool of choice. For instance, one of our Chippewa River Writing Project colleagues, Becky Schwartz of Springport High School in Michigan, has shared many of her resources in an openly available, archived webinar. There are many free notebook-style templates available on SlidesGo. Links to both of these resources are on the book's companion website, and we will see another teacher's take on digital notebooks when we meet Tricia Clancy later in this chapter.

While I was still working over the summer to create a meaningful experience with digital writing notebooks via Google, I was reminded of one big idea from the BIT-ELA statement's Belief #3, "Technologies provide new ways to consume and produce texts." Also, I return to the first line of the preamble of the statement and consider new ideas about "what it means to communicate, create, and participate in society." Without a doubt, our students need to learn how to write for a world that continues to rely so much on computers and smartphones. Further, as the preamble argues, teachers need to "be responsive to such changes in meaningful ways without abandoning the kinds of practices and principles that we as English teachers have come to value and know to work."

Reimagining the writer's notebook as a set of Google Slides was an example of my response to that idea, which has opened up a whole new way for students to think about writing in general, and digital writing in particular. I continue to challenge students' thinking when we use the word "text." Because they often limit themselves to the idea that "text" means words on a page, I try to encourage them to see that, in reality, a text can be a sculpture, a video, a podcast, and, yes, words on a page (either printed on paper or on the web). In that spirit, moving to the digital writer's notebook allowed students to expand their own definition of writing.

As I look ahead, I believe that we will no longer be confined to pencil or pen on paper, though there are times we may still use paper for different tasks. As students form initial ideas in a digital writers' notebook, we see how examples of "writing" can be expanded. While it likely will not happen in one single ten-minute quick write, a student may grow from an initial entry into a digital story that could be embedded on a slide as narrative writing. Or, extending it even further, these initial digital jottings may lead to creating a children's book on Storybird as a form of creative writing. A screencast on Flipgrid or Screencastify can allow students to show how they can write about a process in a series of steps. While the "writing" is in video form, a script or storyboard needs to support the final product. All of these examples showcase how writing in digital spaces opens doors for student writers that didn't exist when using the marble notebook (or, at the very least, were one step away in the imagination given the limitations of format).

With all the exciting possibilities here, Belief 2 and the namesake of the book, "Consider literacies before technologies," reminds us to stay focused on the goals at hand. One of the sub-beliefs encourages us to "explore an expanded definition of 'text' in a digital world which includes alphabetic text as well as multimodal texts such as images, charts, videos, maps, and hypertexts." Yet, with all of these new forms of digital expression, there is the added layer of teaching the skills necessary for successful completion of the task. For example, if a student is creating an infographic as a form of argument writing, there are other skills that need to be taught for student success, not the least of which include some basics on graphic design. Yet another connection emerges then, as one of the sub-beliefs in Belief 3 reminds us that "[t]eachers must consider the principles of design and composition as well as the theories connected to issues of power and representation in visual imagery, music, and sound."

Also, in my current district, there is another specific connection to Belief #4, "Technologies and their associated literacies are not neutral," which ties in with the district's equity statement. We continue to make a concentrated effort to close the gap for our marginalized populations so all students have what they need to participate in a digital society. If this had not been addressed, the limitations of doing a digital writer's notebook would be monumental. For students who don't have the necessary technology to create what is being assigned, we simply would not be able to put the elements of the BIT-ELA statement into practice. In 2020-21 all students had a school-issued Chromebook that was loaded with all of the links students need to be successful in school. Students who would not otherwise have access had also been given a hotspot for their home. This level of access, in turn, provided teachers with the ability to expand literacy practices in the positive ways as one-to-one computing is now enacted.

Notes from Troy

Even with the many millions of dollars that the Coronavirus Aid, Relief, and Economic Security (CARES) Act and Elementary and Secondary School Emergency Relief (ESSER) funds provided for schools, districts, and communities, we understand that gaps in equity and access still exist. While no individual teacher—or even school district's information technology staff—can solve all the problems, there are many organizations that work to promote digital inclusion such as Everyone On, Education Superhighway, and the National Digital Inclusion Alliance which can provide additional resources. A link to each of these three organizations is provided on the book's companion page, and I encourage educators to seek out local and regional community partnerships to further digital equity and access.

While providing computers to all students is a great first step, and there are likely even more connections to BIT-ELA that I could explore, I will pause here. The initial school closures forced a significant shift in the way I viewed my assignments, so everything was going to have to be designed and delivered on a computer. I felt that the challenge of this unprecedented year would be to create assignments that offered students ways in which they could push against stereotypes and connect to the world that needed to be innovative. The digital writer's notebook, then, would be just one example of how my assignments could be re-imagined this year, and in future years. Using the belief statements to guide my thinking about the assignments I create in the future will be pivotal. What I hope will result is that the scope and design of the lessons will provide students with choice and connection to the broader world, so let me explain a bit more about how we accomplished these goals.

Putting Principles into Practice: Enacting Digital Writers' Notebooks in Jill's Classroom

Beginning the year in our Zoom classrooms, just as we would have done in physical space, each student took a marble-covered notebook—or at least a Google Slide deck with many options for building notebook pages and, of course, the first slide with a picture of a composition notebook cover—and made it their own. In addition to the kinds of "stickers" or handwritten decorations that they could have added to a physical notebook, it was also compelling to see the ways in which students found images to represent their identity from the millions of image possibilities across the web. Images 2.1-2.3 below show the creative ways in which three students "decorated" their digital notebooks. (Please note that here, and throughout the book, student names are blurred out in images and replaced with pseudonyms).

For Figure 2.1, we see Molly's notebook with a collage of images that represents her passion for family, faith, and sports, as well as her strong sense of self. To represent her confidence, for instance, she placed in the lower left-hand corner a picture of writing from inside one of her journals that says, "Don't Compare Yourself to Others." She also included images of a basketball, volleyball, and softball, as well as some images from social media that represent faith and the idea of home. She expresses her outgoing nature on the notebook cover, and I have seen this in class, too, as she acts as a leader amongst her peers.

Similarly, Amy in Figure 2.2 shows her passions for music and also represents her status as a first-generation American. As a young woman of Chinese descent, the image of the paper lanterns reflects her cultural heritage. The image of the family, with two children, represents her bond with her parents and sister. She, too, brought in a quote: "If you believe in yourself, no one can stop your victory." She also represents her love for music with images of a piano keyboard and a violin. While Amy is somewhat reserved in class, her writing and the images she chose to associate with her identity are evidence of her breadth of skills at writing and reflecting.

Finally, in Figure 2.3, we see the cover created by Holly. Unlike the first two, Holly integrated photos of herself, her friends, and her family as well as images representing her interest in flowers, gardening, and her family pets. In her initial writings, she was already sharing her outgoing—and socially aware—perspective. These ideas are represented on the cover with one picture of her wearing a face mask and another of her preparing for a performance. As it happens, she continued to write about these themes and used her informational writing project to explore issues about adolescents' mental health, a topic she began exploring in these early days of the digital writer's notebook.

With images representing everything from sports to music, pets to politics, my students were able to create their first visual composition. As we began to use the notebooks at the beginning of a year of remote learning, the students added entries much as they would a physical notebook. For instance, when I kicked off a new unit, I encouraged them to create a new section in their digital notebook, color coding the heading on the page to represent the unit we were beginning. While there were a few glitches along the way—though, it is important to note, students could never claim that they have truly "lost" their notebooks anymore—they did report that they enjoyed using the notebooks. Students could copy teacher-created slides from a day's lesson and paste them into their own digital notebook, and they could make links within their notebook to subsections in the Google Slide deck as well as to outside resources. At least one student described the experience of using the digital notebook as, to paraphrase, "something that I actually want to do, because doing it digitally makes it more organized and interesting for me."

Once these covers were complete, our first prompt was part of our identity unit to open the year. The prompt was built from Taiye Selasi's TED Talk, "Don't ask where I am from, ask where I'm a local" (link available on companion webpage) and was designed to invite students to focus on three elements that comprise their identity: 1) a single ritual, 2) a key relationship, and 3) a particular restriction in their lives. In the examples below, Paige and Bill show the three aspects of one piece of identity through both writing and visuals. In Figure 2.4, Paige describes the importance of her family through the ritual of a favorite meal, the relationships she shares with her parents and siblings, and finally the restrictions of a Jewish kosher diet. Likewise, in Figure 2.5, Bill chose to think about his identity through an annual tradition of spending summers on Lake Superior. In his work we see the daily summer ritual of enjoying sunsets over water, cherishing relationships through time spent with extended family, and the restrictions of Lake Superior on a windy day. Both of these samples show how identity is shaped and formed by family and shared experiences. By breaking it into the three categories— rituals, relationships, and restrictions—students can see that identity is multifaceted.

FIGURES 2.1, 2.2, AND 2.3: Sample Digital Notebook Covers

FIGURES 2.4 AND 2.5: Sample "Where I Am Local" Slides from Students' Digital Notebooks

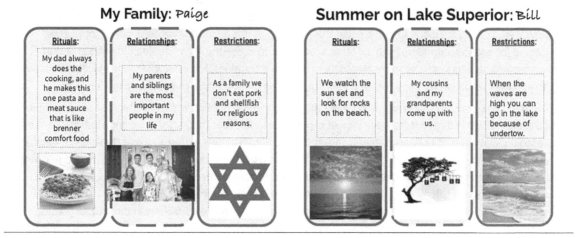

As we read through these examples taken from Jill's first weeks in this totally digital environment, it's worth mentioning one more time that these examples come from a compelling moment in history, the fall of 2020 in a remote learning situation, let alone a small moment in the progression of digital tools and literacies. As noted in our preface, we have written this book during a particular moment, both chaotic and kairotic. As this one example of Jill's use of digital writer's notebook demonstrates, the ideas outlined in the BIT-ELA document provide us with opportunity to recenter our work, to realign teaching practices that—before the vast majority of students had devices at hand, whether sitting at home or in school—felt out of reach.

And we are not trying to default to a view of pure techno-utopianism here, as we are constantly reminded of the point that Belief 4 so succinctly captures: neither the technologies nor the literacies enabled by them are neutral. Even when used creatively, Google Slides still poses limitations in terms of what it can do (let alone the broader critiques of Google's policies related to advertising and concerns about privacy). Still, we are hopeful for the possibilities that improved access to technology can offer our students, and for the possibilities that we can now imagine through deeper analysis and integration of the BIT-ELA ideals into our pedagogy.

Notes from Troy

Jill's students' use of notebooks raises some interesting questions about copyright and fair use. Is it okay, we might wonder, that they simply repurpose images from Google Image Searches into their notebook cover slides? The short answer is "yes." The longer answer is "yes, and . . ."

>

With the short, "yes," answer, I understand that many educators are concerned about the use of copyrighted material, whether their own uses of that material or when their students use that material in their own digital projects. Suffice it to say, copyright and fair use have long-been trouble spots for educators, though media literacy scholar Renee Hobbs would suggest that—so long as it is a transformational use of copyrighted material for analysis, critique, parody, or other academic purposes—the high degree of likelihood is that teachers and students can use these materials in their own creations. For more on Hobbs's Media Education Lab and their resources on Copyright and Fair Use, please visit our book's companion page for a link.

With the longer, "yes, and" answer, I would also suggest, based on Hobbs's work, that the idea of appropriate academic citation is different from the idea of copyright and fair use. That is, teachers and students have all the legal capabilities of fair use at their disposal (the "yes" from above) with the caveat that we still need, in a "yes, and" way, to cite our sources. So, it is appropriate and useful to integrate these images, though teaching students to document their sources is important. All items on the internet, including images, were created by someone and have a URL to identify where it lives on a server. So, teaching students to cite these sources—in addition to transforming them as part of their digital writing—is crucial, especially in the middle grades. In short, it is okay to repurpose existing work in a transformational manner, and be sure to cite your original source, too.

Here, as we consider ways to build community and establish norms with digital writer's notebooks, we hear how Tricia Clancy, a sixth-grade educator and fellow teacher consultant with the Chippewa River Writing Project, like Jill, used the opportunity in 2020–2021 to use these new tools to support her students as writers. She, too, values a sense of community and authentic purposes for writing with digital tools. As we close the chapter, we step into her classroom as students are using their 1:1 laptops in the midst of a writing workshop. The vignette described here took place in the face-to-face classroom, though many of the consistent themes about the importance of notebooks that Jill has already shared resonate for Tricia, too.

From the Classroom: "Digital Writer's Notebooks" by Tricia Clancy

Patricia (Tricia) Clancy has over thirty years of teaching experience. She has taught kindergarten through second grade, Reading Recovery, and middle school English language arts. Her passion for high-quality literacy education has prompted her to take on professional development roles throughout her career. She is a teacher consultant for the Chippewa River Writing Project, has presented at the Michigan Reading Association conference and the Reading Recovery Conference, was a Reading Recovery Teacher Leader, and is now working as an early literacy coach for the Clare-Gladwin RESD.

The classroom is filled with 31 sixth-grade students, but all you can hear is the sound of fingers tapping on keyboards. It's January, and the students have come to look forward to the daily routine of starting the hour writing what they choose in their digital writer's notebooks. I rotate from writer to writer checking in as they work.

"What are you working on in your writing today, Zay?" I ask.

"I'm writing about Gramps. You know, I'm trying to show how awesome he is." I quickly scan Zay's Google Slide to see what he has written in the few minutes since class began. The story of his Gramps beating him in basketball fills the screen. As I jot a note to myself that Zay has grasped the idea of writing small moments to express big ideas, I reflect on how much he has grown as a writer since September.

When we began our writer's notebooks, he was convinced that he couldn't write so he didn't even try. While his classmates wrote descriptions of what they had observed on our nature walk, he sat staring at the blank page. When I told the students that they had writing homework, Zay let out an audible sigh. "Your homework is to continue to see the world with a writer's eyes," I explained. "Come back tomorrow with an observation that you can record in your notebook. You can remember it, or you can take a picture and bring your phone to class."

Zay did his homework. He brought his phone to class and showed me a picture of his dog sleeping on his bed. I taught him how to email the photo to himself, add it to his Google Drive, and insert it into his digital notebook. Underneath the photo, he wrote: "I love my dog." It wasn't much, but it was a start.

From that moment forward, Zay wrote in his notebook every day. For a while, he simply uploaded photos from his phone and added a few words, but he was telling his story. As I reflect on his progress, I realize that inviting Zay to express himself through photos helped him to see himself as a writer.

On that January day, I snap myself out of my reflection on Zay's progress and continue conferring with him. "Zay, I can tell from your writing that you understand that one way to write about big ideas is to write small. That will really help you when we begin our poetry unit today."

Zay looks at me, eyes wide with shock. "Poetry. Ahh man. I can't write poetry."

"But Zay," I tell him, "you already have! Let me show you. Go to your 'From the Heart' section." Using the link on his table of contents slide, Zay navigates to that part of his notebook. I click through a few entries and find one that will work. "Copy this entry you wrote about the school dance and paste it onto a new doc. Now, all you need are line breaks and you'll have a poem."

"What are line breaks?" he asks. I give a quick lesson on author's craft, and we add them where he wants them. He reads the finished poem out loud. "Man, I'm good at this!" he says, beaming with pride.

"Yes, you are," I reply. "And there are more poems waiting to be discovered in your notebook," I add.

As I signal the students to finish their notebook work for the day, I think to myself, "I'll never go back to traditional notebooks." For Zay and for many of the other students, keeping their notebook digitally has made a huge difference. Specifically, they have learned how to use their writer's notebook as a tool for generating future writing. Often, with a simple cut and paste, they have a start on any type of writing. Many more students come to mind.

I think of Lily, who reads online news articles and links the most interesting ones to her notebook. She uses the articles to generate seed ideas for realistic fiction short stories.

Or Kimberly, who is researching how dresses have changed throughout history and has created a timeline complete with photos in her notebook. She plans to turn these notebook entries into a time travel story or maybe a blog about the history of fashion.

And Evan, who inserts tables into his notebook to organize the research he is doing on the connection between exercise and improved school performance. He is planning to create a presentation to advocate for middle school recess.

For these students, writing in their digital writer's notebooks is not an academic exercise; it's a way to express their passions and influence their world. As noted in the NCTE Belief statement, my students use their notebooks to "collaboratively construct knowledge, participate in immersive learning experiences, and reach out to their own community and a global audience."

And, in this moment, for Zay, his digital writer's notebook is a risk-free place to tell his story, construct his understanding of the world, and develop his identity as a writer.

Thoughts from Troy

From Tricia's classroom, we see many ways that students are, indeed, connecting to their local community and global audiences. She welcomes them to write their way into different ideas through their notebooks, ultimately leading them to actionable writing. Her students see the notebook entries not just as "bell ringers" or "warmups," but as a key component that connects to the work that writers actually *do*.

In this sense, the digital writing tools help students iterate on their initial ideas, taking those initial posts and turning them into something worthy of sharing. This is not the kind of off-the-cuff, impromptu kinds of writing pieces that end up in the majority of social media posts. Instead, it is intentional work that builds, one step to the next, as students develop their voice across genres and media, deepening their writing interests over time.

Final Thoughts from Troy and Jill: Establishing Routines with the BIT-ELA Principles in Mind

As it has been said in many other ways, the 2020–2021 academic year brought many changes to the ways that we all experience educational technologies. Whether we want to say that the cat is out of the bag, the horse is out of the barn, or the genie is out of the bottle, there is really no way to go back to previous models of thinking about technology and literacy. When the statement was final completed in October of 2018, the authors of the BIT-ELA could not have fully known the ways in which Belief 4's description—"While access to technology and the internet has the potential to lessen issues of inequity, they can also perpetuate and even accelerate discrimination based on gender, race, socioeconomic status, and other factors"—would come into such sharp focus with the calls for racial justice in the wake of George Floyd's and Breonna Taylor's murders, the 2020 US presidential election, and, ultimately, the insurrection of January 6, 2021. Technology, and social media in particular, has played a role in all these interconnected issues, and we are still only beginning to fully understand what we could—and should—be doing to stop perpetuating these problems and instead address them through critical and proactive literacy instruction. These, in turn, fuel the ways in which we set up routines and build relationships with students.

To guide further discussion and exploration, we encourage teachers to think about the following:

- How might the examples of using digital writer's notebooks documented in this chapter be adaptable in your own middle grades ELA classroom?

- In what ways can you invite students to use images as a key component of their digital writing, all the while encouraging them to document their sources with citation tools available in your school or district?

- With the caveat that controversies in the classroom are always uncomfortable (which is likely why we often avoid them) and that local contexts vary (so we need to introduce contemporary topics in sensitive yet still defensible ways), what are the kind of notebook prompts that you can use to encourage students to write in authentic ways, leading to deeper inquiry?

Chapter Three

Close Reading

Reflections from Jill's Classroom

The conversation around the text was vibrant, the kind of dialogue that ELA teachers hope for.

Students were in the midst of a close reading of Ray Bradbury's "All Summer in a Day" (1954), and we had been thinking about questions that they could ask of the text, which opens with students in their classroom on Venus questioning whether or not seven years of rain would stop and, for only an hour, they might see the sun for the first time in their young lives.

My own students had been asked to read the short story ahead of time, using the district's installation of a PDF annotation tool, Kami, to begin asking questions of the text and to identify elements of figurative language. Before we hopped into our Zoom class session, I had opened a few of the annotated documents, anxious to see if students in this virtual setting were asking the same kind of questions they might have in a more traditional setting. And they did brainstorm similar kinds of questions: Why had Margot's family moved to Venus if they knew it would be so bad? Why were the other kids really so jealous of her? What did she say when the closet door was opened?

These were good questions for getting started, yet I wanted them to explore the ways that Bradbury used the figurative language to heighten the stakes of the story and to highlight the conflict between Margot and William. So, as we gathered back together, I provided a quick overview and then moved students into breakouts, inviting them to engage in a discussion of the sophisticated uses of figurative language, beginning by sharing their own initial annotations via Kami with their classmates. Both through screen sharing on Zoom as well as with a quick link provided via Kami's interface, students were able to share their initial thoughts about "roses" and "weeds," and then make even more connections to what they understood about the typical elements in a narrative, including overall plot structure and the ways Bradbury used imagery to bring us into the Venetian classroom.

Context and Connections to the BIT-ELA Statement

This vignette played out during the early part of the school year, as students were beginning to explore elements of author's craft in the literary works we were reading. My colleagues and I were studying these stories and poems both as literary works as well as mentor texts that students could emulate in their own narrative and poetry writing.

This approach to annotation, which will be described more below, brings me back to the third tenet of the BIT-ELA: "Technologies provide new ways to consume and produce texts." The teacher's role in this, as noted in Belief 3, is to "direct students to use a note-taking tool to post text and images connected to a piece of literature they are reading in the form of a character's diary or a reader response journal." As Troy and I demonstrate in this chapter, technology can help us find new ways to assist students in the process of reading closely. Throughout this unit that focused on how to read closely, I saw students do just this, using Kami as a tool for initial commentary, followed by conversations with classmates via Zoom and in breakout rooms. With this scaffolding in place, they were able to have robust conversations about literary devices, connecting the ways that they saw authors make these moves to their own writing.

Since the introduction of the Common Core Standards in 2010, the idea of "close reading" has undergone critical reexamination and has stirred a great deal of controversy. For instance, Patrick Shannon's collection, *Closer Readings of the Common Core* (Shannon, 2013), gathered a number of ELA leaders—and critics—of the standards. In his chapter from that book, Randy Bomer connects the first writing and reading standards, noting the kinds of writing (argument) and reading (citing specific textual evidence by reading closely) at the center of these standards, arguing that these standards suggest "a certain kind of literacy practice [that] is being valued: A person is expected to read a text and then produce an original text that makes one or more references to the first textual object under discussion" (2013, p. 23). This is but one critique of the concept of "close reading," a form of responding to texts that emerged from New Critical approaches to teaching literature (Poetry Foundation, n.d.). Other scholars who questioned New Criticism included Rosenblatt's transactional reader response theory (1978), and these critiques were subsequently taken up through the broader work of comprehension and strategy instruction that invite readers to question the text in different ways (e.g., Beers & Probst, 2012; Harvey & Goudvis, 2017; Keene et al., 2007; Tovani, 2000).

Put another way, Chris Lehman and Kate Roberts define the traditional view of close reading in this way: it is "the process of trying to tune out everything else while looking at the style, words, meter, structure, and so on, of a piece of writing—letting the text itself shine through" (2013, p. 2). They go on to articulate a view of close reading that includes ideas from other scholars and educators that point toward careful observation and interpretation, as well as extrapolating ideas from a smaller chunk to the text as a whole. Again, though Lehman and Roberts—as well as numerous other ELA educators—have worked to define (and redefine) the idea of close reading to show that it can move beyond the original New Critical intention to focus solely on "attention on the variety and degree of certain literary devices, specifically metaphor, irony, tension, and paradox" (Poetry Foundation), the debate still goes on, amongst members of NCTE and beyond. Close reading remains a contested approach.

Still, even as the definition of close reading is up for debate, ELA educators must consider how they can teach students to be strategic with their reading. Since the 1980s, reading educators have made a concerted effort to articulate specific, actionable teaching strategies for textual annotation that can lead to deeper, more substantive interactions with text, some of which are mentioned above. As NCTE has noted in their many position statements, we as English teachers must make the skills of reading explicit while, at the same time, providing students with choices about what they want to read, too. In 2019, for instance, NCTE's *The Act of Reading: Instructional Foundations and Policy Guidelines* (2019b) articulates the point that teachers must

> Model higher-order thinking skills, using techniques such as think-alouds, to illustrate the range of meaning-making strategies readers utilize in the process of reading, including strategies (e.g., prediction, self-monitoring, reflection) they use before, during, and after engagement with meaningful texts. (para 19)

From general suggestions such as "forming inferences," "making predictions," and "asking questions," to more specific strategies such as "SQ3R" (survey, question, read, recite, and review), we know that it is important to model our own tactics for tackling texts and to ask students to engage in those process. One way in which close reading is described in the Ann Arbor curriculum's overall learning goals is that the "[s]tudent analyzes nuances of word/phrase meanings used in different contexts," and many lessons are centered around the kinds of comprehension strategies articulated by educators like Kelly Gallagher and Penny Kittle (Gallagher, 2009; Gallagher & Kittle, 2018; Kittle, 2013).

If ELA teachers plan to introduce concepts of close reading, then this also raises questions about the kinds of texts we introduce to our students that we choose to then have them read closely. Of course, this raises questions about the literary canon and may, in fact, be part of the reason that close reading, as a concept, remains under attack. At the time that New Criticism came into vogue, the literary canon was decidedly made up of white, male, Western authors, many of whom had been dead for decades, if not centuries. To that end, Troy and I again note that the concept of close reading—and the curriculum in which close reading is enacted—remains fraught.

Thus, all of us need to continue to look to the voices of educators and authors of color to help us reconsider the texts that we bring to our courses. For instance, mentioned briefly in Chapter 1, the colleagues who have developed #DisruptTexts who are self-described as "four women educators of color"—Tricia Ebarvia, Lorena Germán, Dr. Kimberly N. Parker, and Julia E. Torres—have argued that teachers must "challenge the traditional canon in order to create a more inclusive, representative, and equitable language arts curriculum that our students deserve" (Ebarvia, 2021; Ebarvia et al., 2018). Other NCTE colleagues have expressed similar statements through their work, including the NCTE title *Workshopping the Canon* by Mary Styslinger (2017) and *Letting Go of Literary Whiteness: Antiracist Literature Instruction for White Students* by Carlin Borsheim-Black and Sophia Sarigianides (2019). These conceptions of what it means to teach reading, to bring a critical approach to doing so—as well as the texts that we choose to share with students to support their reading—continue to change, and ELA teachers must be mindful of the work of these educators who are moving our field forward. In fact, my work with her colleagues to diversify the literary curriculum is described in more detail in Chapter 4.

The kind of close reading and annotation described in the opening vignette is just one way to experience text. Before delving even deeper into my use of a jigsaw protocol to promote close reading, it is important to gain insights from other middle school teachers on how they use technology to work with their students toward reading closely. Thus, in the next vignette, we look to another one of our Chippewa River Writing Project colleagues, Megan Kowalski, who offers ideas for integrating audiobooks as part of her reading instruction with students, including students with disabilities. Close reading, in an audiobook, is a bit different than what we experience with words on the page, and her story illustrates that point with a dose of humor, too.

From the Classroom: "Inviting Audio Books into the ELA Classroom" by Megan Kowalski

Megan Kowalski is a teacher of English language arts and mathematics to students with disabilities at Walsh Elementary in Chicago. She has been a teacher consultant with the Chippewa River Writing Project since 2009. Contact her at <kowalski. megan@gmail.com> or @MeganKowalski7 on Twitter.

It was one of those late May days. I had a large group of students from mixed middle grades with a variety of disability labels, and we were all tired. I'm a fairly serious teacher and my students will tell you: I hate wasted time. That day, we were all "tracking along" in our copies of *Ella Enchanted* (Levine, 1997), listening to the audiobook. Students had recently finished a research project on "Motte and Bailey" castles (those early castles created on mounds with ditches surrounding them) and were in the last chapters of the novel where the protagonist, Ella, has to find strength inside of herself to break a curse of obedience that has been placed on her. Ella has to put her mind to *not* obeying a command in order to break the curse. Suddenly, the chapter ended with music that seemed far too dramatic for the internal struggle Ella is facing. I couldn't help myself; I burst out laughing. My students stared nervously while I laughed too hard to speak clearly. When I regained some composure, I apologized and said I just felt the music didn't suit the end of the chapter since Ella was getting ready to find internal strength and not go to fight a physical battle.

One of my boys spoke up: "Play it again!" I did and—now in on the interpretation that I had shared—we all erupted in belly laughs.

Who knew that an audiobook could lead to this kind of shared literacy and literary experience? After an impromptu discussion of why we thought the music was funny (instead of adding to the drama, as was intended), we went deeper, talking about audience and purpose and why readers (or, in this case, listeners) might have reacted differently to the music. None of these literacy concepts or literary discussions were in my lesson (or even on my mind) when that class began. Over the years, I've had so many moments like this as my students and I read together through audiobooks. I'll never forget the student who gasped aloud during *The Outsiders* when Dallas confronts the police (Hinton, 1967), nor will I forget the student who yelled out "wait a second!" in *Holes* when Zero reveals his full name is Hector Zeroni (Sachar, 1998). None of these moments would have happened without adding the audio component to our novel studies, reading and listening together.

In all honesty, building my students into digital citizens wasn't a top concern for me when I started teaching at the middle school level in 2011; I was more worried about making them into readers and writers. However, it didn't take long for me to realize that integrating technology and multimedia texts would be a key to this. I work primarily with students with disabilities. Most of the students I get are reading well below grade level and don't self-identify as "readers." Part of my job then is to make high-quality, age-appropriate material accessible while addressing gaps in phonics, phonemic awareness, and fluency.

To that end, audiobooks became an immediate practice in my classroom. They allowed me to help students analyze and discuss texts they had the intellect to talk about and enjoy, but not the basic phonics skills to be able to read independently, without accommodations. In no time, my students loved coming to their reading block with me and were eager to read the next chapter together along with our audio version. I signed up for an Audible subscription and learned how to borrow audiobooks from the library right through my devices. I began collecting old iPods and stocking them with my most recent Audible downloads and student requests. We took a class trip to the nearest public library and each student left with their own library card and—more importantly—access to the Chicago Public Library's vast audiobook and ebook collection. Even more resources for audiobooks include Libro. fm's Audiobook Listening Copy (ALC) program for educators, as well as public domain and openly available audiobooks through LibriVox, Loyal Books, and StoryNory, as well as through district, local, and state electronic libraries with apps like Sora. Resources to gamify vocabulary learning include Kahoot!, Gimkit, and Quizlet (links to all these resources are provided on the book's companion site).

All of these experiences reminded me that there are so many ways to access text, but students may not be aware of all of the tools at their disposal. Developing literacy doesn't just mean that students are reading at a certain level by a predetermined date, but that students have the tools to solve problems, answer their own questions, and access information without support. Integrating technology into the classroom doesn't end by giving students a laptop; it is through teaching about the tools and resources that are available through this device.

Audio versions of novels that we read in class were just the beginning for me. Over the years, I've begun to dedicate more and more time to making use of digital tools to enhance what's happening in my classroom. We now use Flipgrid (now renamed to Flip) for reading fluency tracking—a much more tangible way to show students their own growth. I felt proficient in Flipgrid this fall when I began integrating it into assignments and activities, but one of my students alerted me to the filters and sticky note options, noting that "shy kids might want to blur themselves." Over the course of the year, we've all enjoyed their increasing commitment to creatively using stickers and filters, and I now offer extra credit for students who can "theme" their Flipgrid video through filters, stickers, and backgrounds to match the text they're reading. I like to ask early finishers to listen to their old videos and decide if they can "hear" their own growth from week to week. Sometimes, the movement from one Flipgrid to the next doesn't feel like much, but the students can hear the difference between a Flipgrid recorded in December and a Flipgrid recorded in March.

Similarly, Hyperdocs have become an exciting and much requested part of my practice (Highfill et al., 2016). When I created a Hyperdoc-based "field trip" to New York City, one of the students asked me where I had gotten it from and, immediately after that, "Why haven't you taught me how to make a Hyperdoc like this?" Beyond these interactive documents for inquiry, I also invite students to use platforms like Kahoot!, Gimkit, and Quizlet to "gamify" studying Greek and Latin roots and new vocabulary words. Studying vocabulary and memorizing Latin bases was not a favorite activity in my classes until we began studying online in the 2020–2021 academic year. And, though it is a relatively simple use of technology, students who finish early now ask if they can study their vocabulary cards.

In many ways, integrating technology into reading has been a journey I've taken with my students. While I'm certainly leading them down a path, when it comes to new technology, sometimes I'm not far ahead of them. This caused me a lot of anxiety at first, but I've learned to relax into it and to enjoy the moments when students themselves discover new features, add-ons, or extensions for the technology. The NCTE *Beliefs for Integrating Technology into the English Language Arts Classroom* states that students and teachers should strive to "collaboratively construct knowledge [and] participate in immersive learning experiences." My goal is to help them, or perhaps simply join them, in this process.

The most exciting part of integrating technology into my practice has also been the most daunting. Trying out tools together has given my students a sense of ownership about their place in the digital world. Given the fast-paced and ever-changing nature of new technologies, it makes sense that I'm often mastering the technology right beside my students. While it certainly isn't always easy for me, I hope I'm modeling for them how to navigate the discomfort in trying new things and letting them see that you can learn to move beyond pen and paper at any age.

Notes from Troy

Engaging students in a variety of textual forms can give them encouragement and support for deeply comprehending what they read. As Megan describes her use of audiobooks, I am also reminded of the ways that many educators use podcasts as an entry point into many topics, inviting their students to experience a compelling story in a different manner.

Whether they are just a few minutes long or in upwards of an hour, there are many ways that podcasts can connect with the ELA curriculum. A web search will likely yield thousands of ideas, yet two posts about podcasts in the classroom that could be useful include ELA resource designer Ashley Bible's "Podcasts Pairings for the Secondary ELA Classroom: Podcasts to Use in English Class" (2016) and a list from Erin Wilkey Oh, Content Director, Family & Community Engagement at Common Sense Education (2020). Both are linked on the book's companion page.

Putting Principles into Practice: Reading Closely with Technology Tools in Jill's Classroom

Given the context for teaching close reading—and my overarching goal of delivering mini-lessons that will help our students learn to "read like writers"—I will often look at mentor texts for inspiration: a poem or segment from a short story, novel, or essay. In order to achieve true mastery, a student must be able to reasonably explain why, using textual evidence, a writer made any particular choice related to diction, literary devices, sentence structure, or other aspects of the writing itself. Once I find a mentor text I then need to consider the ways that my students can use a digital tool to notice the moves: the patterns of imagery, the ways that a story can begin and end, the places where time is sped up or slowed down, or ways in which a literary device is effectively used. I want my students to notice and label where these things are happening in a mentor text, and then move into deeper analysis. There are a few tools that serve this purpose particularly well, including Google Docs and Kami.

For mentor texts that are web-based and easy to copy, Google Docs offers the comment tool, which works just fine. With provisions of fair use of copyrighted materials for analysis and critique noted above (Hobbs, 2010; National Association for Media Literacy Education et al., 2018), it is acceptable for educators to copy and paste online materials and share them in a Google Doc as a transformative use of the text for analysis and critique (though, we believe, it is important to use discretion and only choose the portion of the mentor text that students really need for context and the writerly move in lieu of an entire text). Once copied into a Google Doc, I can share that mentor text for analysis through our school's learning management system and—depending on whether I want students to do so individually or in small groups—will change the distribution settings as needed.

Notes from Troy

As we prepare to look at the way Jill moved her students through the lessons in this unit, we take another quick look at questions of copyright, already noted in Chapter 2, and this time in light of literature that has been made available in the public domain including Project Gutenberg and the Internet Archive. These texts are available for use by the general public in any way, including copying and distribution.

We offer this general advice if you are encouraging students to find texts that have been put online in a legal manner: students can copy and paste part or all of those texts into other digital tools such as Kami or Google Docs, and then use them for close reading and interpretation without any concern.

That said, we know that other copyrighted texts are available online. And, well... they may be shared, but not transformed. This raises another ethical issue: should we have students annotate and engage with those texts that are still under copyright? The answer: yes and no.   **>**

I strongly discourage people from downloading illegal copies of copyrighted material. If there is a "born digital" copy of something (like an article on a website or a portion of a book available as a preview), then yes, it is okay to use. Still, there are many materials that are copyrighted and then put on websites where users can download a PDF or other copies. In this case, the answer about annotating an online version of a text is clearly "no." There is no need to contribute to online piracy (nor to get malware or viruses as a result of doing so).

All that said, there are solutions. For texts that are copyright protected, I sometimes see educators encouraging students to, quite literally, snap pictures of a relevant passage of text using their smartphone, and then annotate that image with tools like Google Slides or Google Drawings. These are strategies that I have outlined in another Principles in Practice book that I coauthored with Kristen Hawley Turner, *Connected Reading* (2015), and with Andy Schoenborn in *Creating Confident Writers* (2020). Another educator who describes a unique strategy for annotation is Tara Martin, who popularized the idea of #BookSnaps (2016).

Another unique take on looking at copyrighted materials in a new manner comes from Tom Liam Lynch's work on *Plotting Plots* (2021). Here, he describes how "[m]ixed literary analyses introduce students to computational text analysis techniques by exposing them to the ways quantitative data about literature can deepen one's qualitative interpretations" (Lynch, 2021). This approach allows teachers and students to pull the corpus of words from many novels and, in turn, search through those books with keywords, generating line graphs to show frequencies and relationships between words. Lynch has offered numerous teaching resources, too, to describe the process in more detail. This use of these texts is, indeed, transformative, and raises even more questions about the nature of close (and, as Lynch notes, "distant") reading.

For more about the way that educators and students can employ elements of transformative use with copyrighted materials, a brief reminder from one of my previous notes is that there is a link to the Media Education Lab's resources on copyright from this book's companion page.

To avoid spending an inordinate amount of time fiddling with a PDF to format it correctly for Google Docs (or going through a file conversion service), our district has adopted a tool which has become particularly valuable: Kami. As a Google Chrome extension, Kami allows users to collaboratively annotate PDFs with a great deal of functionality for users, including a robust toolbox that allows for text, voice, and even video comments, as well as tools to add highlights in multiple colors (so students can choose a particular color for their annotations). Figure 3.1 shows how I introduce the use of Kami with a publicly-available version of the story we read together that I referenced above, "All Summer in a Day" by Ray Bradbury (1954).

Bradbury's story provides us with the opportunity for analyzing literary devices including simile, metaphor, hyperbole, and personification. In addition to being included in countless literature anthologies, the story is widely available online (which does raise copyright concerns for those who posted it originally, though makes it easier for educators to have students access, given the transformative nature of the activity; see Troy's notes above). In the past, I would have had students use the "jigsaw" strategy (School Reform Initiative, adapted from Spencer Kagan, 2017) to read a segment

FIGURE 3.1: Image of Annotated Text in Kami

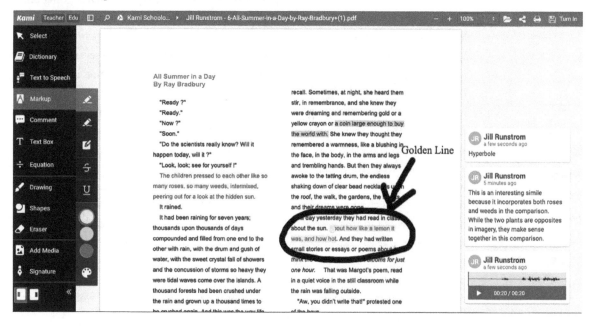

of a text and report back on what they had discovered in their reading. I have used
the jigsaw strategy numerous times in the past, both in professional development
and classroom settings. Traditionally, jigsawing is used to help a group get a broader
understanding of a longer text: each group is assigned a chapter or section of reading;
then, after discussing it in their group, they report to the whole class.

Since students already had some experience with the Bradbury story in a previous
grade, I decided that—instead of having students jigsaw the reading itself—I would
have them reacquaint themselves with the text and then jigsaw the literary devices that
Bradbury used as part of his author's craft. For this assignment, then, I deviated from
the way I had been taught to use jigsawing. Students, in this case, read the entire piece
and then each small group focused their discussion on one of four literary devices that
contributed to the author's craft: simile, metaphor, hyperbole, and personification. Each
group was tasked with a second reading of the story with emphasis on noting the places
where Bradbury used the literary device assigned. Thus, students would read closely for
a specific literary device, analyzing how the device contributed to the author's craft.

In this sense, I think it's important to give kids the experience of "the deep dive"
into analysis, a step that is easy to overlook. When giving students multiple literary
terms to juggle and identify in a reading, oftentimes we rely on our strong students
to articulate the deeper analysis through discussion or another technique to make it
seem like the "analysis box" has been checked off in our ever-growing list of teaching

points. Instead, I like to find ways for students to become literate in the author's craft by giving them small pieces to chew on, to really pull apart and explain what is going on. Jigsawing the literary devices and using Kami to have the students demonstrate their learning did that quite nicely.

For instance, even in the opening paragraphs of the story, we see several examples of simile (e.g., "like so many roses, so many weeds," and "how like a lemon it was"). Bradbury, however, doesn't present them in a one-sentence comparison or with a single item compared to another single item. Giving students time to focus only on simile, and the support of a group allows students to experience the nuance of the use of simile as well as how it can be adapted in a more sophisticated way in their own writing. When looking specifically for similes, these opening examples can be easily overlooked. Thus, when those examples are broken into chunks, students do the deeper thinking as it relates to the assigned literary device. If I had asked students to label all four literary devices presented in this lesson, some of the similes—for instance, "The children pressed to each other like so many roses, so many weeds, intermixed, peering out for a look at the hidden sun"—may be glossed over because it uses two plants in its comparison, plants that are opposite in connotation. When students looked at these examples more carefully, however, they noticed how the use of both "roses" and "weeds" work together to create a bigger kind of imagery in Bradbury's prose.

In the next section, I elaborate on the steps taken to deliver this lesson in a remote setting. As a district, we had been given a number of Google Slide templates that encouraged us to use a particular color scheme and heading format in order to help students understand what we expected of them and to maintain that consistency across all of their courses. At first, I thought this requirement was going to be confining, yet the creative constraint ultimately allowed me to focus more on content and instructional design as compared to fiddling around with countless numbers of slide templates.

Notes from Troy

Jill's use of Kami as a tool and jigsawing as a strategy aligns with a number of elements in the BIT-ELA document. For instance, as noted in the opening statement for Belief 3, "students can collaborate virtually on their reading (e.g., annotating a shared text even when not in the same physical space)" and they are attuned to the "unique purposes, audiences, and contexts related to online/e-book reading."

In so doing, she is aiming to foster "substantive discussion about issues of plot, theme, and character development." And, as the explanation about copyright and fair use above indicates, this lesson connects to the BIT-ELA point that we talk about "issues of intellectual property and licensing in the context of multimodal reading." Inviting students to interrogate a text in this digital manner offers many opportunities to think about the purposes and processes for choosing the text itself, as well as the tools.

In short, this activity, like others described in the book, is nuanced and offers a number of key practices related to the BIT-ELA, all worthy of further exploration.

Extending the Principles: Reading Closely during Remote Instruction

I started the lesson by defining the literary device terms. Using the Marzano vocabulary structure of defining the term, offering an illustration, and providing an example (2009), we jumped into our exploration of literary devices. Beginning with examples (Figure 3.2), the lesson was then shaped with additional context, introducing Ray Bradbury as an author. Next, the students were given time to asynchronously read or listen to the audio of the story. I always tell my students when looking at an author's craft to "read like writers" so they pay closer attention to the elements of the lesson we are studying for that day.

While they were reading, I put them in breakout rooms of four to have students meet first to discuss only the assigned literary device in the story. They were given ten minutes to scour the story and label all of the instances of their assigned literary device they could find. Together, they decided which example was going to be the "golden" one to share with others in the second round of breakout groups—the jigsaw. If this segment of the jigsaw protocol is done thoughtfully, the student has to become an expert for this short story in the assigned literary device before moving further along in the jigsawing process. After this first round adjourned, they immediately moved to a second breakout room where they met with an "expert" from each of the other literary devices.

FIGURE 3.2: Screenshot of Jill's Slide Introducing Personification, Using Covers from Jory John's Books, *The Good Egg* and *The Bad Seed*, blurred due to copyright restrictions. (Screenshot taken by Jill Runstrom)

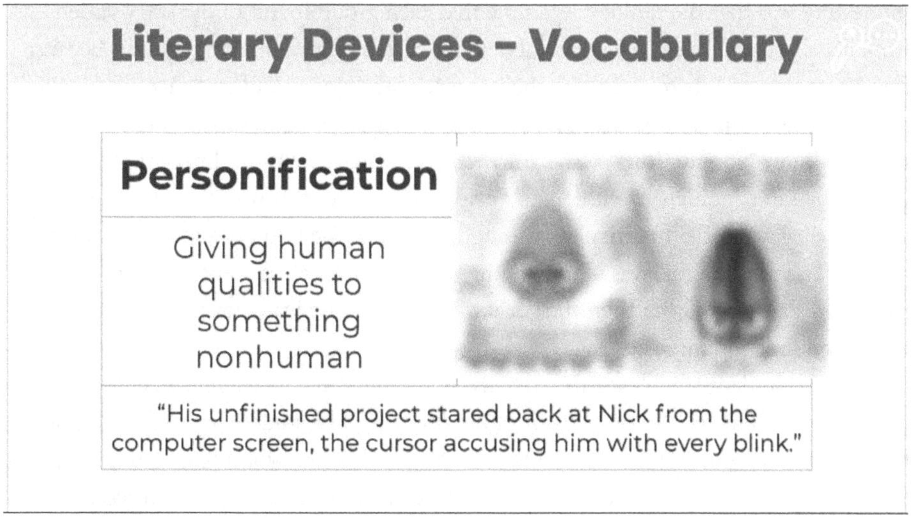

Literary Devices – Vocabulary

Personification

Giving human qualities to something nonhuman

"His unfinished project stared back at Nick from the computer screen, the cursor accusing him with every blink."

The jigsaw group—which was comprised of one of each of the members from the original literary device groups—allowed students to talk about simile, metaphor, personification, and hyperbole, topics in which they were now "experts." Together, they worked through their ideas, offering examples of the best evidence of the author's, sharing why they felt that way. Moreover, they were considering how this particular use of the literary device helped to move the story forward. This process pushed their thinking to analysis and became the "deep dive" I was hoping for. While each student did not necessarily become an expert with all four of the literary devices for this story, taking the time to really explore one literary device bolstered their confidence and continued this line of thinking when looking for literary devices in other texts or working on their own author's craft moves.

Of course, one goal of this collaboration is to bring along the reluctant students who may not have the confidence (or interest) in examining literary devices. As all teachers know, we constantly walk a tightrope between giving students complete choice in their partners/groups and assigning those groups outright. In this case, I did make group assignments both for their content-knowledge and leadership (not to mention the point that Zoom's breakout room functionality made it pretty seamless to move them into these configurations). The darker gray lines embedded in the charts on the slide below represent purposeful placement of the stronger English students. That way, I knew that there would be at least one content leader in each round of breakout rooms. While I do sometimes allow students to pick their groups, this was not one of those instances; that said, I of course deleted the bolder lines around the student names before introducing this slide to the class in our Zoom session (See Figure 3.3).

Finally, the lesson ended with a whole class share out. I was amazed at the deep thinking the students were able to employ in their analysis of this story. What I found interesting was that the "golden" example that each group found in the story varied from class to class. This is a wonderful demonstration of their literary analysis because the students were able to articulate their choice with reasons and evidence, all of which connect to the mini-lesson that launched the class session and broader themes about what we know "good writing" to be. Further, even when groups in different classes shared the same "golden" example, their evidence to support it was different. Again, because they were able to articulate through the use of their voices and connections to the text, I felt like this was a more authentic way to get all students to do the deep thinking of analysis rather than the vocal minority that typically loves to lead class discussion (See Figure 3.4).

Some students didn't see this activity as anything much different than any of the other mini-lessons we had done in this unit. However, the students who don't consider themselves strong in English indicated that they really liked working in groups first to find and label their text. The discussion to select the "golden" example required all of

FIGURE 3.3: Screenshot of Jill's Slide Introducing Breakout Rooms, with names blurred for privacy. (Screenshot taken by Jill Runstrom)

Jigsaw Discussion – Breakout Rooms

Round 1 - Meet with your literary device group. Notice and note all of the examples of your literary device in the story. Why did the author put them in the story? Which one is the best one and why? Use an **audio annotation** to explain this in your own words.

Round 2 - Meet with your number group. Take turns sharing your literary device with your group so they may note it on their copy. Discuss any overlap or duplications. Mark the "Golden Literary Device" in each category on your document. Why did it earn this? **Make an annotation** to mark the best example of each device and the reason why.

	Simile	Metaphor	Personification	Hyperbole
1				
2				
3				
4				

	Simile	Metaphor	Personification	Hyperbole
5				
6				
7				
8				

FIGURE 3.4: Screenshot of Jill's Slide Introducing the Share Out Activity. (Screenshot taken by Jill Runstrom)

Share Out

Breakout Room

Report:

- Each breakout should have a spokesperson
- Share the example of your literary device that you feel was most important and why.

them to listen and ask questions because they knew that they all would be responsible for sharing out in the next group where no one else had done the same work they had. "I like working in the breakout groups because I wasn't really confident with finding and explaining metaphors," one student commented, and it reminds us that thoughtfully scaffolded instruction and opportunities for collaboration can be powerful, even for reluctant students.

Notes from Troy

As a long-time fan of protocols—defined by the National School Reform Faculty (NSRF) as "structured processes and guidelines to promote meaningful, efficient communication, problem solving, and learning" (2018)—I often use these tools from NSRF in classroom instruction and professional learning contexts. Similarly, the Visible Thinking Routines from Harvard Project Zero (n.d.) and community build activities from Equity Unbound and OneHE (n.d.) can all be useful ways to think about structuring discussion-based lessons. Links to these sites are on the book's companion page. These can be adapted, too, for online discussion activities whether through a discussion forum, a Flipgrid dialogue, or as annotations on a document. With a little flexibility, protocols can help support a variety of synchronous and asynchronous lessons across a variety of digital tools, including Google Docs, Kami, and more.

Given these many ways that students can talk about—and experience—texts, it is worth noting that annotation on a digital document followed by discussion, in the classroom or in a Zoom room, can happen in other ways, too. Before concluding this chapter, we welcome another educator to share her insights on teaching reading. Towanda Harris describes her experience working with a group of six Black girls in an online book club. Her vignette reminds us that our uses of technology can, sometimes, put us back into a routine, one that teachers have relied on for decades. Instead, with a little listening and creative thinking, we can also invite our students into innovative approaches, presenting them with many paths to learning.

From the Classroom: "Learning Ways: A Path to Student Connection" by Towanda Harris

Towanda Harris has been a teacher, staff developer, and instructional coach. Currently a consultant and adjunct professor at Clark Atlanta University, she brings almost twenty years of experience to the education world. Towanda is the author of The Right Tools: A Guide to Selecting, Evaluating, and Implementing Classroom Resources and Practices *(2019). Her passion to elevate teachers' voices through her podcast, "My Two Cents," provides a space for educators to share their personal stories with each other. In addition, Towanda is a Heinemann PD provider, a member of The Educator*

Collaborative, an advisor for the #G2Great Twitter chat, and an advisory board member of the We Are Teachers organization.

Learning is a two-way interaction. At times, we shift to a "one-way" type of learning because of the need to share new learning quickly; however, this one-way process restricts us to simple compliance and forces us to forsake the liberation born out of two-way teaching. Dr. Rudine Sims-Bishop's work acknowledges the urgent need for books to be the windows, the mirrors, and the sliding glass doors for our students (1990), and I am reminded of a summer book club that I facilitated with a group of sixth graders with big, beautiful personalities. This book club was designed to be a virtual experience that would engage six Black girls over a period of four weeks.

For some, this was the first time I met them, so I was eager to jump right into the exciting learning that would take place and hear their brilliance. I planned for hours the perfect questions, the ideal technology platform, and the best writing opportunities. Yet, to my surprise, the first session didn't start so perfectly. You see, I was so excited to share the things that I planned that I failed first to pause long enough to connect to the very students who read the book. The structure of my class didn't center my students. My questioning, my technology platform, and my writing opportunity did not organically create a space for the brilliance behind each of the virtual squares on my screen. I was committed to being responsive to the students, so I continuously adjusted throughout the learning experience, stretching over the course of the four weeks and three sessions. Reflecting on the process, here are some of my takeaways.

One-way:
Oh, no! The "one-way" process of learning began to emerge. As the class started, I noticed that the students waited for me to ask all of the questions and naturally began to raise their hands to answer one-by-one. I slowly began to feel myself being the "sage on stage" as I began to hear myself fill the silence with my thinking. I knew that continuing with this type of teacher-centered Q & A would make our time together long and arduous. So, how could I switch it up in real-time? I introduced Nearpod to the students and decided to use it to bridge the reading to the reader (link available on the book's companion website). Nearpod is a virtual platform that aims to help educators make any lesson interactive by inserting true/false, multiple choice, and open-ended questions, among other kinds of digital activities; however, I knew that it was up to me to provide the opportunity to help the learner make connections to the lesson. I quickly created a poll that allowed students some more "think time" before responding to my questions. I was then able to use the group's responses as a guide for the direction I needed to go; however, I still wanted students to be able to dialogue and learn from each other, so this feature had its limitations.

Two-way:

Even with Nearpod, I still needed to make a hard left; the setting required a transition to a more collaborative way of learning, a "two-way" type of interaction. But how could I be responsive in my teaching so quickly? The clock was ticking! I must admit that I feared this would be a super failure that would make for a tough comeback, yet I was willing to take the risk. During our meeting times, I used a Google Jamboard (link available on the book's companion website) to create spaces where students could silently share their thoughts, comment on their peers' thinking, and connect them with their classmates by affirming similar experiences that arose. After that experience, I noticed a shift in their engagement. They made better connections with each other and were more motivated to share their learning and ask questions.

For instance, from the book we talked about the Black Panther movement and their influence on improving the community. To help students understand how instrumental they were throughout the book, I showed a YouTube video in which young students interviewed former members of the organization. Afterward, I could see their eyes widened as they began to discuss how that organization influenced the characters' actions throughout the story. This wouldn't have happened if I hadn't used technology to share other perspectives from the interview and provided a safe space for them to share their thinking. And, as noted in the *Beliefs for Integrating Technology into the English Language Arts Classroom*, I was working to "advocate for equitable solutions that employ technology in culturally responsive ways, drawing on students' and teachers' existing funds of knowledge related to literacy, learning, and using digital devices/networks."

In her book *Culturally Responsive Teaching & The Brain* (2014), Zaretta Hammond said, "[a] good number of teachers who have asked me about cultural responsiveness think of it as a 'bag of tricks.' Far from being a bag of tricks, culturally responsive teaching is a pedagogical approach firmly rooted in learning theory and cognitive science." In all of my planning, I did not consider how I could create spaces that valued their input, ways that our learning could grow together in the process, and practices that I could build on their intellect. I realized that when I planned for what I could give them—and not what we could gain together—the learning was one-way. Being responsive in my instruction—in the moment—allowed me to use technology to provide students with a safe space that welcomed their voices and valued their experiences, and as a result the learning became two-way. Students were connected to the text itself—as well as one another—in new ways, and our summer book club reminded us that technology can be a way to draw us together, even in a time of remote learning.

A Note from Troy

Like Harris, I have spent some time with Nearpod (and other similar tools), thinking about how to make the traditional "one-way" instruction into something more interactive. And, like her, with the "hard left" that she describes in her vignette, I have talked with many teachers about how—even with the best of intentions at being more engaging and collaborative—the use of a tool like Nearpod is, ultimately, a teacher-centered practice.

This is not to say that we cannot find meaningful times and places in our instruction to use Nearpod, even for what they describe as their "student-paced" lessons. It is, however, worth looking again at BIT-ELA Belief 4, in which we are encouraged to prompt conversation about "conceptual, procedural, and attitudinal and/or value-based knowledge" in lesson design and curriculum planning more broadly.

Just because we have a nifty tool that builds in some interactive components, this does not mean that we have fundamentally changed our approach to teaching (nor should we always accept broad claims about tools that suggest they will change our teaching for us).

Final Thoughts from Troy and Jill: Close Reading with the BIT-ELA Principles in Mind

For this chapter, we again recognize that the term "close reading" is still highly contested both as a framework for literary analysis based on New Criticism as well as a specific set of instructional practices that are tied to limited notions of literacy learning promoted by the architects of the Common Core State Standards. Still, this is the term that Jill's district has used to define the six-week unit, and we think that there is still some value in starting with a "close read" of a text and, as we have shown, move into additional comprehension strategies, reader responses, and interpretive lenses.

Thus, as we come to the end of this chapter—and as we will come to this point of remaining chapters—we return to the BIT-ELA statement and look at opportunities to extend and adapt the ideas presented by Jill and our NCTE colleagues. We will also provide additional resources that can support the kinds of lessons presented.

As noted in Belief 1, our goal should be to help students "collaboratively construct knowledge, participate in immersive learning experiences, and reach out to their own community" and to push students toward more nuanced analyses of "portrayals of individuals in terms of gender, race, socioeconomic status, physical and cognitive ability, and other factors." As students highlight and annotate their texts in purposeful ways, they are invited to continually rethink these portrayals and question the author's (or authors') intentions and biases.

Then, from Belief 2, we can really begin to explore "the unique purposes, audiences, and contexts related to online/e-book reading" and "explore an expanded definition of 'text.'" To some extent, we are able to even "discuss issues of intellectual property and licensing" given that students are reading some canonical texts, available in the public domain, as well as contemporary, copyrighted materials that they are examining under provisions of fair use. In fact, this kind of close reading in which students are intentionally focused on a single segment of a text is a prime opportunity to talk about transformative uses of copyrighted material as they interpret and analyze these segments of text. Also, as we move away from traditional textbooks and into digital documents, sources like Newsela, Commonlit, and Readworks are helpful for high-interest texts. Then, we are reminded—as great as web-based text is, it shifts around a lot—that sharing the texts as PDFs is easier, as they remain consistent for viewing across platforms.

With Belief 3, this series of activities demonstrates that we are immersed in "new ways to consume and produce texts" and to rethink ways that our students can "interact with both the texts themselves and with other people" as they "read, annotate, and discuss both alphabetic and visual texts, leading to substantive discussion about issues of plot, theme, and character development." The functionality of tools like Kami is, in and of itself, a powerful incentive for teachers to invite students to use them to talk with one another about the texts. These conversations don't just happen organically, however, and we are reminded that structured protocols for discussion can be valuable for scaffolding students' interactions.

And, finally, from Belief 4, we note that we must "choose technology products and services with an intentional awareness toward equity, including the affordances and constraints evident in free/open source, freemium, and subscription-based offerings." Additional tools beyond Kami that can be used for annotation of texts include Edji, Perusall, and NowComment. Additional places to get Lexile-leveled texts include Tween Tribune, Read Works, and Common Lit. Finally, additional tools that support screen reading include Read&Write for Google Chrome, Snap and Read, and Microsoft's Immersive Reader. Links for these tools are available on the book's companion website.

Close reading remains a debated term and, even though her school district still uses that term as the name of this unit plan, we can also think of "reading closely"—with all the strategies and tech tools that it entails—as an alternative. Throughout this chapter, we have worked to show how Jill scaffolds the process of close reading, still drawing on socio-collaborative approaches to learning, all the while encouraging students to engage in substantive dialogue about the text. There are many places to access free, high-quality texts in a variety of forms, and we encourage our readers to review the first tenet of the first principle in the BIT-ELA, noting that students should "collaboratively construct knowledge, participate in immersive learning experiences, and reach out to their own community and a global audience."

To guide further discussion and exploration, we encourage teachers to think about the following:

- What are the texts that you and your colleagues are "required" to teach? In what ways are those texts potentially problematic? In what ways could these texts be paired with other texts, especially contemporary and multimedia texts from diverse authors?

- Even without premium subscriptions to tools like Kami, in what ways might you be able to repurpose tools like Google Docs to engage in close reading and annotation? How might you invite them to use screencasting and screenshots?

- As you consider the possibilities for other forms of response—especially for texts that are available in the public domain—how might you ask students to create brief movies, podcasts, timelines, maps, or other multimedia to stretch their initial close reading into a more complex and nuanced literary response?

Research, Inform, Explain

Reflections from Jill's Classroom

As my students scanned the two pages, they started to discuss time-tested techniques for analyzing website credibility.

"Both are .orgs," one student noted.

"Yes, and both are really well designed with clear navigation," added another student.

As an entry point to our new unit, "Research, Inform, Explain," students had been given links to two medical societies, the American College of Pediatricians and the American Association of Pediatrics. A casual reader of each site would, indeed, agree with my students' initial assessment of the two sites.

Each one is designed effectively with clear navigation, catchy visuals, bold headlines, and invitations to click for "more information" on a variety of topics. A quick overview of each shows how my students' initial response was warranted (though, as we will see below, their conclusions needed to be investigated further). I had asked them to review both sites, looking for information about same-sex couples adopting children.

So, they began with a scan of the two sites, overall, to get a sense of what each provided, and then the conversation really began to take off.

By now, it is no secret to any ELA teacher that the internet is full of amazing, accurate, and useful content, as well as misinformation and outright lies. The two sites mentioned here bring this dichotomy into sharp focus.

Context and Connections to the BIT-ELA Statement

Teaching students to examine the veracity of websites is nothing new at this point, yet the extent to which mis- and disinformation has become ever-present online has become more and more of a problem in an era of social media. Even in this one lesson, I believe that there are many layers of complexity to unravel with the two websites being examined.

For the unit "Research, Inform, Explain," the idea is to pay attention to and utilize information that is trustworthy; the result is that the students will add to the conversation with ideas that accurately inform their readers, thus making a community of well-informed writers, readers, and citizens. This connects to a broader theme: students need to think about the World Wide Web as, well, a web. It is not a book that readers take from top to bottom, with one consistent voice. Instead, it reads like an interconnected collection of ideas. Some of those ideas are positive, useful and strong, while others are negative and not really worthy of consideration. Connecting to the BIT-ELA, Troy and I see many points of overlap between the statement and this unit, especially the goals under Belief 1 that ELA teachers "develop information literacies to determine the validity and relevance of media for academic argument" and "foster critical media literacies by engaging students in analysis of both commercial media corporations and social media."

There are, of course, other models for website evaluation, fact checking, and understanding the underlying ideologies that drive content creators (see the next "Notes from Troy" for more on this). So, as I work with my students, I boil it down to three main ideas. If students are able to look at online information and answer the following questions, then they can truly interrogate the ideas and think about what they might discover:

- Who is behind the information?
- What is the evidence for their claims?
- What do other sources say?

Based on these three questions, students will be able to begin to sort out the truths from the untruths and base their inquiry on reliable information.

Notes from Troy

In thinking about the ways that we might teach students to fact check, there are a number of resources we might pursue. Here, briefly, are just a few that are worthy of further exploration:

Mike Caulfield's "SIFT" model, in which he describes the "four moves" for fact checking that include stopping, investigating the source, finding better coverage, and tracing "claims, quotes, and media to the original context" (Caulfield, 2019).

The Stanford History Education Group (SHEG) and their Civic Online Reasoning curriculum, which aims to "teach students to evaluate online information that affects them, their communities, and the world" (Stanford History Education Group, n.d.a). They introduced the concept of "lateral reading," which we will explore more below.

And the Association of College and Research Libraries' "Framework for Information Literacy for Higher Education," which is "based on a cluster of interconnected core concepts, with flexible options for implementation" that include concepts like "Authority Is Constructed and Contextual" and "Scholarship as Conversation" (Association of College and Research Libraries, 2015).

There are, of course, other models for website evaluation, fact checking, and understanding the underlying ideologies that drive content creators. Also, it is worth noting to our students that journalists are held to a variety of professional standards, including the Society for Professional Journalists' *Code of Ethics* (2014), though going into a full discussion and analysis of journalistic standards is beyond the scope of this book.

Finally, the NCTE Task Force on Critical Media Literacy released a report in 2021 calling for five key recommendations, including the goal to "[i]ncrease the visibility of media texts, authors, and pedagogies," with the goal that there is "a more deliberate expansion" of multimedia forms across the NCTE community, as well as a "focus on the diversity of authorship practices." For more, click on the book's companion page to be taken directly to the report.

For instance, the American College of Pediatrics (ACP) website (as of the time of this writing) features a bold, blue banner and theme, with a video in the space "above the scroll" that feature an embedded video with a smiling African American boy on the image, along with the ACP logo. Their site is available at <acpeds.org>. Their slogan, "Best for Children," with the caption, "Enabling all children to reach their optimal physical and emotional health and well-being," is featured prominently. Further scrolling yields additional information about their stance on adoption, fetal pain, and ethical vaccine development, with invitations to read more on sub-pages of their own site. Images of medical professionals and children feature prominently on the page, with links along the bottom for physicians to learn about—and sign up for—membership. And, like most websites, prominent links for the "About Us," "Resources," "News," "Contact Us," and even a "Donate" button were featured in the banner. Figure 4.1 shows an image (slightly blurred for fair use and copyright concerns) of the entire homepage.

As a comparison, my students also looked at the American Association of
Pediatrics (AAP) page, as shown in Figure 4.2. Like the ACP website, the AAP
provided links for similar, standard elements such as resources, policies, membership,
and an "About" page. Their site is available at <aap.org>. With the slogan "Dedicated
to the Health of All Children" in the banner, the AAP site also features information
on immunizations, fetal growth, and adoptions, as well as other policy documents and
resources for parents. Notably, they also include a section for "Professional Education"
as well as for "Advocacy & Policy" and links to other companion sites including
HealthyChildren.org. Given the window of time in which my students were searching
the site, it was notable that information on COVID-19 featured prominently in a
banner on the homepage. With many more links present on just the homepage—as
well as links to outside resources—the AAP website provided students with a slightly
different experience than the ACP one, with many more resources and links to
additional information, both on their own site and externally.

Through their readings of the websites, students started to see some words
and phrases that they began to wonder about yet didn't have a clear way to discern
exactly *what* it was that they were finding. For instance, on the ACP page, they noted
phrases like "a healthy family environment" and "low-conflict, married mother-father
households." While it leads naturally to see how a "healthy" environment could still
be accomplished without all the elements in the second phrase, students began to ask
questions about "low-conflict," "married," and "mother-father," since these were not
phrases that they were seeing on the AAP site. Even with these phrases, students were
not quite ready to push back against the ACP site with any critical questions. In short,
it all still looked quite credible.

It was then that I asked them to open a new tab and—like professional fact
checkers who engage in lateral reading—do a Google search on "American College
of Pediatricians." Of course, the ACP webpage came up first in the listing, and a
Wikipedia entry came up in the right-hand margin of the search results. The snippet
from Wikipedia begins, "This article is about a socially conservative advocacy group . . ."
(Wikipedia Contributors, 2021). Then, students noticed another page that showed
up in second place (but no lower than third place in most of their search listings), one
from the Southern Poverty Law Center (SPLC). While my students didn't know this
initially, they came to discover that the SPLC is a group that tracks hate groups, and
the snippet from their site began: "The American College of Pediatricians (ACPeds)
is a fringe anti-LGBTQ hate group that masquerades as the premier U.S. association
of pediatricians . . ." (n.d.a.). Upon seeing these two outside sources, Wikipedia and
SPLC, my students began asking more questions, which is exactly where I wanted their
thinking to go.

FIGURE 4.1: Screenshot of the
American College of Pediatrics
website on January 26, 2021
(Screenshot by Troy Hicks , blurred to
protect copyright)

FIGURE 4.2: Screenshot of the American
Association of Pediatrics website on
January 26, 2021 (Screenshot by Troy
Hicks , blurred to protect copyright)

Notes from Troy

As it relates to the ever-increasing challenge of mis- and disinformation, there are times when we simply need to point students to resources where they can immediately see that certain organizations and websites are, indeed, not what they seem to be. As noted in the vignette, the Southern Poverty Law Center maintains a set of "Extremist Files" (n.d.b.) that can be a source to double-check the nature and ideology of groups that may appear to be relatively innocuous. Also, the concept of "astroturfing" (having a corporation or political party create what appears to be a "grassroots" organization) can cause confusion, such as the case with the "Restaurant Workers of America" group advocating against minimum wage (Thielman, 2018). Other examples can be found in Wikipedia's entry on "Astroturfing" and ThoughtCo's "What Is Astroturfing in Politics? Definition and Examples" (Longley, 2020), linked from the book's companion website.

At the heart of this unit is one key goal: asking students to discover information and to question it, ultimately helping them to become careful consumers of information. This is the context around which all of the lessons are designed. If there is anything that we have learned in an "alternative fact" or "post-truth" world, we know that it is no easy task to have students simply "derive meaning" and evaluate "the validity, reliability, and/or relevance" of any web-based source. This is challenging work, even for adults, as we are likely to give in to the whims of confirmation bias and our own echo chambers.

Thus, the application of the skills from this unit connecting to the real world is easy for them to understand. I will often tell students that they will be the generation that puts a stop to disinformation and misinformation because their careful habits of fact-checking will put a stop to it. I often repeat an important line, spoken from John Green, during a Crash Course video we watch, "The Facts about Fact Checking," from the "Navigating Digital Information" series. Green says that "[B]etter information leads to better decisions, which leads to a better world" (Green, 2019). Another John Green mantra echoed in many of his videos is the idea that the internet can be a force for good; we talk about the many positives that come from connectivity, despite the challenges of mis- and disinformation, let alone cyberbullying and other negative aspects of life online.

Putting Principles into Practice: More on the Research, Inform, Explain Unit in Jill's Classroom

To assess my students' prior knowledge, I used the sites of the American Academy of Pediatrics, founded in 1930, as well as the American College of Pediatrics, which was founded in 2002 and labeled by the SPLC as a hate group. As a quick exercise during a real-time class session, I asked students to use whatever skills they had for evaluating these two websites and to then report on which site they felt presented the most reliable information. After dropping the links to the two sources in the chat room, I provided them with about ten minutes to review the sites, yet I didn't provide any particular criteria that they should use in their evaluation.

While this may appear to be in contrast with the BIT-ELA idea that we "foster critical media literacies," this is exactly where I wanted them to be, at least for the moment. In other words, this is a "show what you know" moment, and I am aiming to create some cognitive dissonance for them. That is, while they had likely looked at some incredibly fake sites before—like the rare Pacific Northwest Tree Octopus or the incredibly dangerous-sounding Dihydrogen Monoxide (find links on the book's companion page)—my students were having trouble discerning websites that were not meant to be overtly humorous or subtly sarcastic. And, as noted above, we know that recognizing our own ideologies and seeing how those manifest themselves in different sources—like these two well-presented sites by official-sounding organizations—is tough.

After those few minutes, when they were done with their initial analysis, their comments fell in line, and students made similar remarks about each site, both by taking the microphone and dropping some ideas in the chat:

- "The website was laid out well."

- "It was easy to use and to find things."

- "They were both '.orgs,' so that means we can trust those sites."

- "Both of the sites had links to additional resources."

As my students debriefed their experiences in a breakout room conversation with their peers, they were providing their initial impressions of two websites. In many ways, the responses that they offered were quite reasonable, given their prior experiences with website evaluation checklists and what they understood about the medical profession.

In many ways, this is what I had expected. In fact, as both an ELA teacher and as a former librarian, I had taught all of the strategies they were sharing—but that was many years ago.

Looking at a website in isolation is no longer enough to make a decision about the reliability of information in today's world. There are too many amateur web designers out there who can make a bogus or radically biased website that "checks all of the boxes" for website evaluation, the same set of checklist ideas that my students were sharing in our discussion. Therefore, teaching students to look at a website on its own is not enough nor the best way to begin.

This segues to the skills behind fact-checking. Fact-checking is a habit that needs to become second nature for students; evaluating a website by only looking at the site itself is analogous to thinking you know everything about a person based on what they share on their social media. Let's face it, we share our best version of ourselves and the good things we do. Likewise, websites don't give all the information or what other people may think about it. This is a hard-learned lesson in life, though it is also something that can be taught in the context of academic research.

Therefore, students must employ the fact-checking strategy of lateral reading. As outlined by Sam Wineburg, Sarah McGrew, and their team at the Stanford History Education Group (SHEG), lateral reading can be described as the process of "leaving a site to see what other digital sources say about it" (Stanford History Education Group, 2020, n.d.b.). This process encourages students to not spend too much time on a source that seems reliable, and instead, to click open a new tab (or two) in order to read not "vertically" (on the page itself) but "laterally" across sources. Again, our natural instinct is to start at the beginning and read something vertically, from top to bottom. If you think of the World Wide Web visually as a network of interconnected sites, it makes sense that trying to evaluate what's on it by reading vertically just isn't logical. Therefore, students must break this analog reading habit and toggle between different tabs as the first line of defense for online information reliability.

Notes from Troy

The Stanford History Education Group's Civic Online Reasoning (COR) curriculum and brief video clips are a useful set of resources for exploring many of the issues described here (Stanford History Education Group, n.d.a.). Built on the research cited above, their website offers resources centered on three main questions: "Who's behind the information?"; "What's the evidence?"; and "What do other sources say?" Moreover, they have multiple iterations of lessons related to the concept of lateral reading that can lead to a deeper exploration of that skill in multiple contexts. Like other sources mentioned in the book, a link to COR is available on the book's companion website.

As we prepared to begin the unit, then, we saw that yet another one of John Green's truisms resonates: all information is created by someone, and those people have a particular perspective on the information that they are presenting. If it really were ever the case that we might find objective facts in a source like an encyclopedia, a periodical or newspaper, or a book from a reputable publisher (and it is questionable that, indeed, it ever was) it is certainly now the case that searching for information is multifaceted, nuanced, and layered. Looking at something, anything, online requires that we must examine other sources to ensure that the information is accurate. And, as the BIT-ELA statement reminds us about the goal, from Belief 1, we help students "develop information literacies to determine the validity and relevance of media for academic argument."

Over the course of the unit, many of my students were willing to rethink their previous approach to information literacy. They began to understand more about the ways that they were receiving information from multiple inputs, including social media, and to begin thinking about when, why, and how they might find more information about the news items they were receiving in their news feeds. This then connects to Belief 4, and the idea that students "promote and demonstrate critical thinking through discussion and identification of the rhetoric of written and digital materials."

As they started their work in this unit, their confidence about their own website evaluation skills dipped, based on our initial analysis of the ACP and AAP websites. After that initial mini-lesson where we had looked at the two websites together, they chose their own topics (and websites) to examine. With topics ranging from personal interests like the chemistry of baking bread and how to train a horse to topics that had a more universal appeal such as the effects of globalism and climate change—as well as COVID-related topics such as vaccines and mask-wearing—my students were able to find many different ways to research, inform, and explain.

With the introduction of the ACP and AAP websites as background knowledge, students were primed to learn more. We drew from the Civic Online Reasoning lessons, produced by the Stanford History Education Group, who note that their free, openly available curriculum is designed to "provide free lessons and assessments that help you teach students to evaluate online information that affects them, their communities, and the world" (n.d.a.).

As noted above, an interesting companion piece for the SHEG COR lessons comes from author, activist, and content creator John Green, who many of my students already knew through his books and many other media channels: the VlogBrothers YouTube channel, Nerdfighteria, and more. Another angle of his work comes through producing, and sometimes starring in, videos for the ever-growing collection called Crash Course. Founded originally as a part of YouTube's $100 Million "Original Channel Initiative," Crash Course was founded by John and Hank Green, and "transforms the traditional textbook model by presenting information in a fast-paced format, enhancing the learning experience" (Crash Course, n.d.). An opportunity to watch this video and use it as a launching point for lateral reading then led to students creating their own essays and, ultimately, infographics, as described below.

Using EdPuzzle to Prompt Lateral Reading

One particularly useful video from their series on "Navigating Digital Information" is Episode 2, released on January 15, 2019, called "The Facts about Fact Checking" (link available on book's companion page). In this video, John Green opens with the idea that the internet is a big place, and some bad things happen on, with, and through the web. While we could dwell in these negativities and ask about what can be done to fix it, he pivots to ask a new question.

Instead, the better question might be, "How can I make the Internet a more positive force in my life, and the lives of others?" and, part of the answer, I think, is that better information leads to better decision-making, which leads to a better world.

My goal was to have students pursue this question, using this video, in the context of a block-scheduled, 105-minute class session (taught in a remote setting via Zoom).

In order to do this, I decided to make use of EdPuzzle—a tool designed for building questions and interactions over an existing video—to help students dig more deeply. Oftentimes EdPuzzle is used as an accountability tool to ensure that students watch a video that a teacher deems valuable to their learning. An EdPuzzle task could easily be assigned as homework for the lesson about fact-checking; however, I made a different move. Because we teach and learn in a block schedule, one of the elements of planning is finding ways to successfully break up the time into chunks in order to allow students to engage in meaningful activities to support their learning. Therefore—both as both a break for students from listening to me and as a way to engage with the lesson content more meaningfully—I used EdPuzzle as more than an accountability quiz and instead as a tool in a key instructional moment.

Think for a moment about how we might traditionally get students to view and respond to a video like this in an in-person setting. In order to help students really chew on the information presented, in addition to enjoying John Green's quirky humor and interesting graphics, we might stop the video in key places to think, write, pair, share, or tease out important ideas by providing a graphic organizer. This is how I would slow this process down, all in order to foster deeper thought. However, because my students were at home, and so was I, most of the options I would normally employ didn't allow me the ability to guide my students through the video. If I asked them to stop, think, and write to process and organize their ideas, most of them would do this in the context of our Zoom session. However, there would also be a small contingent of students who would get up from the computer to get a snack, take a bathroom break, or pursue any other form of distraction that learning from home provides. EdPuzzle was the tool I found that would help me keep my students engaged. It provided a way for students to watch the entertaining and informative John Green while providing answers to questions at key spots of my choosing.

One way to use EdPuzzle could be to employ multiple choice questions at different spots that asked students to recall the content. While I could see that this might be useful as one kind of check for comprehension, as part of an overall lesson, I wanted my students to do more—to not just comprehend, but to connect to the information and examine their own digital identities as well as the world around them. Instead, I chose to create short answer questions with sentence stems to push students to analyze their thinking as well as slow down John Green's rapid-fire delivery. In this sense, I wanted to get students to process the information in a timely manner and monitor their thinking, so I used EdPuzzle as a way to encourage writing-to-learn in the midst of a Zoom class session, as shown in Figure 4.3.

Notes from Troy

Though a truism about video length and student engagement has been shared often as a part of teaching lore—one minute of video for students at that grade level (e.g., six minutes for a sixth grader)—it is difficult to know exactly how long any one video of any length will keep any particular viewer paying attention. A first grader, for instance, is likely to pay attention to more than one minute of video just as a senior in high school could tune out way before the twelve-minute mark. The goal of tools like EdPuzzle, then, is to force students to engage with the video. On the one hand, this is good instructional scaffolding.

On the other hand, an EdPuzzle activity, too, can be a distraction. With so many interruptions, learning could be disrupted. To that end, it is also worthwhile to share a link to the video so students can, if they choose, watch it all without disruption. Particularly useful for that task are sites like VideoLink (formerly "SafeYouTube") and SafeShare, which allow you to generate a URL for a video that is shown in a clean viewing space, with no ads, autoplaying of more videos, or extraneous links.

On the book's companion page, you can find links to these tools.

FIGURE 4.3: Screenshot of a quiz question in EdPuzzle (Screenshot by Jill Runstrom)

🔲 OPEN-ENDED

Respond to <u>ONE</u> of the big ideas presented so far:

1. Is the Internet a net positive or net negative in my life and the lives of others?

2. How can I make the Internet a more positive force in m life and the lives of others?

3. What does, "better information leads to better decision-making, which leads to a better world" mean to you?

Write a 2-5 sentence response.

Sentence stems to start my thinking:

I see the Internet as ...

While the Internet is viewed by many as _____, I think that _____.

I think the quote in number 3 means...

As we talked about this question shown in Figure 4.3, one student shared that he felt the internet was a positive force in his life by keeping him connected to his friends. His family had recently moved back to Ann Arbor after a two-year stint in Germany, and he still had many German friends with whom he wanted to keep in touch. The way this group of kids decided to do that was to have an established Saturday every month where they would play video games together.

When thinking about how better information leads to better decision-making, which leads to a better world, another student responded:

> This [quote] is saying that if you use the internet to find good, credible information then you as a person will know more and understand the world around you better with those correct facts. This will then lead you to make better informed decisions instead of guessing. This will then lead to a positive impact on the world based on real information.

As a reminder, John Green features the ACP and AAP websites in the Crash Course video, and I did not want my students to just glance over those quickly without interrogating them. I connected the websites the students had evaluated before watching the Crash Course video in order to activate their prior knowledge. Since they had already spent some time looking at and thinking about them and the information they provide, I then used EdPuzzle to continue their evaluation of the sites.

Then, when John Green presented the main ideas of website evaluation, I used EdPuzzle to pause the video and to give students time to think about it. For example, when John Green states that a good fact checker knows who is behind the information, I asked students to open a new tab and revisit the ACP and AAP sites to see if they could find the names of the authors who presented the information. What they should deduce is that all of the information in the conservative ACP site is created by the doctors who belong to the ACP. When they stop and look at the AAP site, what they realize is that additional, reputable agencies and medical practitioners are supporting their claims. As mentioned earlier, these two sites are visually appealing and well organized, so it is this deeper dive into what is presented that offers students the ability to conclude that the information on the ACP site is strongly conservative and biased in the information that it presents.

EdPuzzle also allowed me to engage them in a deeper form of lateral reading. As the video continued, the questions I created in EdPuzzle had students return to the two medical websites to test the strategy of lateral reading. As John Green presented his three big questions all fact-checkers use to validate information, I had EdPuzzle stop the video and ask students to employ the fact-checking skill on our two pediatric sites. The three questions good fact-checkers ask are as follows:

1. Who is behind the information?

2. What is the evidence for their claims?

3. What do other sources say about the organization and its claims?

As students worked to evaluate both the AAP and the ACP for the answers to these questions, they ended up opening new tabs on their computers instead of spending time reading the sites themselves (See Figure 4.4).

FIGURE 4.4: Screenshot of a quiz question with feedback in EdPuzzle (Screenshot by Jill Runstrom)

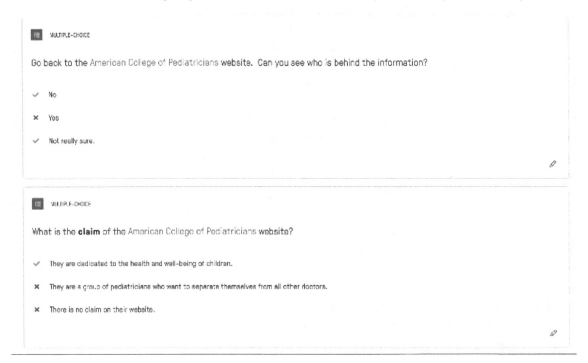

The teaching move, then, was to inspire students to think critically about what reading means while online. Using the two websites as touchstones allowed me to create pauses in the Crash Course video that then provided me with pivotal formative assessment data in the following areas:

- What is a student's view on the internet's impact on their lives and the world around them?
- How might I supplement students' thinking about the internet—as a force for good and a student's role in contributing to that—in subsequent lessons?
- What strategies do students use in evaluating a website's credibility?

Also, of note, I used EdPuzzle to monitor their engagement during the lesson—this was more than a "gotcha" kind of check in. This was the equivalent of walking around the room, in real time, to check on students, as shown in Figure 4.5.

FIGURE 4.5: Screenshot of a teacher dashboard in EdPuzzle, showing student progress (Screenshot by Jill Runstrom)

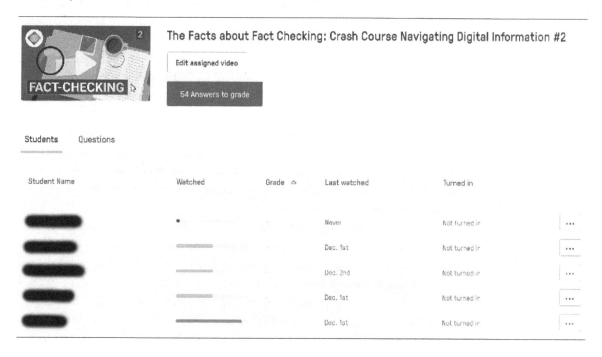

As always, my students teach me more about their thinking and the context of their world by using examples; they shared how they use the internet, as well as ways they could limit their internet use to benefit themselves. One student offered this:

> I can make the internet a more positive force in my life by being responsible with how long I use it. Also, I can limit my daily screen time to make more time for things like completing homework, practicing soccer, and spending time with family. I can make the Internet more positive for others by checking up on them daily.

What the EdPuzzle questions during the video did was scaffold this new idea for students to show them that their initial claims about the websites being organized, easy to navigate, and visually pleasing really did nothing to add to their credibility. Those comments were generated from vertically reading the websites. What the students discovered is that when a site seems like something that will work for their research, a good fact-checker does not invest much time reading the site, at least not initially.

Instead, when a site seems viable to student research, the student should open a tab or two laterally on the computer and visit Google, Wikipedia, Snopes, FactCheck.org, and other sources. Validating the reliability of an online source by using lateral reading saves students time when researching. Juliana, a student in my class, was able to quickly assess the two practice sites and responded, "Wikipedia says that the AAP site was flagged that it reads like an ad. Does that mean that they pay for its good reviews?"

Another student, Ben, discovered in Wikipedia that the ACP is "a socially conservative website." Further, Wikipedia states, "For the professional association of pediatricians, see American Academy of Pediatrics." After reading this, Ben concluded, "The AAP is the more reliable source because it is referenced as *the* professional organization for pediatricians. The ACP is only for pediatricians with conservative views." If they had this skill at the start of this lesson, they would have quickly discovered the bias of the ACP in its ultra-conservative views and may have abandoned it as a reputable site.

This process organically opened the door for interesting conversations about bias. What students realized by analyzing the two websites using lateral reading is that bias is present in everything they read. What they need to decide is if the bias makes the information unreliable or not useful for their research. I talk with my freshman students about the differences between what they learned in middle school and how freshman year is a transition from middle school thinking to a more nuanced, sophisticated understanding and application of the skills they already have. This lateral reading lesson allowed them to see that there is so much more to online information than making judgements about a .com versus a .gov website, or a website's readability as a measure of validity. While those ideas may have served them in the beginning stages of research, by ninth grade students need to start thinking: "What kind of information am I looking for to support my claim? How will I know when I find something online that supports my thinking as well as holds up to the test of lateral reading?" In short, this approach helped them move beyond a simple checklist to understand that, in the end, every source has a perspective.

In sum, the use of a digital tool like EdPuzzle during my class allowed for my students to test the strategy of lateral reading in the moment it was presented. John Green's fast-paced style was intentionally paused at key spots so when Green asked "What do other sources say about the organization and its claims?" students were allowed time to implement and process that part of fact-checking to prove its worth. Just listening to the video presents the information without time to apply it and using EdPuzzle allows them to synthesize the knowledge they just learned.

Notes from Troy

As noted earlier in the chapter, simply having students move through a checklist to determine a website's credibility does not—as Jill demonstrates here—help them thoroughly compare and contrast the ways that various sites employ multiple forms of persuasion in order to get their point across. Indeed, this kind of deeper, more ideological work is what we are aiming for in BIT-ELA Belief 4, where we want to "promote and demonstrate critical thinking through discussion and identification of the rhetoric of written and digital materials." As we will discuss later in this chapter, there are sites like AllSides, ProCon, or media bias ratings that can help students begin how to understand the ways in which these ideologies are at play across various media, yet it is an ongoing conversation that requires an open mind and critical thinking to fully understand.

Moreover, Jill's skillful adaptation of EdPuzzle for an in-class, formative activity makes the use of the tool especially unique. Like reading, we can assign video viewing, though we don't know that students will fully engage. In some ways, this is the reason EdPuzzle exists: to ensure engagement. That said, there is little social purpose in completing multiple choice questions on your own. In this lesson, Jill approaches EdPuzzle from a different angle, and lets students know that their engagement with the video will immediately come into play in their class discussion, adding at least some level of motivation for doing the EdPuzzle in the first place.

From Lateral Reading to Composing an Infographic

Once students had made progress on lateral reading, it was time for them to put that skill to use in their own research. When planning information writing tasks for students, I try to give them as much choice as possible. It's been my experience that students create a better product when they have choice and a vested interest, much more than if I were to assign the whole class one topic. In order to help students find and narrow their topics effectively, I rely on a technique I adapted from Kelly Gallagher's *Write Like This* where students take large, broad topics of interest and turn it into 18 topics more suitable for a school writing assignment. According to Gallagher, "The 1 Topic = 18 Topics chart works with any topic and has value in that it enables students to see the various angles from which a writer may approach a topic" (2011, p. 13). The adaptation made for our middle grade students was to take a broad topic and turn it into six inquiry questions that tie into the different modes of information writing.

To help my students make the transition into writing their essay, I began with the idea that students would first create an infographic. To help them get started on the project and to organize their infographic, one of my colleagues—Alaina Feliks— developed a graphic organizer for all ninth graders to use. I then provided them with a link to this as an assignment in Schoology, our classroom management system, so students could begin to explore a general topic by transforming it into six inquiry questions. As our interpretation of the Gallagher assignment noted above, Alaina made the graphic organizer in such a manner that it centered on creating inquiry questions.

To model this process for students, I created a mentor text on the topic of the COVID vaccine (this lesson was being taught in December 2020, just as the vaccines were becoming available). There was so much transpiring as this unit took place, so the vaccine questions were easy to formulate. My colleague Alaina had provided her own example of moving from a topic into a set of inquiry questions and—during our Zoom class sessions—I was able to model my process with the topic of vaccines. The results of our group brainstorming and modeling session is also shown in the Hyperdoc in Figure 4.6, which included many resources for students, including a screen recording in which Alaina modeled the process for students.

As students came to the end of the brainstorming, they explored infographics as a form of digital information writing. From there, students chose the best inquiry question for the task. The highlighted question, in pink in Figure 4.6, is what I decided to explore as I created an infographic alongside my students. I was focused on the "How-To" or "Describe the process of" modes of information writing, arriving at the inquiry question of "Who will get the vaccine first and how is that decided?"

During a subsequent class session, after students had created their research questions using this graphic organizer, they started thinking about moving the answers to those questions into a visual representation through the form of an infographic. Again, I was aiming to have them write an essay, of course, yet wanted them to visualize the information first. This move required them to consider the kind of research that would be required to answer the question as well as how to translate this answer into a visually appealing image. For instance, as I modeled the process for them—based on my question of "Who will get the vaccine first and how is that decided?"—I used Piktochart to generate one segment of an infographic showing the order of vaccination (Figure 4.7).

One of the ways that I decided to visually represent numerical data I

FIGURE 4.6: Screenshot of a Hyperdoc lesson for the "Research, Inform, Explain" unit created by Alaina Feliks (Screenshot by Jill Runstrom)

Select a big topic and write it in the box below

COVID Vaccine

Here is a video demonstration of how to do this.

Mode	Essay Topic
Definition **What makes X, X?** *Infographic Example*	How are the COVID vaccines different from traditional vaccines used in the past?
Classification **What are the types of?** *Infographic Example*	Are the different companies that are coming out with a vaccine producing drastically different vaccines?
Cause **Why do we...?** *Infographic Example*	Why do we need a vaccine — can't we just let COVID run its course?
Effects of **What are the effects of?** *Infographic Example*	What are the side effects of the COVID vaccines?
How-To or Describe the process of.. **How to do X?** **How does X work?** **What is the process of?** *Infographic Example*	Who will get the vaccine first and how is that decided?
Compare and Contrast **How are X and Y the same?** **How are X and Y different?** *Infographic Example*	Which company's vaccine is best for people? Easiest to distribute?

found about the rollout of the vaccine was to create a chart. Within the Piktochart interface, there is a way to enter spreadsheet data. While not all of my students chose to do this, I felt like it really helped me understand what information was important for me to display as well as make the moves necessary. My goal was to create the kind of graph that would easily make sense to the reader. In addition to the chart here, I also modeled for students how to compose a meaningful paragraph describing the data in each image and its importance. I was, in a sense, shaping the answer to my question—in words and through the chart—to make it clear and specific.

For instance, in this version of my paragraph, a "rough draft" of what I would then model for students and transition into the full essay, I shared the following:

> We have lived with COVID-19 at the forefront of our lives for ten months. The vaccines are coming, so we are all excited about the idea of life regaining some sense of normalcy. The problem is we all cannot get vaccinated at once—there aren't enough vaccines to go around. So how does our country decide who goes first?

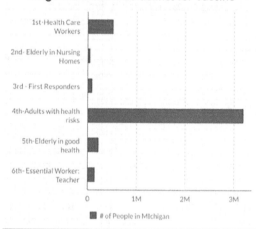

FIGURE 4.7: Screenshot of a sample infographic for the "Research, Inform, Explain" unit created by Jill Runstrom (Screenshot by Jill Runstrom)

This paragraph, of course, didn't fully explain the data in the chart, yet it was enough to demonstrate for them how they could extend the ideas around their research question and begin to make connections. From there, students also had to describe their decision-making as it related to the design of the infographic. They looked at information that was relevant and talked about what "relevant" means in the context of presenting info both graphically, as well as in writing in their essays. Also, I reminded them that they should get facts and statistics from reputable sources and that their infographic should represent the most accurate data that they had at the time. As shown in the examples below, there were some great connections that students made, first writing something in their essay and then making a connection to the idea in their infographic.

Notes from Troy

In this use of Piktochart, Jill is taking advantage of a key feature that may, in some ways, be overlooked. That is, with a built-in spreadsheet for data entry and manipulation, infographic tools like Piktochart, Infogram, and Easel.ly actually allow us to create both the "info" and the "graphic," and to do so as more than just a glorified poster. In fact, I would argue that we *must* have students enter data into a spreadsheet, building both their literacy and numeracy skills.

For more on infographic creation, a web search will yield many tutorials and ideas. For even more inspiration, the site Information is Beautiful offers countless examples of infographics on relevant topics. Also, ReadWriteThink offers "A Picture IS Worth a Thousand Words: Using Infographics to Illustrate How-to Writing," a middle-level lesson by Kathy Wickline. Links to both are available on the book's companion website.

First, in Figure 4.8, we see Sarah's example of plastic in the ocean and effects on marine life. In her essay, Sarah wrote about the idea that marine animals can be negatively impacted by this debris and, in her infographic, she chose images that would convey this message in even more direct terms. With icons of a turtle stuck in a bag, a plastic bottle inside a dolphin, and a laceration on the side of a fish, Sarah was able to make a compelling visual argument that accompanied her words. While she didn't add specific statistical data in her infographic, she did make her claim stand out in clear, if not stark, images.

In a similar manner, we see DeeAnn's example of the number of power plants present in the United States as of 2019 in comparison to their overall output (Figure 4.9). In her writing, she is making an argument for the necessity of nuclear power, especially given the fact that the small number of plants produce a significant and consistent energy output when compared to other sources. In her infographic, which was constructed in a series of "Pros" advocating for nuclear energy as well as a few "Cons," one segment puts the information from the writing into a broader context. Here, with two images, she shows the total percentage of nuclear energy in the pie chart (~20%) in relation to the total number of nuclear plants (<100). This makes her point that nuclear energy provides a major source of America's power and stands out in a visual form.

Students were then invited to write a reflection about the process of writing their essay and the infographic, comparing and contrasting the processes that they went through. The prompt for their reflection was "What do you notice about the differences between your infographic and your essay and the purpose each serves?"

In response, both Sarah and DeeAnn had insightful comments about the process. Sarah noted:

> The infographic is for an audience who are looking for a quicker way to get information. It's more fun and engaging. As writers, we don't have

FIGURE 4.8: Segment from Sarah's essay and image from her infographic about the effects of plastic on marine life. (Permission granted by student and parent)

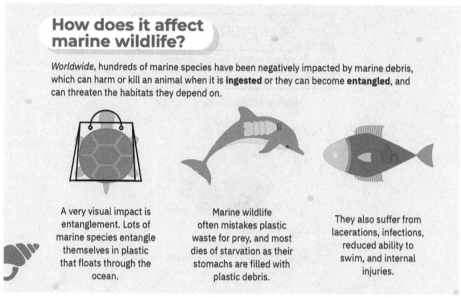

How does plastic in the ocean affect marine wildlife?

Worldwide, hundreds of marine species are adversely affected by marine debris, which can be harmful or even lethal when an animal ingests it or is entangled in it. The most visual and frightening consequences of marine plastics are the ingestion, suffocation, and entanglement of hundreds of marine species. Marine wildlife often mistake plastic for prey, and most die of starvation as plastic debris accumulates in their stomachs. These animals can also suffer from lacerations, infections, reduced ability to swim, and internal injuries if they become entangled in plastic debris. Additionally, floating plastics contribute to the spread of invasive marine organisms and bacteria, which disrupt ecosystems. For these reasons, it is increasingly important to keep plastic out of the ocean and make a better environment for marine wildlife.

much work to do. We have to research facts, but we don't have to write out paragraphs because an infographic shouldn't have long blocks of text. On the other hand, the essay is for an audience who are trying to get a more thorough and deep understanding of the topic. We have to do much more work in this part because we need at least five or more fully formed paragraphs. It's also a challenge for us to make the essay appealing because people have a harder time remembering words compared to simple graphics, like those in our infographic.

FIGURE 4.9: Segment from DeeAnn's essay and image from her infographic about the effects of nuclear energy. (Permission granted by student and parent)

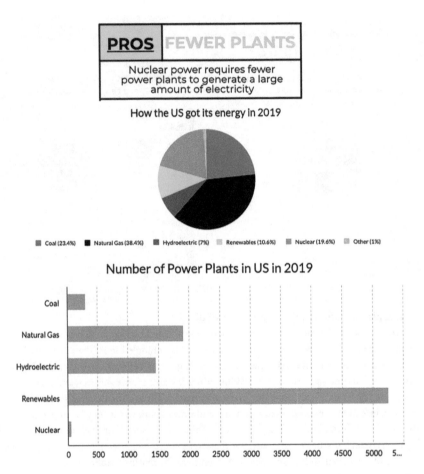

The argument for nuclear power gets even stronger when nuclear is compared to its contenders, like solar, wind, and hydroelectric power. One major problem with renewable energy is that they can't constantly produce power. Solar arrays can't produce power in the night, and wind turbines can't produce power when it isn't windy. On the other hand, nuclear plants produce power year-round, except for when they have to undergo maintenance. (Rhodes). In fact, data from the US government's energy report shows that nuclear plants were fully operating for 92.4% of the time, in 2019. In the same year, solar arrays operated for 24.3% of the time, wind turbines operated for 34.3% of the time, and hydroelectric dams for 41.2% of the time ("Electric Power Monthly: Table 6.07.B"). Even coal plants only operated for 47.4% of the time. ("Electric Power Monthly: Table 6.07.A."). If countries shut down nuclear plants, like many activists say they should, renewables wouldn't be enough to give everyone constant energy. Coal and gas plants would have to be run for the rest of the time. Some suggest using massive batteries to store energy to use, but that isn't close to possible with our current infrastructure. Nuclear power is necessary since it's not only efficient but also reliable.

Also, DeeAnn believed that:

> One difference that I notice between my infographic and my essay is that
> my infographic uses much less writing and more visuals, and my essay uses
> only writing. I notice that my infographic serves the purpose of giving
> information and guiding the reader through that information with visuals
> and graphics. It is meant to be easier to read because there isn't as much
> information thrown at your face all at once; it is more spaced out and
> accompanied by a visual that represents the information. I notice that my
> essay serves the purpose of informing the reader about my topic through
> writing and presenting reliable information.

As the unit came to a close, I asked students a "chicken or egg" style question: Which
should come first, the infographic or the essay? Though certainly not a scientific poll,
the comments in Zoom chat and from those students who took the microphone to
speak suggest to me that we might have actually been better off to have written the
essay first, transitioning to the infographic, rather than starting with the infographic as
we did this time. As with all teaching, I continue to learn with my students, and this
feedback will help make improvements to the next iteration of this unit.

Notes from Troy

I deeply appreciate Jill's process of moving students recursively from infographic to essay and back again in
this unit. As I noted in *Crafting Digital Writing* (2013), "With digital writing, we need to think with words, of
course—yet we also need to begin thinking like artists, web designers, recording engineers, photographers, and
filmmakers" (18–9). The intentional choices that she and her colleagues made align with part of BIT-ELA Belief
3, where they were able to "investigate their stance on social issues through the multimodal inquiry methods"
as well as demonstrate the process as digital writers themselves. In this sense, they thoughtfully scaffolded
their students in an entire digital writing process, making the most of the two primary forms of media—text and
graphs—in their efforts to create both the essay itself and the infographic.

For even more on infographics, please explore the book I've written with Jeremy Hyler and Wiline Pangle on
these ideas: *Ask, Explore, Write! An Inquiry-Driven Approach to Science and Literacy Learning* (2020 Routledge/Eye
on Education).

Before moving into the conclusion of this chapter, we look again to an ELA
colleague to see additional ways for engaging students in research. There are any number
of possibilities that we might explore, as well as stances toward project- or problem-
based learning that we might employ. This is, however, not just something that we bring
to our students as a one-off idea, something to simply try quickly and then move on.
This kind of teaching takes time and intention. Here, Blaine Smith offers ideas for
expanding inquiry through digital multimodal projects in her "Project Imagine the

Future (Project IF)," showing us possibilities for how this kind of work can be nurtured over time.

From the Classroom: "Project Imagine the Future" by Blaine Smith

Blaine Smith is an associate professor in the Department of Teaching, Learning, and Sociocultural Studies at the University of Arizona. She is also the co-director of the Digital Innovation and Learning Lab in the College of Education. Dr. Smith's research examines bi/multilingual adolescents' digital literacies across contexts, with special attention to their multimodal composing processes. Her research also focuses on developing scaffolded instructional strategies for supporting teachers' integration of technology in diverse classrooms. Her work has appeared in Reading Research Quarterly, Research in the Teaching of English, Written Communication, *and the* Journal of Literacy Research, *among others.*

During the Project Imagine the Future (Project IF) summer academy, a small group of middle school students brainstormed how to effectively integrate visuals, sounds, and text into the conclusion of their science fiction (sci-fi) narrative, "A Turtle Tale":

> Claudia: At the end we can have a part called "Our voice!" Like a call to action ... humans can save cute turtles together.
>
> Brian: Sounds great!
>
> Claudia: We can explain a little bit that sea turtles are in danger.
>
> Rachel: We can have pictures to show that.
>
> Claudia: Also, some music to show something in danger? Like a nervous music?

Claudia, Brian, and Rachel's final multimodal sci-fi narrative detailed how a sea turtle traveled in a spaceship back in time to Earth to enlist the help of humans in saving his species from endangerment. They interwove written narrative with photographs of sea turtles and their habitat, Pixton comics depicting key events, sound effects, and music into a creative and engaging interactive flipbook that was shared online.

Project IF was designed to support young adolescents in developing disciplinary expertise and identities while working with peers to create multimodal sci-fi narratives. It connects to the NCTE *Beliefs for Integrating Technology* by providing opportunities for middle school students to explore local socio-scientific issues through multiple modes, connecting to the principle that we "design assignments, activities, and assessments that encourage interdisciplinary thinking, community and civic engagement."

Co-developed with Ji Shen at the University of Miami, Project IF involved multiple iterations as a summer academy for middle schoolers and a sixth-grade elective course. The culminating project for Project IF was a sci-fi narrative constructed through multiple modes (text, visuals, sound, and animation) and digital formats (e.g., hyperlinked text, Scratch animations, Pixton comics, infographics, and interactive flipbook). Situated in Miami, Florida, many students participating in Project IF chose locally relevant climate issues to tackle in their sci-fi narratives, ranging from global warming, sea-rise, flooding, to superstorms that have impacted their local community. The project challenged students to choose a relevant socio-scientific issue to explore and suggest solutions through their narrative. Socio-scientific issues are controversial, ill-structured social problems with multiple solutions and perspectives (e.g., decisions on practices and policies related to climate change).

During Project IF, students participated in a scaffolded workshop sequence (Smith & Shen, 2017). First, we provided disciplinary sessions to learn more about various socio-scientific issues, including web-based science units, hands-on activities, and field trips (e.g., university science labs and botanical garden). Second, students read and analyzed sci-fi mentor texts to understand the genre and gain inspiration for their own narratives. Students then learned principles of multimodal design and how to effectively use various modes for different purposes and audiences. Third, students participated in a variety of sessions where they learned from "experts"—ranging from practicing scientists to sci-fi authors, filmmakers, and professional game designers. Fourth, many sessions included a short tech tutorial where students learn how to use new digital tools or programs such as Pixton, Scratch, and MovieMaker (note that MovieMaker is no longer available as a program for Windows 10, and the Photos app has taken its place).

During the multimodal composing process, students developed individualized roles within their collaborative teams to complete their multimodal sci-fi narratives. On the first day of workshops, three main roles were presented for students to potentially represent: 1) the scientist could contribute by integrating all scientific content into the project, 2) the writer developed the narrative, and 3) the designer created the multimedia for the story. To promote interest-driven composing, we wanted students to have the freedom to select which digital tools and online programs they used for creating their projects. Students also shared their sci-fi narratives with multiple audiences. They participated in peer workshops and in-process presentations to gain feedback on their work at different stages. Students' final projects were shared with a broader audience; they were posted online, and students presented their work at a local sci-fi film festival.

We found this type of multimodal composition offered students unique opportunities for leveraging their interests into their digital narratives, as well as demonstrating creative solutions for climate issues. For instance, one group explored issues of climate change through remixing the powers of Disney princesses in their written narrative and comics. Other creative solutions ranged from using giant sponges to sop up water to save people in the path of a tsunami to designing a machine that could generate oxygen to combat increased carbon dioxide from burning fossil fuels. The communicative freedom offered through multiple modes allowed students to share their work with authentic audiences and express themselves in a variety of meaningful, creative, and individualized ways.

Notes from Troy

Project IF, from its title to its implementation, invites students to ask critical and creative questions, further emphasizing the ways in which they might take up digital literacy practices in their own lives and communities. Even when introduced through elements of science fiction, it is clear that Smith and Shen's students were taking aim at real-world issues. Moving even further beyond the idea that they would see their ideas represented in digital spaces for school-based projects, these students were moving toward action.

There are likely many opportunities to connect to our colleagues in Social Studies, whose College, Career, and Civic Life (C3) Framework encourages students to take "informed action" and our colleagues in the STEM fields who, similarly, are looking to have students design solutions to problems. In nearly any content area, the connections between the BIT-ELA principles and other standards can be a way to help encourage more dialogue both amongst students who are involved in the projects as well as with colleagues who are helping to plan them.

Final Thoughts from Troy and Jill: Researching, Informing, and Explaining with the BIT-ELA Principles in Mind

As we look ahead at other ways to structure the "Research, Inform, Explain" unit and design other opportunities for students to share their work with a wider audience, it is important to remember that the infographic elements of this assignment were not an add-on, a bonus for students to do just to have fun or take a break from the work of writing. Indeed, they were writing their essays and composing their infographics at the same time, and this reciprocal process was meaningful for them to test out new ideas and put them into action, both in words and image. Connecting back to the BIT-ELA statement, we are reminded that we can help students, as in Belief 2, "explore an expanded definition of 'text' in a digital world." In this sense, they were creating the visuals for the infographic while then preparing to put ideas into sentences, paragraphs, and their final essay.

With the adaptation of EdPuzzle, we can see ways to take content-rich and fast-paced John Green Crash Course videos (and others of similar style that will catch students' attention and are full of great content) and allow the teacher to insert metacognitive questions to promote comprehension and deeper analysis. Again, connecting to the BIT-ELA, we see ways to repurpose tools, like EdPuzzle, that go beyond their "fixed uses" and encourage a more creative approach for helping students engage with, comprehend, and then utilize what they have learned from viewing what otherwise would have been a fast-paced and entertaining—though perhaps not immediately applicable—video. In other words, we needed to help students pause long enough in their viewing and comprehension of the video to make it stick, and EdPuzzle—when used to provide strategic questioning—allowed them to do just that. Moreover, this could be created as a lesson that students could do in the classroom, too, perhaps with a thinking partner to discuss and then answer the questions.

As an extension, we can imagine using a variety of additional resources to help students explore contemporary—and potentially controversial—topics. For instance, *The New York Times* has an ever-growing list of argument writing prompts (Gonchar, 2017), and KQED offers a variety of youth-oriented media on "The Lowdown," though it is not being updated (KQED Education, n.d.b.) and their ongoing video series, "Above the Noise" (KQED Education, n.d.a.). We also look to sources like AllSides, ProCon, Kialo EDU, and Gale's Opposing Viewpoints in Context database for opportunities to explore different topics (links available on the book's companion website). By introducing topics to students in a way that encourages debate and dialogue—rather than just jumping in to do an initial Google search and agreeing with the first result—students are able to adapt the process of lateral reading from the get-go.

And, while it was valuable that we did the infographic and the essay together at the same time, we could have looked at other informational modes, too. Returning to Kelly Gallagher, he suggests that the critique/review genre can be a powerful option for students to write when exploring, informing, and explaining. Also, Barry Lane provides a number of alternative genres that could have provided students with different options—from "top ten" lists to wanted posters—in his book *51 Wacky We-Search Papers* (Lane, 2003). Depending on exactly what our goals for the unit might be tweaked and adjusted to in any given academic year, providing students with these different genres to write in (and then represent in their infographics) could have also been useful.

Thus, as we complete the "Research, Inform, Explain" unit and prepare for our next steps, students are primed for deeper discussions about source reliability. Moreover, they had a new set of lateral reading and fact-checking skills to, as John Green reminds us, make better decisions that can, in turn, make a better world. They would need these skills as we made the transition to literary analysis, which we take up in Chapter 5.

In an era where the phrase "doing my own research" has taken on a negative, even sarcastic, tone, and where individuals (our middle level students as well as adults) have taken to the web to find answers to life's simple challenges and more complex societal problems, ELA teachers need to reaffirm their commitment to teaching the research process in critical and creative ways. This involves more than simply finding existing documents, websites, or other materials and doing fact checks, though this is a part of the process. Instead, as we have shown here—and see in the vignettes from our colleagues—we need to embrace a research process in which students become active knowledge constructors, employing surveys, interviews, and other qualitative and quantitative methods, and moving into the role of being youth participatory action researchers (Mirra et al., 2015).

To guide further discussion and exploration, we encourage teachers to think about the following:

- As you consider your own media and information literacies, where might you feel that you are most able to recognize mis- and disinformation? What sources are ones that you typically trust (and why)? Where might confirmation bias lead you as you consider the intersection of your own cultural, religious, gender, racial, community, and educational backgrounds?

- Given the many challenges that are being presented in American communities during school board meetings and at the ballot box, how will you open opportunities for—and maintain expectations for—civil dialogue? As students engage in the research process, when and where in that process might you anticipate moments where you will need to provide more time and space for conversation?

- As students prepare to share their research with broader audiences, what additional opportunities might present themselves for digital writing? Along with infographics, what other multimodal compositions could be appealing for your students? What kinds of mentor texts might you need to find to provide as models?

Chapter Five

Reading Literary Texts in Substantive Ways

Reflections from Jill's Classroom

As I hopped into my third breakout room conversation during the second period's literature circles, the group leader was skillfully facilitating their work.

"Thanks, Jed," said Isaac. "That's a really good point. I see that Ben put something in the chat, too, so let me read that."

Though the vast majority of our time in Zoom rooms had, so far, been spent with cameras off, the two weeks students spent in literature circles provided a refreshing change to synchronous classes. As a district, Ann Arbor Public Schools made the choice during virtual learning to offer literature circles in place of whole-class novels. While I had some experience with literature circles, planning and thinking about how to best deliver them had me working again with my Skyline ninth-grade TLN. As teachers, we had talked about what books to offer and a theme they might have in common; this approach would provide all students with an element of choice coupled with a common theme that could be discussed across all of the selected titles. As we worked through the planning stages, we returned again and again to the fear we all shared that having students meet in groups would be a giant failure. How will we inspire them to turn their cameras on? Will there be lots of issues with video lag and audio cut out? Will the introverts participate at all? We had already shared our frustrations about getting students to talk to us; how would they fare when left for long periods of time in a breakout room together to talk about their books?

Still, we moved forward. The students selected their books and groups were formed. As the breakout room literature circle meetings began, the ninth-grade teachers collectively held their breath and crossed their fingers. Each literature circle meeting allowed time for students to share their notes taken while reading and preparing to talk together. Additionally, groups were given a common task to complete as it related to the section of reading assigned. While students were in their breakout rooms, I would drop in and out of all of the rooms to monitor what was happening. I predicted that I would have to inspire, cajole, and require that kids talk to each other. What happened instead was really wonderful.

Each group had its own personality—some with all cameras on, some with half on and half off, and only a select few that didn't turn cameras on at all. As I stayed and listened to the conversations, I realized that Zoom provided a way for all of the students to participate in the modality that was comfortable for them. For example, one neurodiverse student, Ben (a pseudonym, as all students' names in the book are), who isn't very verbal, used the chat function to add his ideas to the conversation with his group. This group had a student who led the conversation and monitored the chat. When Ben added a comment, the group leader would read his contribution aloud, giving him a way to make a positive addition. This group inspired me in their creative use of Zoom's breakout rooms to offer all group members a way to be part of the conversation. If this group was doing the same activity in person at school, the outcome likely would have been much different. Ben would have most likely sat quietly, and if prompted to talk by another student, there would be a large lag of silence as Ben collected his thoughts and struggled to verbalize them. Most likely, the students would have moved on with the discussion out of empathy for Ben, not wanting him to struggle any longer. Ben's contribution would never be heard and his feeling of being different from the others would be magnified even further. Instead, the Zoom breakout room allowed a space for conversation in a different way. What the ninth-grade teachers expected compared to what really happened in many groups were two very different outcomes.

What we, as teachers, learned from Zoom breakout literature circles was that students really wanted to be together and talk to each other. This was the closest thing they had experienced to in-person interactions since they left their school in

March of 2020. In so many of the breakout rooms observed by all the ninth-grade teachers, students were excited to talk to each other, turn their cameras on, share their screens, and work collaboratively on the tasks assigned to them. What we couldn't predict was the impact of the technology, specifically the Zoom breakout room features, to reach those students who are less verbal and outgoing. They liked literature circles too, and the Zoom space allowed them a new way to participate that was a comfortable, hybrid form of in-person discussion. The students embraced it, and literature circle discussions became one of the more rewarding experiences of the virtual classroom—for everyone.

"So, Ben says that…" Isaac began, and the group's dialogue continued.

Context and Connections to the BIT-ELA Statement

Defining the work of "literary analysis" is challenging for all English teachers and especially for those of us teaching in the middle grades. As my ninth-grade students continued moving from understanding the basic elements of literary form, they were also working to understand that the stories, novels, plays, and poems they read can be interpreted in many ways. Helping them to see that there are many lenses through which they can elaborate on their initial, close readings (as shared in Chapter 2), most ELA teachers can agree that the shift from these initial, somewhat superficial literary interpretations into a deeper analysis is challenging work.

And, while they don't come along very often, there are times I know that the above ideas are resonating when I get an email from a student like this one:

Dear Mrs. Runstrom,
I was just looking at your feedback for my MASTERY analysis on *The Glass Castle* and was wondering if I would be able to make those changes you suggested before I put this piece in my Mastery Portfolio? I'm not as satisfied now with my analysis and feel that I want to make some changes.

This email not only warmed my teacher-heart, showing me that my student wanted to improve the analysis of Jeannette Walls's memoir (Walls, 2006) but proved to me that students do have the potential to make great progress when a series of skills is taught through the lens of analysis. In some ways, I could argue that all of the writing and reading done in my class allows students to practice the process of literary analysis. This leads to portfolio pieces that go in a student's mastery portfolio that is created using Google sites; the mastery portfolio showcases student work from each of the units we study that are considered examples of mastery. Of course, students know that they can take these assignments and revise until the mastery standard is met. In order for students to meet the mastery standard for literary analysis—explaining how the structure of a text impacts the meaning of that text—their writing must show that they understand the text and use the skills learned throughout the unit to support their claims about the author's craft.

The student who wrote me this email is also exhibiting the habits of mind needed to do this kind of difficult work. Ann Arbor's district rubric for literary analysis states that the following habits of mind should be examined during this unit, drawn from the *Framework for Success in Postsecondary Writing* (Council of Writing Program Administrators et al., 2011): curiosity, openness, engagement, creativity, persistence, responsibility, flexibility, and metacognition. The student who sent me the email regarding her writing is showing mastery of the skills we practiced for literary analysis, while at the same time she is demonstrating the habits of mind necessary to be a successful writer. Unlike the many emails I get asking for clarification of something I already stated in class, this email was diving into the learning and labor of good writing—a great joy for any teacher to see realized. It was my pleasure to reply to this email, which provides a good way to jump into the unit.

Notes from Troy

Though there will be descriptions of a "literary analysis" unit that Jill notes throughout the chapter, this phrase—one that ELA teachers have used for decades—is not in the title of this chapter. As we reflected on the notion of "literary analysis," we realized that we wanted to embrace the BIT-ELA statement's idea that we should be "moving beyond historical conceptions of literature and composition in more narrowly defined, text-centric ways." Thus, we revised the working title of this chapter many times, finally landing on "Reading Literary Texts in Substantive Ways."

This, then, begs the question: what do you mean by "substantive ways?" First, we would respond to that by returning to the BIT-ELA, noting that the document still outlines many aspects of what we would look for in a typical study of literature, including an analysis of plot, characters, and theme. Moreover, the idea of "substantive ways" asks students to annotate and respond to texts in an ongoing manner (and not only through an essay), instead inviting them to develop new interpretations through options like a "photo essay, a timeline, and an interactive game." And, as this chapter demonstrates, Jill was able to embrace these multimodal options as students were invited to choose a book for their literature circle and then create responses in media as varied as book trailers, podcasts, and even Spotify-style playlists.

We have many opportunities to engage students in substantive reading practices, especially when we offer them choices in what they read and how they respond.

Putting Principles into Practice: More on Reading Literary Texts in Jill's Classroom

The literary analysis unit while teaching remotely provided many interesting challenges that technology helped solve.

First was access to books. Prior to teaching online, most teachers selected a whole-class novel, and used it as the text for analysis. With a physical copy provided for each student from our school's book depository, the whole-class novel allowed students to have a copy of the book to carry with them during the unit. Through whole-class discussion and other activities, the skills of analyzing good literature were established. During remote instruction, though, things had to change. Because no teachers or students had access to the buildings or the books inside, a different access point to books was offered through Sora: an ebook library paid for at the district level. Due to the cost associated with purchasing the number of digital copies necessary to provide a whole-class novel to over 400 students, it was decided at the district level to instead consider an alternative; thus, the online literature circle unit was born. Because teachers planned as collaborative teams, the timing of literature circles was the same for all ninth-grade teachers. Consequently, teachers did not flex the teaching of literature circles—we all taught the literature circle lessons on the same schedule. Budget concerns aside, there were many teachers in the Ann Arbor Public Schools who used literature circles in their classrooms prior to this pivot, and they served as mentors and advocates for the rest of us. Our district English department spent many meetings learning about how to effectively teach literary analysis through literature circles.

Notes from Troy

In addition to the subscription services that Jill's school was able to provide, there are times where access to even these subscription services can be limiting. Though not guaranteed to have all the contemporary literature that Jill and her colleagues provided for their students via Sora (listed later in this chapter), state electronic libraries often do contain links to provide their own residents with access to collections of digital books.

Michigan, for instance, offers students free access to a number of premium services with ebooks such as Britannica School, EBSCO, Explora, Learning Express, and NovelList Plus. While we can only attest to what is available here in Michigan, a list of "State Electronic Libraries" curated by the Tennessee State Library and Archives is available on our book's companion page.

And, while it may be difficult to find some texts after searching across multiple ebook collections, it could be a worthwhile endeavor to curate your own "digital bookshelf" using a tool like Wakelet or Symbaloo (also linked on the book's companion page).

The second challenge in our learning path was how to get students talking about books, uncovering necessary literary elements, and doing the work of analysis when the whole class was not reading the same text. The collaborative team that I planned lessons with decided that we needed a series of "Big Ideas" to explore that would serve as lenses through which students could process and analyze their literature circle novel—whatever that novel was. All of the books chosen for this unit had these big ideas among them:

- Community—as will be explored a bit more below, the topic of "community" emerged as a major topic with questions about group belonging, perspective-taking, and being an outlier, all coming from my students.

- Intersectionality—as students thought about the many communities to which they belong and identities that they inhabit, they began to think about the overlaps and, sometimes, the contradictions present in these connections.

- Hyphen-Americans—as students think about people who descend from immigrant families or immigrate themselves from another culture, they explored ways in which people feel embraced—and sometimes rejected—in American society.

These big ideas helped students activate their own schema, allowing them to have meaningful conversations with each other about their books in their literature circle groups as well as whole-class discussions.

The third challenge was the dilemma of how to get students to work in small groups when we were all in different spaces and only together online. The use of Zoom and its breakout room feature was a terrific technology tool to aid in this process. Zoom allows the teacher to create group spaces that can be monitored by the teacher. The teacher can join and leave a breakout room using the functions provided as the host of the Zoom meeting. Additionally, students in breakout rooms function independently from the large group Zoom class; they can request help from the teacher by clicking on a request function provided to breakout room participants. The assigned breakout room feature worked really well during the lessons the students had literature circle meetings. What this means is that the teacher, as Zoom host, can assign the student names to groups and save them for future group work. Creating 5–7 groups per class while students are waiting can take up to five minutes. The assigned breakout room allowed the teacher to create the groups outside of class, one time, which allowed students to transition from the whole-class Zoom meeting to their small literature circle groups with no lost instructional time.

Once the students were in the breakout spaces, they were given questions to discuss as well as group activities to complete. At first, this all seemed strange because so much of what I do as a teacher is based on what I observe in the classroom. For example, when students work in groups while in a face-to-face environment, I learned from walking around: listening to conversations, observing group members' body language, and chiming in with questions to move group conversations forward. It happened easily, and I observed many groups of students at the same time. Thus, breakout rooms in a digital space felt awkward at first. I gave the students directions for the literature circle discussion time, answered any questions students had, and clicked the button to open the breakout rooms. What I was used to in the face-to-face classroom was noise and movement as students would physically put themselves in groups and begin their group discussions. In the digital classroom, students took the breakout room invitation that pushed to their screens, and in the main Zoom space, I was alone. I was left with a black screen and no students to observe. "What are they doing?" I wondered. This was the exact opposite of what my experience taught me is supposed to happen, so I had to adapt. What I learned was that technology provided some really powerful tools for students to read and discuss a novel in literature circles.

Here's what I did: I gave the students a few minutes to get started, and then I dropped in to listen to what was happening in the breakout room discussions. Gone was the ability to eavesdrop from nearby because my presence was announced to the students with a tell-tale "doorbell" sound as I joined their breakout rooms and turned on my camera. What I witnessed, though, were students taking leadership roles by using the technology provided to them. Most literature circle meetings would include an activity that the group was responsible to work on together. Effective groups would often have one student share their screen to allow everyone else the opportunity to see the Google Doc or slide deck that was involved in the activity. Oftentimes a scribe, either a volunteer or (often) someone elected by the group, would be the screen sharer so everyone else could see what was being typed. This allowed them to write as a group, offering revision suggestions on the fly. Students reported that this was a meaningful activity by telling me, "I liked it that someone else shared their screen. I don't feel comfortable doing that myself, but it really helped me see what we were doing in real-time." Other groups would share the group document so every group member could have "editing" access to the assignment. I also saw students helping each other during the discussion time. One student would lead the discussion, and group members were allowed, through the features of Zoom rooms, to participate in different modalities. Most students participated by unmuting their microphones, turning on their cameras, and talking to each other. This was what I expected all students to do because it closely imitated what we all remembered from the face-to-face classroom.

What I didn't expect was the discussion leader using the chat feature that allowed the students who don't feel comfortable speaking in a group to offer their input in a different way. This was powerful. These were the students who in the traditional face-to-face environment were underperforming—contributing to discussion only when prompted or not at all. In this digital environment, introverted students had time to think about what to say and compose it in the chat space. I also had a few students, one or two in any given class, who had connectivity issues that they overcame by leaving their camera off and microphone muted. Participating in the chat allowed these students to still contribute while conserving precious bandwidth.

Another interesting way that I monitored student discussions was through group recordings—a tool offered to students while in a Zoom breakout room. Students were responsible for actively participating in group discussions of the text. Most of the time they were given broad questions to consider that revolved around the "big ideas" that were talked about earlier. A discussion leader was elected by each group, and that person would record the discussion, making sure to read any comments offered along the way in the chat. This allowed me to confirm that all groups were productively engaged in the discussion, something that I used to do by observing and eavesdropping in the face-to-face classroom. The recordings also served as an archive of the students' evolving understanding of the novel and its themes. Additionally, the recordings could be linked to students' digital portfolios as evidence of mastery for this unit.

All of the aforementioned examples were not planned or expected; instead, they evolved through the students' collective curiosity about how to use Zoom as a learning tool. What we all discovered was this unit and the small group discussions in literature circles turned out to be many students' favorite unit for the year. Zoom's breakout rooms allowed students to talk to each other and share the labor of the unit in ways that a traditional classroom cannot offer.

Many of us began teaching and learning remotely with a touch of skepticism, believing that learning online would not benefit students in the same ways that the tried-and-true traditional classroom did. However, as this unit in particular progressed, what I learned was that technology can create new ways of learning—especially for those who felt marginalized in the traditional classroom. The best part was watching the students learn how to do this for themselves and each other.

Notes from Troy

We recognize that when it comes to breakout rooms—no matter how much we might try with team-building activities, protocols for discussion, or expectations to contribute to a Google Doc or other shared space—not all students will be willing or able to participate. As we consider the reasons when, why, and how we might expect students to participate (and they may not be), I am reminded of Maha Bali's blog post from June of 2020, just as many emergency remote teaching situations were coming to an end, entitled "About That Webcam Obsession You're Having . . ." (Bali, 2020). In her piece, she posits that "I am assuming having camera on is mainly a proxy for engagement," and then goes on to offer a number of reasons why students may choose not to participate (including personal reasons or a slow internet connection), as well as other ways to engage students during real time, video-based class sessions.   **>**

For instance, Bali suggests that we ask questions and provide time for students to respond in the chat. Here, too, some students may be quick to respond while others are still thinking/typing, so we can use a strategy called a "waterfall of chat" or a "chat fall" where everyone types their response, yet then waits for a countdown before posting (Dinwiddie, 2020). That way, everyone has a chance to finish their message, and then all messages are posted at once so they can be read and interpreted at the same time.

Bali also encourages the instructor to be judicious about when and how they use the recording function. Certainly, one of the advantages (and, sometimes, necessities) of working with Zoom or similar video conference tools is that sessions can easily be recorded for students who must miss for any number of reasons. That said, the red "recording" light blinking on screen does, without a doubt, change the dynamics of the class sessions, sometimes for better and sometimes for worse. So, breakout rooms are certainly a space where students could enjoy a more open conversation without the recording going on in the background.

Finally, as we think about the ways to best engage students in conversation during a video chat, sometimes the best methods are the ones that we can adapt from face-to-face settings. The classic "draw a name," especially the "draw a name written on a popsicle stick from a coffee cup" is one way to invite students to talk. There are some software programs that help with this, built right into a learning management system or other app. Similarly, the free and openly available Flippity.net, created by a teacher and educational technologist, Steve Fortna, has a "random name picker" tool that can be customized in different ways, including the option to choose a single name or put students in a "line up," where they will see their name coming up in a list.

No matter how educators work to build interactivity into real-time video class sessions, we need to remember that there are times where students (just as they might in the face-to-face classroom) choose not to participate. As we think about productive and proactive ways to engage students in dialogue, I am reminded of BIT-ELA's Belief 4, noting that "While access to technology and the internet has the potential to lessen issues of inequity, they can also perpetuate and even accelerate discrimination based on gender, race, socioeconomic status, and other factors." For those reasons, we need to be mindful of when, how, and why we invite our students to participate with cameras on (or not), and to be creative in our approaches to breakout room conversations.

Beginning the Literary Analysis Unit: Building toward Literature Circles

This unit began with a pretest, based on a student's reading of one of *The New York Times* 100-word "Tiny Love Stories" in which students were asked to analyze the theme and structure of the piece. I learned from my reading of their analyses that they did need some intentional guidance through a process of examining text structure, something we hoped they could learn through literature circles. We relied on the ideas outlined in the BIT-ELA of ways to integrate digital writing opportunities within the study of literature. Specifically, Belief 3 contends that we should "ask students to repurpose a variety of digital media (e.g., images, video, music, text) to create a multimodal mashup or explore other emerging media genres (e.g., digital storytelling, infographics, annotated visuals, screencasts) that reflect concepts in literature such as theme, character, and setting."

So, the two mastery standards the students worked on are the following:

- Literary Analysis—Mastery Standard: Analyze how an author's choices concerning how to structure a text, order events within it (e.g., parallel plots), and manipulate time (e.g., pacing, flashbacks) create such effects as mystery, tension, or surprise.

- Speaking and Listening—Initiate and participate effectively in a range of collaborative discussions (one-on-one, in groups, and teacher-led) with diverse partners on grades 9–10 topics, texts, and issues, building on others' ideas and expressing their own clearly and persuasively.

As noted in the opening vignette, it is challenging to ensure that students are reading and comprehending text at an initial level where they can summarize and recall important details from the story. Pushing them into literary analysis—though they are familiar with the concepts of simile and metaphor, personification and symbolism, and more—is difficult. As their brains are moving from a more literal interpretation of the world in the text to a perspective that can allow for abstract thinking, we need to be mindful of the skills students need to practice that will aid them in analysis. As the unit progressed, I frequently showed before a mini-lesson that included what had already been covered, and the focus for the day. As the unit went on, the lists got longer and longer as students built a literary bag of tricks. By the end of the unit, the slide included a full set of skills and big ideas (as shown in Figure 5.1).

In addition to skills like looking at structure, pacing, and plot elements, students also considered some of the "Big Ideas" (or, in more literary language, the "themes") in their thinking and discussions. Students were asked to notice themes that developed throughout their books on the topic of "community." In addition, they were asked to keep track of perspective: the author's, the characters', and their own. Each is a complicated element that makes reading the same book a community-building exercise as well as eye-opening experience as students consider perspectives different from their own.

As stated in Belief 1, we know that literacy means *literacies*: "Literacy is more than reading, writing, speaking, listening, and viewing as traditionally defined. It is more useful to think of literacies, which are social practices that transcend individual modes of communication." Our work around the "Big Ideas" we presented to students thus supported this idea. Through the social practice of a small learning community within the class (literature circle groups), students were able to explore and think about issues of race and perspectives that, I believe, would have been difficult for me to explore in a teacher-led classroom.

One compelling moment happened during a full class discussion about the "Big Idea" of being a "hyphenated" American. Students had been sent to Zoom breakout

FIGURE 5.1: List of Skills and Big Ideas in the Literary Analysis Unit

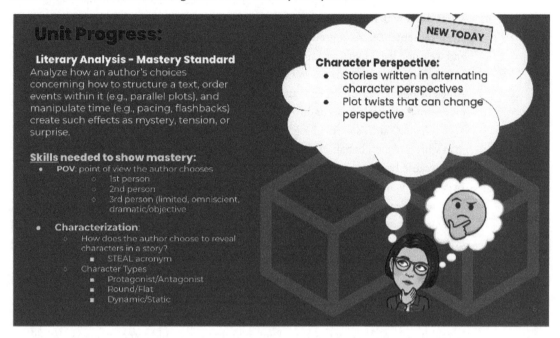

rooms to watch an assigned video from a *New York Times* project called "Hyphen-Nation" (Ross Smith, 2017). Each video offered a different perspective regarding communities of people that get "hyphenated" in America and what being American means to them. Before they went to breakout rooms, students were told that when they returned to the main room, their task would be to share their experience of watching one of the nine videos, using the "word, phrase, sentence" protocol from Harvard Project Zero (linked on the book's companion page). This protocol asks students to identify at least one word, phrase, or sentence that stood out in the video they watched.

Notes from Troy

"Hyphen-Nation" was produced by Bayeté Ross Smith, whose website describes him as "an interdisciplinary artist, photographer, filmmaker and education worker, working at the intersection of photography, film & video, visual journalism, 3D objects and new media." A link to his homepage, from which these quotes are drawn, is available on this book's companion website. His portfolio includes a number of additional projects including "Our Kind of People," a project that "examines perception based on appearance and deconstructs how clothing, race, gender, and class signifiers affect our daily interactions and social systems," and other film and virtual reality projects (Ross Smith, n.d.).

For instance, some groups reported that they had to watch parts of the video multiple times to get the proper wording of a sentence, and some even joked a bit about the way that they worked to discern the difference between just a phrase and an entire sentence. Most groups were able to identify at least a few words or phrases, and we came back together for a full class discussion. Then, they began to share their impressions. The group that watched an African-American man named Jason was struck by one powerful sentence that he spoke: "Here in this country, I am a Black man—first—American second."

Given that this particular group was comprised of all white students, the young man who spoke on behalf of this group said that Jason's sentence was so powerful for him because he had never thought of this perspective from the eyes of a Black man. Because he is white, the idea of skin color and gender as a threat to one's identity have never been an obstacle for him. What I found so genuine and compelling in this student's response was the way he shared his thoughts with such awe and honesty, drawing directly from Jason's spoken words in the video. This, in turn, opened space for the "hyphenated" students to offer more about their own experiences.

After this first group, the door was open for the other groups to genuinely share what was compelling to them from the stories they viewed. The group who watched Wendy's story were surprised when she described her experience as an Asian American in middle school. Wendy was teased and told that she would someday marry the only other student in the class who was also Asian American, for no other reason than they were both Asian. It was through these stories that my students began to recognize the effects of prejudice and implicit bias and how we all have it.

What I told my students is that it is not bad to have implicit bias—it's human nature—yet we can learn to overcome it with practice. We all need to know and recognize what our implicit biases are and mentally take note of them when one creeps into our thinking. As each group shared their word, phrase, and sentence, gathering perspectives from a different person on the "Hyphen-Nation" website, the students talked about perspective and bias and how it shapes our thinking. Across all of the stories, students heard a common refrain: "Where are you from?" This phrase, too, echoed in so many of the stories on the "Hyphen-Nation" website that were similar to the stories that my own hyphenated students described.

With this lesson, we can see just one example of how my students—like many other middle grade readers—continue to try on new perspectives and literary lenses, learning how to think critically and carefully about the texts that they read/watch, as well as the responses that they offer. Having a website like "Hyphen-Nation" is a powerful example of how technology can present texts in a new way that can't be re-created in an analog environment. As we consider the complexities of Belief 4,

"Technologies and their associated literacies are not neutral," we can see how a site like "Hyphen-Nation" can "provide exemplars of technology use for educational equity that expand beyond gender, race, and socioeconomic status to include mental health, ableism, immigration status, exceptionality, and (dis)ability."

The short video vignettes provided students the ability to understand the role of white privilege in American society and identify the ways in which people are marginalized. For students of color or those facing marginalization in other ways, the video vignettes provided a way to see their stories in ways that they might not have the courage to express on their own. There are many great print texts available that students could read, but the video texts allowed students to hear the emotion and see the expressions of the people featured. As evidenced by the student who confessed, "I never thought about this before," the power of video engaged my students in ways a printed text could not. My students used this as a mentor text and then pushed their thinking further through their group discussions and analysis. The "Hyphen-Nation" video lesson paved the way for students to talk openly with each other about the lenses through which they viewed their world.

Could reading a story in print have had the same impact? I would hope so, but in this instance the video experience gave students the opportunity to view a selection of nine different but related videos, thus allowing for differentiation and choice. We continued this work as we began our exploration of African American authors in Black History Month.

Notes from Troy

Understanding bias—let alone admitting that we all suffer from it—can be a fraught conversation to have with our students. One collection of resources that deals with many aspects of how we evaluate online information, including issues around bias, is the "Crash Course" series on "Navigating Digital Information" hosted by author and vlogger, John Green.

We took a closer look at one of the videos in this series back in Chapter 4 (a link to the series is available on the book's companion page). For now, it is worth noting that—even in a unit where we invite students to engage in the substantive dialogue around literary works—we can also be thinking about the intersecting literacies that are required of our students, including connections to issues like bias.

Celebrating African American Authors during Black History Month

My colleagues and I also used technology to curate author spotlights that included video clips, book covers, quotes from the author, and more. Videos included TED-Ed offerings that helped inform students about authors, like James Baldwin, who many students had never heard of (Figure 5.2).

FIGURE 5.2: Slide Celebrating Black Author James Baldwin with an Image from TEDx

In addition to honoring Black authors and their work, author spotlights also helped students better understand one of their final project options—a choice board of literary analysis projects—described in more detail below. And while we know that these spotlights were not a substitution for the more intentional study of Black authors, they did start many conversations amongst students and primed them for our work to come in literature circles. These author spotlights were created by the teacher who built the slides for that week (we all took turns creating lesson slides, a week at a time, in an effort to lessen the workload). Over the month, a total of eight author spotlights were created, two by each of the four teachers on my team. We each considered contemporary African American authors and those from the past, as well as a balance of men and women, and included Elizabeth Acevedo, a woman who is described in intersectional terms as "an Afro-Dominican poet and novelist" (Beete, 2021).

Continuing to Build: Literature Circles

A second way that my teacher-team responded to the district's call to spotlighting marginalized populations was by replacing the canon of literary texts with culturally responsive choices that showcase authors and characters of color. This served two purposes:

1. To disrupt the typical white hero stories that dominate the canon with texts that have diverse characters who work through modern conflicts of race and identity.

2. To offer students choice in their reading through the use of Sora, the electronic library service described above, thus providing equity of access for all students.

In prior years, students had access to the school's book depository that allowed us the ability to do whole-class novels. Last year, I taught *To Kill a Mockingbird* (Lee, 1960), and all of my students had a paperback copy of the novel to use both in and outside of the classroom. In this sense, we were provided with an opportunity to reevaluate our curriculum both because we were unable to distribute physical copies of the books that were available and to build on recent professional development that we attended which introduced Dr. Rudine Sims Bishop's ideas about books as windows, mirrors, and sliding glass doors (Bishop, 1990). Thus, to offer students equal access to books, Sora, the ebook service was purchased for all students, K–12. A committee that included student volunteers, the school's media specialists, and the English department chair worked to generate a list of titles the district purchased for students. District media specialists handled the logistics of purchase and electronic distribution through Sora.

This process resulted in six titles from which students could choose:

- *Everything I Never Told You* by Celeste Ng (2015)
- *Speak* by Laurie Halse Anderson (1999)
- *Unwind* by Neil Shusterman (2009)
- *Aristotle and Dante Discover the Secrets of the Universe* by Benjamin Alire Sáenz (2014)
- *Patron Saints of Nothing* by Randy Ribay (2020)
- *Born a Crime* by Trevor Noah (2016)

I created literature circle groups in which students worked together to manage the reading and complete group assignments required. Once students electronically received their books, our classes established a predictable pattern for our time together. Over the span of three weeks and three 105-minute synchronous class sessions, we followed this format:

1. The lesson opened with a teacher-led, skills-based mini-lesson where we looked at literary elements such as point of view, plot, and character development (20–30 minutes).

2. Literature Circle Meetings met in breakout rooms created by the teacher in Zoom (30 minutes).

3. Reading time at the end of the class period for students to read the next section of the book according to the literature circle reading schedule (approximately 15 to 30 minutes, depending on the time remaining in class).

In a mini-lesson, skills of identifying theme, author, character perspective, and pacing were taught and practiced, one per lesson. The "Big Ideas" provided a context for students to practice and apply the skills taught in the mini-lessons. As noted above, students began to raise questions about community, intersectionality, and what it means to be "hyphenated" in modern American society. The "Big Ideas" helped supplement the conversations about characters and plot, allowing students to make connections with the characters and the world around them. As I explain in the next section, we used a strategy called "hexagonal thinking" to help students brainstorm and articulate questions. These are the kinds of questions that are not easily answered in the text and pushed my students to dig into literary analysis in subtantive ways.

Also of note, as they continued to read the digitized versions of the book, students found out some interesting ways to use the tools that were available while reading in this mode. First, they could put back into practice the close reading techniques they learned earlier in the year by using the highlighter tool and notes feature. While in their Zoom breakout rooms for literature circles, students would contribute to the group conversations by sharing their screens and showing each other what they highlighted and notes they recorded. Additionally, the Sora service allowed students to look up the definitions of any words they encountered that they didn't know. Students could then compare their vocabulary lists by highlighting words they did not know and writing down their definitions. In short, using the tools that Sora and Zoom allowed them, they were able to mimic as closely as possible a "connected reading" experience that was, if not exactly the same as sitting next to one another in the classroom and pointing out passages in the text, pretty close (Turner & Hicks, 2015).

Thinking about additional ways to engage students in their reading, we transition here to share an example of how Justin Stygles flexed some of his asynchronous learning time and, indeed, used the "off day" to connect with students and engage them in conversation about their reading through online conferences.

From the Classroom: "The Space Between: Engaging in Online Reading Conferences" by Justin Stygles

Justin Stygles is a fourth-grade teacher at Lyseth Elementary in Portland, Maine. He's spent eighteen years working in rural Maine school districts. His accomplishments include National Board certification, as well as several digital articles published on the ILA Today blog and Choice Literacy. He's also written feature articles for the New England Reading Association Journal and Voices from the Middle.

Remember when teaching five days a week didn't feel like enough time? Pandemic teaching altered my perception of urgency and reminded me of the ever-necessary investment of interpersonal transactions with my students around the incorporation of reading into their larger lives.

Back in the day, that being preCOVID, I took reading conferences for granted. I'd forsaken conferences trying to immerse students in the breadth of content and curriculum within the mere ninety-minutes I'd been given to teach integrated reading and writing. I'll be even more honest here: I passed on conferences, albeit the most integral part of a reading workshop, because the students were "always" there. If all else failed, and I couldn't confer with them today, we'd meet tomorrow.

Until tomorrow didn't happen.

Tomorrow came six months later. "Social distance" became the norm as did layers of facial coverings. Conferring with readers became challenging, to say the least. How was I supposed to engage with my readers devoid of their facial expression and affect—their physical responses to reading—the unspoken language of their reading interactions and comprehension?

October 2020. A Wednesday morning started, our fully remote day. Like the six previous weeks, I taught a whole-class reading and writing workshop via Zoom. Only this time, I'd had enough. If anything, the students and I were merely being procedural. They showed up. I "taught." We checked off the box. This was not acceptable. I knew I could be more resourceful.

Technology has advanced our abilities to communicate across space and time more than ever. In this case, I taught from Back Cove in Portland, Maine, 40 miles from school, back in Wiscasset, Maine. Overall, evidence suggested that students weren't "learning," nor were they engaged with school beyond the obligatory Zoom meeting. That needed to change.

Recognizing the simple fact that I wasn't conferring, I made a seemingly progressive move—I repurposed our day to schedule personalized ten-minute reading conferences with every reader. In this manner, I could see their faces again, their responses both cognitively and affectively to reading. I could also give back something the students had lost—someone genuinely interested in them and their lives as readers. Remote learning days were about to become a saving grace in a time of crisis and a gift I wasn't ready to overlook. I started conferences at 8 AM and ran non-stop for hours.

It didn't stop there. I reformatted my traditional after-school reading commitments.

In fact, at the time of this writing, I just finished conferring with a student. The student's been reading the book *Nowhere Boy* (Marsh, 2018) for some time. Level-wise, the book is appropriate. Content wise, he's struggling. Places like Pakistan and Lebanon are new. So, too, is the author's use of French and Arabic. That doesn't include extensive identification of unfamiliar vocabulary uncovered by the student's use of "clarifying." So how was I going to help him carry this burden—the one of learning how to handle more complex books, of one's own choosing—in a distant setting?

Like many of his classmates, he had little support to read at home. Remote learning was to be on his own initiative, his responsibility, and his alone. Such is the nature of working-class families in rural New England.

But why must this be a time to be confined within the limitations imposed by the school day? I reinvented my after-school programming to support my kiddos where they needed help the most—at home during their true independent reading. In this case, we just completed reading and discussing *Nowhere Boy*, together, to scaffold his nightly home reading expectations. He was my last session, now 5 PM. Since mentoring readers hadn't been happening effectively in the classroom due to social distancing, I decided to make time for him when he needed it most. Perhaps for one significant reason and one alone, he wanted someone to read with, over a digital platform; this is nothing short of a miracle. How can I acquiesce to such an opportunity? Pandemic teaching was no reason to abandon a child's maturing reading life. Otherwise, I would have lost my students to their own devices. I had a reason to try this new way of teaching—the kiddos wanted it!

I can't deny there remained "a space between," literally and figuratively, but remote learning revolutionized my role as a reading mentor and my students benefited greatly. Nothing will ever replace the interpersonal transaction between reader and student in rich, authentic discussion about books that can happen when I sit side-by-side with students. Yet, as the NCTE *Beliefs for Integrating Technology into the English Language Arts Classroom* contend, we can and should "collaboratively construct knowledge, [and] participate in immersive learning experiences." If anything, digital meeting platforms have allowed me to reach students on a more personal level, devoid of peer pressure, comparative perceptions, and risks to social capital. It's just me and the student. We bridge the space between by laughing, talking, and focusing on the most important person in the world at that moment—the reader.

Notes from Troy

Though we have known this for decades, since the dawn of the "educational industrial complex" (Brightman & Gutmore, 2002; Picciano & Spring, 2012), teaching and learning has often been dictated by disciplinary silos, disrupted days filled with bell ringing and constant transitions, and many other distractions. As anyone who works in middle grades education knows, there have been many ways that we try to counter these challenges, with team teaching, flexible scheduling, and project-based learning. Still, the simple fact that we do not have time to meet with individual students on a regular basis is one of the distinct challenges of our current structure of schooling.

Stygles' reminds us that—when used strategically—a reorganization of time and purpose during remote learning can be incredibly powerful. In addition to the goals from the BIT-ELA mentioned in his vignette, Stygles pushes back against technologies that "often reduce pedagogy to the mere coverage of shallow content and completion of basic assessments," instead modeling the way to offer "robust innovation for students to creatively represent their learning," as noted in Belief 4. This critical stance shows how time and technology can open up new spaces for substantive teaching.   >

Even when real time conferences are not available, some teachers report that they are using Flipgrid for asynchronous conferring sessions. Christy Rush-Levine, in a post on the *Choice Literacy* blog, suggests that "as our students have gained one-to-one access to Chromebooks, I have added video-recorded responses to my menu of options" for reading responses (Rush-Levine, n.d.), and many other edubloggers have echoed this idea. No matter how we do it, technology provides us with new ways to connect with students through real time or any time dialogue, and we would be wise to take advantage of these opportunities.

Deepening Literature Circle Dialogue with Hexagonal Thinking and Google Slides

With my TLN teacher team, we worked to find a visible thinking routine that would work to help our students engage in a deeper level of literary analysis. I first heard of the strategy of "hexagonal thinking" from Betsy Potash in a blog post and podcast for *Cult of Pedagogy* (2020). In the post, she describes it as a "method for considering the connections between ideas and finding the nuances in those connections." In order to move beyond a standard discussion protocol, this would instead have our students do a deeper analysis.

The main idea behind hexagonal thinking is that students will take a number of ideas represented in hexagons—traditionally done with paper cutouts, yet more recently adapted for Google Slides—and then explore the ideas that come out of the intersections. These interactions (as shown with the arrows in Figure 5.3 below) visibly showed where connections among ideas occurred and offered places for writing to learn as well as discussion. As they engaged in dialogue and quickwrites around these intersections, the ideas that emerged could become a foundation for their deeper analysis in an essay. This thinking routine can be offered in different ways. To start, I had the hexagons filled in with terms and concepts, allowing students to do the thinking and discussion needed as they moved the hexagons around on the screen. In the second round, as will be described below, students generated their own terms for the hexagons.

After practicing hexagonal thinking with the terms and concepts provided, in the next class session our students used the same thinking routine to move through their discussion. The second time students developed their own topics for the hexagons based on their own literature circle books. As a class, we had been examining questions such as:

- What does it mean to belong to a community or group?
- What are people willing to do in order to belong?
- What are the benefits of community membership?
- What are the drawbacks of community membership?
- How do community memberships impact our perspective on the world (what do we learn from our communities)?
- What is it like to be an outlier in a community?
- How does your community shape you?

FIGURE 5.3: Screenshot of Hexagonal Thinking Slide Developed in Google Slides

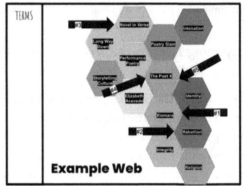

Hexagonal Thinking Routine

Your first writing assignment will ask you to do analysis through a strategy called Hexagonal Thinking.

By arranging your hexagons so that they touch other hexagons where you see a connection, it will guide your thinking to writing process.

From this broader analysis about community, we explored the idea of characters' intersectionality specifically. In their group's copy of the Google Slides with the hexagonal thinking routine, students had terms about identity and intersectionality that they could use—including gender, race, socioeconomic class, religion, age, ability, occupation, passions (like musician, athlete, artist), family dynamic, appearance, nationality—or they could develop other characteristics of their own. Since they understood the idea that they needed to dig into detail on the "Explain Your Thinking Here" intersections, the results were wonderfully varied, even with lit circles that examined the same book. Even though students had approximately fifteen minutes of their literature circle to do the hexagonal thinking exercise, they were able to produce some compelling ideas.

In the examples below, we see how two different groups were able to explore Trevor Noah's *Born a Crime* (Figure 5.4) and Neil Shusterman's *Unwind* (Figure 5.5). For the group that explored Noah's book, it was interesting to see how they were connecting identity, religion, and racial politics in South Africa. Their response, composed as a group writing during the lit circle time, answered the key question, "How do community memberships impact our perspective on the world and what do we learn from our communities?" In their map, I noticed that they did not include Noah's mother, who is a main character and clearly a driving influence on his life. As a formative assessment, their writing is a bit rough yet demonstrates a line of thinking that moves from broader community issues (such as "struggle" and "ideology") into individual morals (with ideas about "right" and "wrong"). In the end, this group shows that they were making some connections between Noah's relationship with his mother, and their shared relationship with religion, race, and Apartheid-era politics.

In the second example, the group reading Shusterman's dystopian *Unwind* were exploring what it means to be an outlier in a community. Children under the age of eighteen can be "unwound," which is described in one segment of the book from the first person through the eyes of a character experiencing this painful event. Because the main character, Risa, is seen as an outsider in the community, she herself is likely a candidate for being unwound. Through their hexagonal map, the group identifies a number of intersections including being an orphan, a ward of the state, and a fugitive as well as traits such as caution and independence. This group's writing in the formative assessment does tend to look a bit more polished than the first—and, to be honest, also has a more typical literary analysis-like feel to it—though it still shows the growth that the group made through discussions of these intersections. See the examples in Figures 5.4 and 5.5.

FIGURE 5.4: Group Hexagonal Analysis of Trevor Noah's *Born a Crime*

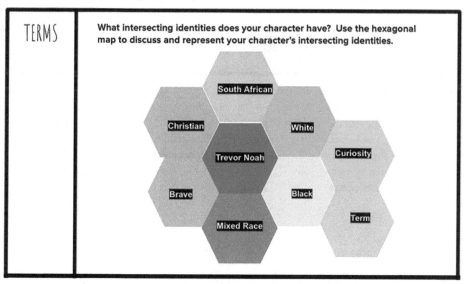

How do community memberships impact our perspective on the world (what do we learn from our communities?

Communities we are a part of have a lot to do with our perspectives on the world and certain things, every person in every community shares something in common with others within their community whether it's a struggle or an ideology. For example in our book *Born a Crime*, the main character's mother is a Christian, a hard devoted Christian, she believes in going to church multiple times a week, and her everyday life is impacted by God. This is the situation for many religious people, like using the Bible (or any religious reading) as a guide for life, like to help you decide which is right and which is wrong.

FIGURE 5.5: Group Hexagonal Analysis of Neil Shusterman's *Unwind*

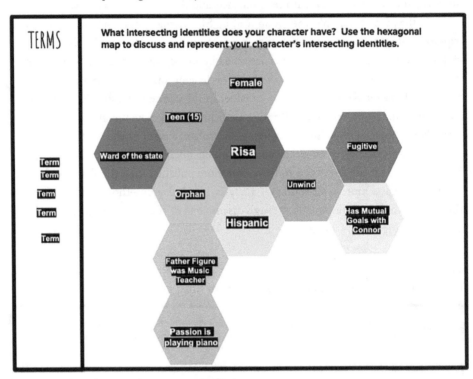

What is it like to be an outlier in a community?
Risa has been an outlier to society her whole life. She grew up as a ward of the state in a state home and along the way she has learned to survive on her own. As an outlier in her community she has learned to be independent and has learned to be careful with her actions. A quote from the book that proves this states, "Risa Megan Ward watches everything around her closely and carefully. She's seen enough at StaHo [State Homes that serve as orphanages] to know that survival rests on how observant you are." This quote alone shows her experience about being an outlier in society.

After this lesson, one student offered the following:

> [H]exagonal thinking allowed us to label which identities the main
> character has, and how it impacts her. The paragraph towards the end was
> also interesting, as our character didn't really belong to any community.

Another explained:

> I liked the hexagonal slides assignment because of how visual everything
> was. I could see clearly how everything branched off of the main character
> and intertwined together.

As they moved from the lit circles activity where they engaged in hexagonal thinking, it was clear that they were moving through their analysis in more nuanced, complex ways. From the intersections that they explored, they then turned their attention to the work of the final project, which offered them a variety of options for sharing their thinking about the book, all packaged in the form of a choice board.

Notes from Troy

As we consider the wide variety of voices that can be brought to our literature circles and a deeper dive into literary analysis, the four teacher leaders who have founded the #DisruptTexts movement—Tricia Ebarvia, Lorena Germán, Dr. Kimberly N. Parker, and Julia E. Torres—provide us with a call to action that we should "challenge the traditional canon in order to create a more inclusive, representative, and equitable language arts curriculum that our students deserve" (Ebarvia et al., 2018). With their website, linked from this book's companion page, they provide blog posts and other professional development materials, as well as links to eight teaching and learning guides for books that align with their mission and principles. Their "Publications and Media" page, too, provides links to many interviews and articles from the four leaders, giving teachers even more insight into their principles and pedagogies.

In Addition to the Literary Essay: Multiple Modes for the Final Project

As they move toward the final project, we provided students with a choice board of activities including:

- Book trailer
- Poster
- Soundtrack
- Letter to the author
- Book choice for character
- Great lines
- Traditional literary analysis
- Video book talk
- Social issue collage (record a response)

Of all of these projects, we found that most students—probably about 50 percent—created a poster to advertise their literature circle book. This poster was accompanied by short pieces of writing, including a brief synopsis of the book without spoilers and two key quotes from the book that captured the essence of the author's craft, with a brief annotation. What is interesting to note is that only 5 percent of the students—perhaps simply because it was familiar—chose the option of the traditional literary analysis essay. The remaining 45 percent of students took the chance and made some other choices.

One particular example that was compelling to me came in the form of a playlist. Students were asked to select 5–8 existing songs and put them into a playlist, with each song representing a unique element of the book's characters, events, or overall theme. Students were asked to find a segment from the lyrics and then offer a brief elaboration, in a short paragraph, resulting in the amount of writing that we might typically expect to see in an essay, though in an alternate format. Students were especially interested in writing their analysis of the lyrics, as they were able to share some of their favorite songs in a different way. For instance, in Figure 5.6 one student created a playlist for Anderson's *Speak* (Anderson, 1999), and was able to blend a variety of hip hop, country, and pop songs into his playlist. (For links to a variety of "social media style" Google Slides presentation templates from the *Ditch That Textbook* site, visit this book's companion site).

FIGURE 5.6: An excerpt from Jud's final project: A playlist

Speak, Laurie Halse Anderson

Songs that Represent by Jud

Speak by Laurie Halse Anderson is a story about a girl who has gone through the traumatic experience of being sexually assaulted. Below are some songs that I believe she could relate to.

"Boy in the Bubble," Alec Benjamin

Lyrics: https://www.musixmatch.com/lyrics/Alec-Benjamin/Boy-In-The-Bubble
Song: https://open.spotify.com/track/60cYr5uuMoxvyuIx45rGEW?si=ZkWYha4EQkKC_5hsopkQvg

I think that this song is a good representation of the book because of the self-deprecating lyrics, and the references to a toxic household; which are two of the biggest ideas in the book. Some of the lyrics that I think pertain the most to the story are:

"Well, there's no excuse for the things he did
But there's a lot at home that he's dealing with
Because his dad's been drunk since he was a kid
And I hope one day that he'll say to him
Put down those bubbles and that belt buckle
In this broken bubble"

This verse shows a lot of the issues which are going on within their home and family. While Melinda's parents aren't alcoholics, they are blind in an emotional way, which does its own damage.

"And my heart was pumping
Chest was screaming
Mind was running
Nose was bleeding
Put my hands up
Put my hands up
I told this kid I'm ready for a fight"

The verse before this talks about how they got into fights and how they got in trouble for it. While Melinda wasn't exactly in the same position, she was raped, and she was the one who got punished for it. This verse is also what I imagined Melinda felt like when she was trapped in the closet with Andy, and he was about to assault her. This is a really powerful verse, and really connects to the story.

This example shows a way in which technology has the power to allow students to showcase their analytical skills through music links and lyrics. Technology makes this project stronger because it allows the teacher to listen to the music referenced. There is no simple way to re-create this in a traditional classroom; it is the student's ability to link the music through technology that makes this such a meaningful project. Another byproduct of this kind of project is that it allows me to make personal connections with students through their choice of music.

Students also had the choice to write a letter to the author. In this case, they would share their response to the book in a more personal manner, pointing out similar literary elements (theme, plot, characters) and unique connections or questions. Then, students had to find a way to contact the author, even if they chose not to send their letter. This task—finding an author's contact page on a website or, in a few cases, an actual physical address to mail the letter—brought a sense of purpose to the task that a normal essay would otherwise have lacked. Of note, at least one student from another classroom did get a response from Anderson, which brought excitement to the project for all of us.

A third creative option was offering one of the characters in the literature circle book itself a personalized list of five additional book titles that the student would recommend for the fictional character to read. The writer would find the cover art and write a brief paragraph to explain why they were recommending this book to the character from the lit circle selection, drawing out connections to the thematic elements and the needs of the character to whom they were writing.

And, in relation to the BIT-ELA, we see elements of at least three of the beliefs enacted here. In Belief 1, we see that literacies are part of social practice, and students have worked diligently to collaboratively construct knowledge by building their own hexagonal thinking map and sharing it. From Belief 3, students were able to "read, annotate, and discuss both alphabetic and visual texts, leading to substantive discussion about issues of plot, theme, and character development." Finally, with Belief 4, we note that this project helped students to "promote and demonstrate critical thinking through discussion and identification of the rhetoric of written and digital materials." There were multiple ways for students to engage in the reading and response of their literature circle book, all of which also tied back to themes in our study of Black History Month.

Final Thoughts from Troy and Jill: Reading Literary Texts with the BIT-ELA Principles in Mind

As we have shared in this chapter—and as all ELA teachers know—there are many students who are "aliterate," in that they know how to read in thoughtful ways yet often choose not to do so for a variety of reasons including a lack of access to high-quality materials as well as the many distractions present in our modern world. During the 2020–2021 school year, the main challenge in Jill's district was working to ensure that most students were able to access ebooks through the app Sora, and they were fortunate to have the funding and technology available to do so. Still, there are lessons learned from this experience—and more technologies and openly available resources to explore—that can help ELA teachers with these types of tasks in the future.

Though one could look at the BIT-ELA principles and see that such an intense focus on using technology might prevent us from teaching our students to read and enjoy literature, we contend that the principles provide students with new ways to think about approaching, analyzing, and interpreting texts. For instance, in Belief 3, we are encouraged to "ask students to repurpose a variety of digital media (e.g., images, video, music, text) to create a multimodal mashup or explore other emerging media genres (e.g., digital storytelling, infographics, annotated visuals, screencasts) that reflect concepts in literature such as theme, character, and setting." These forms of interpretation do not supplant a more traditional literary analysis in the form of an essay and should be considered as a complement. In short, students can do the intellectual work of literary analysis both through a thesis-driven essay and with other modes.

To guide further discussion and exploration, we encourage teachers to think about the following:

- In what ways are we able to provide students with some choices for their reading while also meeting the curricular standards we have in place? How can we use literature circles—especially with contemporary texts—to make connections to broader themes that our students will want to explore?

- In addition to having them write the more typical kinds of literary analysis essays (that, no doubt, they will still be expected to be able to write in college), how might we provide opportunities for them to express their understanding of literary devices, the plot and characters, and their interpretations of these texts in different forms? How can they show their own connections to these texts in new ways, showing how they see themselves in what they read?

- How might we leave space for creativity in our uses of technology (like Zoom breakout rooms for jigsawing or the use of Google Slides for hexagonal thinking), inviting our students to come up with their own ideas for using tech in more nuanced ways? When might we rely on them to demonstrate a particular use of technology that pushes the boundaries of what we might have typically done in the past?

Chapter Six

Arguing and Persuading across Media

Reflections from Jill's Classroom

We were about two weeks into our "Argue and Persuade" unit, and I could hardly believe what I was writing. "While it's true that most Americans would feel the same as I about eating bugs, I have learned that bugs are a sustainable, environmentally friendly food source that should be considered." Eating bugs has never been offered as a food source in my world, but this unit and the text set used forced me to consider the idea.

In many ways, writing this thesis statement—at the end of a brief kernel essay— had been meant to serve only as a sample for my students. I value the process of doing the same writing I ask of my students, engaging in the same labor. It provides me with context for what will come and allows me to share the struggles and successes with my own writing before they try it.

What I discovered, however, was that through the process of writing, I also embodied the learning I hoped my students would do; I considered all sides of an issue through reading a text set—a series of readings that represent different aspects of an issue—and formulated a thesis statement. In doing so, I changed my mind about what I initially thought about eating a bug.

Writing to discover my own ideas uncovered my internal bias and challenged me to reconsider my thought that eating bugs would taste bad and sounded disgusting. I was amazed when presenting this to my students that many of them come from cultures that embrace bugs as a delicacy, and they were frustrated by how American culture doesn't consider bugs as part of the food chain. Through writing and sharing ideas we challenged each other to be open-minded to what the claims of each text were asking us to consider—eating bugs is good for the environment.

While this topic was fun, my experience points to the impact of crafting an argument. A writer should consider their own initial views and opens their mind to the other perspectives, creating space for a new perspective.

Context and Connections to the BIT-ELA Statement

Our English teacher planning group was brainstorming around what to do to start our Argue and Persuade unit. Spring had arrived, student (and teacher) motivation was waning, and we knew that this unit—perhaps more than all the others that came before it—would be the most impactful for students moving forward in school. We believe that understanding the elements of building a compelling argument along with the rhetorical devices needed to make it persuasive is the basic building block to effective communication, for creating an informed electorate, and for encouraging civil discourse. And so, we couldn't coast to the end of the year; this unit had to be really engaging.

To that end, my colleagues and I at Skyline HS turned to the National Writing Project's College, Career, and Community Writers Program's (C3WP) unit on, of all things, eating bugs (n.d.c.)! The C3WP, as will be explained in a bit more detail below, is a set of instructional resources that help educators provide mini-units and individual lessons on a variety of aspects related to argument writing. This connects with one of the components of Belief 1, in that ELA teachers should "design assignments, activities, and assessments that encourage interdisciplinary thinking, community and civic engagement."

Not only was this unit engaging for the students, it opened a channel of connection with colleagues that I didn't know was there. At first, the topic of eating bugs, from my perspective, didn't seem like a great topic to argue. My midwestern, white diet was conducive to the foods that were harvested around me. I eat fruits like apples, cherries, grapes, and cantaloupe—all grown in Michigan. Additionally, my choices of animal proteins were what one might consider American staples: chicken, beef, and basic fish like salmon and whitefish. So, when faced with the idea of eating bugs, my knee-jerk reaction took me to the TV series *Survivor*, where contestants would eat crunchy, gooey, large bugs in order to have the chance at getting food they wanted to eat: pizza, burger and fries, and peanut butter. This only fueled my thinking that eating bugs would have all of my students feeling grossed out like I was. In addition, this reinforced my confirmation bias that everyone eats food like I do.

What I learned—in conversation with my colleagues as we planned the unit as well as through my work with students in the initial exploration of what it really means for our palettes (and our planet) to eat insects—was that I had a lot to learn. Not only is eating bugs widely accepted outside of the Western world, it is a healthy, sustainable food source that can be really delicious. As I created the lessons for this unit, I became more interested in healthy food choices, the impact my current choices were making on our environment, and how I, personally, could do better. These conversations continued in the virtual classroom and through collaborations with colleagues.

And, in a bigger sense, this is the heart of good argument writing: considering all the facets of an argument and then forming a claim based on evidence that comes from good research and expert testimony. Not only does this process build a good essay, the act of adding commentary and articulating one's reasons for the claim may even change the writer's mind. The National Writing Project's C3WP program encourages students to layer reading and writing into an argument to establish a stance. We ask students to think of an argument as a conversation that has already started around a circular table. There is an open spot left for students to enter into the conversation by pulling up a chair and adding their unique perspective, which is where we begin.

Notes from Troy

Along with the eating of insects—as a source for protein and also to understand the implications for food insecurity, climate change, and social justice—there are many other topics that can push students into even deeper understanding of a small, focal concept that can then be moved into a more nuanced, compelling argument.

To help students think about the ways that these local issues are more broadly connected to larger ones, I encourage ELA teachers to explore resources around the United Nation's Sustainable Development Goals (SDGs). In addition to the main SDG website, there is a website created by educators, "Teach SDGs," both linked from this book's companion page.

With the BIT-ELA goal that students "collaboratively construct knowledge, participate in immersive learning experiences, and reach out to their own community and a global audience," the resources provided by the UN and Teach SDGs can help ELA educators inspire critical thinking and move their students' arguments from personal concerns to more complex social issues.

The National Writing Project's College, Career, and Community Writers Program (C3WP)

The C3WP is described as "an intensive professional development program that provides teachers with instructional resources and formative assessment tools for the teaching of evidence-based argument writing" (National Writing Project, n.d.d.). Rather than positioning the C3WP as a curriculum (though it does contain instructional materials), NWP describes it as a set of resources that teachers can use flexibly to support the teaching of argument throughout the school day and across the school year. In an ideal implementation of the C3WP, teachers would use at least four of the units in their ELA classroom throughout the year.

The C3WP is designed around the core idea that argument is not an "either/or" proposition. Instead, the goal is to see argument as dialogic and that we need to develop claims that are debatable, defensible, and nuanced. The core of this perspective comes from Kenneth Burke's idea of the "parlor" and an "unending conversation" where a writer will come to the table, listen, contribute a bit, and then step away in order to come back another time (Burke, 1974). The C3WP also ties in the work of Joseph Harris, who describes ways in which "rewriting"—or taking ideas from other writers to further your own writing—can help establish an argumentative stance (Harris, 2006; 2017). One of our CRWP colleagues and co-directors, Elizabeth Brockman, too, has considered ways to frame our writing prompts to push students toward more nuanced thinking by adding the phrase "to what extent" as a way to help push students' thinking (2020).

Often, students think of "argument" as something that evokes anger and winners and losers. One of the key components of C3WP is that argument is positioned as conversation, not as a win-lose proposition. In this sense, the C3WP materials build on the idea of dialogue in the following way:

> Young writers are invited to a metaphorical table where they "chat" with experts in sources and discuss with classmates how "authorities" in sources influence student thinking. Through teacher facilitated conversations, students gather their thoughts, process information, and contribute their own voices to an argument-in-progress by composing informed claims and writing a kernel essay draft. (National Writing Project, n.d.b.).

As noted above, a foundational text for the C3WP work now in its second edition, Joseph Harris's *Rewriting: How to Do Things with Texts* (J. Harris, 2006; 2017) lays out key elements that comprise the C3WP curriculum. In order to become an effective academic writer, he argues, we do of course need to think about citing sources and avoiding plagiarism. Yet, these practices do not fully capture what it is that academic writers *do*, a term that Harris defines as "*rewriting*—as drawing from, commenting on, adding to—the work of others" (p. 2, emphasis in original). He goes on to explain how the creative work of academics is bound up in "response, reuse, and rewriting" the work of others. It is through this kind of dialogue and ongoing interaction that arguments are composed, and Harris outlines the kinds of "moves" that writers can make in order to accomplish their goals, two of which include "forwarding" and "countering." The action of "forwarding" is actually composed of four separate subactions, "illustrating," "authorizing," "borrowing," and "extending." Without going into extensive detail on each of these moves, we encourage you to look at the "Argument as a Highway" slide deck that has been shared on the C3WP website, with a link from this book's companion page.

Since we first began this work over six years ago, teachers connected with the CRWP—and many other sites around the country—have implemented the units (over three dozen of them that range from upper elementary into high school). Jill, in particular, has implemented approximately seven of the instructional units from C3WP in over 35 classes including seventh, ninth, tenth, and eleventh-grade students, including an iteration of the upper elementary unit entitled, "Practicing Writing Recursive Claims" (National Writing Project, n.d.c.) that we describe in this chapter. We continue to stay connected with and learn from other teachers at our local site and in the broader national network, all of whom are bringing argument to life in new ways.

Finally, one of the great things about the C3WP is that the text sets are, for the most part, interchangeable. For instance, in the deeper dive below, Jill used the unit for "Connecting Evidence to Claims," yet drew an article from the text set "Eating Bugs," which was part of another unit (links to each are available on the book's companion page). The C3WP also offers resources for teachers to build their own text sets, and we encourage readers to think about both the subscription-based services (such as Newsela and Gale's Opposing Viewpoints in Context) and other openly available texts (such as ReadWorks, CommonLit, AllSides, and ProCon) from which text sets can be built. We now move into a deeper dive of the unit that Jill and her colleagues created, with connections again to the BIT-ELA, bringing her voice back into focus.

Notes from Troy

Teaching argument writing and moving beyond the "five-paragraph essay" has long been a conversation amongst ELA teachers. One might even say that the question of why, how, and even *if* to teach the five-paragraph essay is an argument that our field is enmeshed in still today.

In addition to the sources noted above, there are many other professional resources related to alternative audiences, genres, and purposes for academic writing. From Campbell and Latimer's aptly named *Beyond the Five-Paragraph Essay* (2012) to Traci Gardner's *Designing Writing Assignments* (2011) to Cathy Fleischer and Sarah Andrew-Vaughan's *Writing Outside Your Comfort Zone: Helping Students Navigate Unfamiliar Genres* (2009) to more recent works that move students toward social action such as Cornelius Minor's *We Got This* (2018), there are many resources that can help, as the BIT-ELA reminds us, to "articulate ideas related to authentic writing experiences beyond the classroom, including a better account of audiences for whom students are writing and purposes other than [strictly] academic argument."

>

In my own work with other educators including Dawn Reed (Reed & Hicks, 2015) and Jeremy Hyler (Hicks, Hyler, & Pangle, 2020; Hyler & Hicks, 2014), we have considered ways to push argument writing in different directions. Also, with Kristen Hawley Turner, I have explored multimedia argument (Turner & Hicks, 2016), and I am grateful that Jill and her colleagues have taken up some of that work in their teaching, too, moving students toward digital writing practices.

In short, we need to help students understand that academic argument can spill over, well beyond five paragraphs and even into multimodal formats.

Putting Principles into Practice: More on Arguing and Persuading in Jill's Classroom

In this section, Jill provides an overview of four lessons that led students from their initial attempts at argument writing all the way to their mastery assessment project.

Lesson 1: Exploring the Idea in Real Time

To visually demonstrate how an argument evolves, I had the students use their writer's notebooks during real-time instruction via Zoom. At this point of the school year, some students had adapted to and preferred their digital notebook, yet others still gravitated toward the analog paper version. Students were asked to make their thinking visible by having two separate places in their journal to write—one to respond to a text (Reading) and the other to record their thoughts about the argument that they were formulating (Writing). Students using a paper notebook labeled two facing pages while I provided the students who used their digital notebooks with a slide to copy and paste into their notebooks. The slide replicated two facing pages in a paper notebook—two adjacent text boxes with a heading at the top of each to label the spaces where students should write about a text and the other for their own thinking as shown in Figure 6.1.

Beginning on the writing side of their notebooks, I asked students to record their thoughts and feelings about the idea of eating bugs as shown in Figure 6.2. Students had five minutes to record their answers to the following questions:

- Would you ever eat bugs?
- What do you think?
- Why or why not?
- Would there be a certain situation where you would—or people should—eat bugs?
- What made you say that?

FIGURE 6.1: Image from C3WP Slide Deck with Writing Prompt

Reading	Writing
Click to add text	Click to add text

After a sharing of their initial thoughts about eating bugs, students then used the "reading" side of their notebooks to record ideas about texts. The first text was a picture of a person working in a commercial kitchen preparing a plate of bugs to eat (Figure 6.2). (From what we can tell, this image was placed in the C3WP text set from the original source of Minnesota Public Radio's episode of *The Current* [linked from the book's companion page], originally aired on May 13, 2013, and this photo taken by Dario Lopez-Mills of the Associated Press has since been used in many news outlets. We share it here, then, having given much consideration to issues of fair use of copyrighted material.)

FIGURE 6.2: Image of chef serving cooked insects in a restaurant kitchen from Minnesota Public Radio's The Current (May 13, 2013). Image credit: Dario Loez-Mills/AP.

I showed this three times in succession, each time with a different prompt at the bottom:

- Jot down what you see.

- What would you think if the school's cafeteria served this? Would you eat it? Why or why not?

- As you look at the picture, what questions do you have about eating bugs?

Students then had 1–2 minutes to answer the questions on the reading side of their notebooks. As a whole class, we discussed what we wrote down. Uniformly across all sections of this class, students said they would not eat this if served in the cafeteria! What was surprising was it wasn't always because of an aversion to eating bugs but rather the quality of the cuisine served in a school cafeteria. Many students were interested in trying it—they just preferred to go to a restaurant that had bugs on the menu. Additionally, students were interested in the cooking process of bugs—were they fried, baked, served cold/raw? What seasonings were used to make them taste good? Students recorded their thinking thus far using a sentence stem as in Figure 6.3.

This process of layering many skills—thinking, writing, and reading—allows students to follow how their thoughts and new information formulate a stance in any argument. Instead of starting with a claim, the C3WP program encourages students to do this layered approach to allow the evolution of thought with texts that challenge students to record their thinking along the way.

And even though it is just a start, this layering is a useful place to begin. In her book, *Reviving the Essay: How To Teach Structure Without Formula* (2005), Gretchen Bernabei

FIGURE 6.3: Prompts for writing response

On the **writing** side of your notebook . . .

Use one of the sentence stems below, and finish the sentence with your thinking so far.

- The photograph makes me question...
- Now I am thinking...
- I'm wondering...
- Just as I was thinking earlier...

provides organizational structures for what she calls "kernel essays," or the sentences that can then be expanded into paragraphs and full essays. Similarly, from the perspective of college-level writing, the "moves" that writers make provided in Graff and Birkenstein's bestselling *They Say/I Say,* now in its fifth edition (2021), show dozens of ways that we can help writers introduce their own ideas in relation to other sources.

After students selected and completed one of the sentence stems noted above, the beginnings of a claim were starting to emerge.

Students continue to think more about eating bugs when they go back to the reading side of their notebook and write down their ideas about this infographic from *Scholastic Magazine,* published in September of 2013. And, while the infographic is available as a link in the mini-unit "Practicing Writing Recursive Claims," a direct link to it is no longer available. Moreover, we chose not to reprint it here due to concerns about copyright, namely that it is a reprint of an article that was only available by subscription and not publicly available on the web. That said, a brief description of the infographic is worthwhile.

As part of their "You Write It" activity, in which readers are invited to look at background research and then develop a story, the infographic is an invitation to a writing contest sponsored by Scholastic. With a white background and a thick red border around the entire page, the title of the infographic is "The Perfect Meal." That said, a typical American viewer might cringe at this title because, at the center of the infographic, the outline of a human's lips and teeth are biting down on a large grasshopper, so big that it will not even fit in the person's mouth. Around this main image, a number of other icons and interesting facts—facts about how plentiful, popular, nutritious, delicious, and earth-friendly insects are—pepper the page, including the point that over 2 billion people eat insects on a regular basis. Along the bottom, images of a stink bug, a tarantula, a wasp, and a termite suggest that these insects taste like apples, shrimp, pine nuts, and carrots, respectively. In sum, the infographic has the right combination of "gross factor" appeal and interesting informational tidbits, drawing teen and tween readers into this topic in a compelling manner.

Again, students recorded what they saw and evaluated their thoughts/stance on eating bugs. The lesson ended with students adding more to the writing side of the notebook:

- Can you find a place to add one of the facts from the infographic?
- Can you add a whole new idea from the infographic that you do not yet have in your writing?

Once students complete this lesson's writing tasks thoughtfully and completely, they have the building blocks of a well-crafted argument under way. Though students would soon choose their own topic—again, one that would be considered debatable, defensible, and nuanced—we continued to use the topic of eating insects as a model topic that we could explore together, as will become clear when returning to my whole class instruction in Lesson 3.

Lesson 2: Digging Deeper with Asynchronous Work

After the first lesson in which students looked at two texts, an image and an infographic, students were able to work on their own using their new skills to take notes on an assigned article, "Eat up! Insects may truly be the sustainable food source of the future" (again, links to these resources are available on the "Practicing Writing Recursive Claims" page of the C3WP website). This was assigned for asynchronous work, providing students with the time needed to read carefully and add to the notes already started from the first two texts. Additionally, they were asked to consider topics for research and argument that would soon come in later lessons. Giving students choice in topic—and time to think it over—is helpful when the time comes for them to buckle down and write an argument that is not teacher-led and highly scaffolded. And, even though we kept circling back to the topic of eating insects together, that served only as a model from which they could watch me make the "argument moves" in a common writing topic.

Then, during the asynchronous Wednesday work (a shift in our district's calendar, as noted in the opening chapter), students took what we had done with the initial text set on eating insects and then looked for their own topics of interest using Gale's "Opposing Viewpoints in Context" database. Their goal in this individual work was to not only think about potential topics to argue, but to experience with one of the popular databases used for middle grade argument research. In Michigan, we have access to this resource through our state e-library, and it is likely that many districts or states provide similar access. The database has a page of clickable links where students can search for topics that they already have in mind. This comprehensive list also provides food for thought because there are many topics students wouldn't think of on their own. Students perused the list of topics noting not only the ones that they thought of on their own but noticing the topics that they never considered yet find intriguing.

By the time they get to high school, we expect that students can research a topic to find the facets of an argument on their own. There are many ways they can begin to gain insights on these topics, above and beyond the typical practice of beginning with a Google search. In fact, we strongly encourage students to skip the search engine and start elsewhere. As noted earlier in Chapter 5, many states' electronic libraries provide access to vetted research databases that allow students to explore a topic easily. The *Opposing Viewpoints in Context Database* gives students the ability to do the same thing without needing the extensive research skills necessary to find articles from various perspectives and presenting ideas. Additionally, the *Opposing Viewpoints in Context Database* allows students to consume its content in ways that support different learning styles. For example, articles can be translated into different languages allowing English language learners the ability to read in their language of choice. Additionally, all articles are offered as audio for students to listen, and the reading rate is also adjustable.

Beyond this, we may still need to give students new ways to begin thinking about current and controversial topics. Additional sources that could help in a similar way with this include ProCon.org, AllSides, and Living Room Conversations. ProCon.org gives a brief overview of the issues presented, followed by lists of additional resources on both sides of the issue. AllSides, in addition to presenting the news of the day, has both "Topic Guides" and a "Dictionary" for helping students understand the background—as well as additional key words connected to—a variety of issues. Finally, the "topic guides" on the Living Room Conversations website offer brief, one-paragraph overviews of different perspectives on topics that could serve as a launching pad for those students who are still unsure about the nuances of a particular issue. It is important for us to consider that these are introductions to understanding complex issues, and there are even more conversations for students to have once their research is underway.

Put another way, as they review these sources, students also need to discover the ways in which particular ideologies are represented. Students who are still trying to discern the ideological stances of particular news outlets or commentators could also work to compare sources and their bias. Both AllSides and a separate organization, Ad Fontes Media, offer their own media bias charts. These charts, too, should be investigated and explored so students understand how they were created and what contributes to a media bias rating for both AllSides and Ad Fontes (e.g., issues of veracity as well as the use of partisan language). That said, using these charts as a starting place for ongoing dialogue about media bias and the sources that students are drawing from to build their argument is a good start. (All resources mentioned here are linked from the book's companion page.)

Once students had a chance to dig into their own topics, and as we prepared to return for whole class instruction, they shared their thinking in their writer's notebooks, and we prepared them to return to the idea, again, that argument is not an "either/or" proposition but instead an ongoing conversation. Again, in the spirit of the C3WP, we wanted students to create claims that are both debatable and defensible, as well as compelling and nuanced. The traditional thesis statement, one that is one-sided and absolutely firm, does not allow for our students to engage in the full range of critical thinking that this approach might allow.

Notes from Troy

In this stage of the lesson, Jill has worked in the spirit of the BIT-ELA to "choose technology products and services with an intentional awareness toward equity, including the affordances and constraints evident in free/open source, freemium, and subscription-based offerings." Yes, some districts are able to afford a number of premium services for access to ebooks, articles, streaming videos, and more. This is, of course, a local choice and—with a variety of services available and strong pedagogical rationales for doing so—I cannot fault them for making these choices for their students.

However, even with the influx of funding that has been granted to districts, many are still not as fortunate. As noted above, Michigan's electronic library (MEL.org) offers many databases for all residents throughout the state. And, while I am not entirely sure how often these resources are actually accessed by K–12 students, my strong suspicion is that they are vastly underutilized. Many times, when I talk to teachers in the state, they are unaware of MEL and the fact that they can use it for personal and academic purposes.

My hope is this gentle reminder that all educators reading this book will look to their school and community librarians/media specialists to ensure that they are utilizing resources that are made available to them. To quickly search for your local or state library, visit <www.usa.gov/libraries>.

Lesson 3: From "Would You Rather?" to a First-Draft Claim

The third lesson of the week began the same as Lesson 1, gathered back together in our Zoom room, which offered students a lighthearted way to think about argument—answering "would you rather" questions in breakout rooms. The two rounds asked students to take a stand on the choice of either "reading an awesome book" or "watching a good movie." Students talked about how books offer a longer lasting experience, whereas a movie is taken in during one sitting. They also discussed how a book allows one's imagination to create the characters and setting while a movie makes those interpretations for you. This was a simple, low-pressure way to get the conversation going.

The second round then asked students if they would rather "end world hunger" or "establish world peace." While both seem like noble pursuits, some of my students were very passionate about ending world hunger as the answer to establishing world peace. "If people are not hungry, some of the desperate, violent things that people do will no longer be an issue," one student argued. Others argued that money and the struggle for power are what fueled wars and that hunger didn't have anything to do with it. What started as a philosophical "would you rather" ended in students formulating claims for their stance that could be supported with evidence.

Even in these short bursts, opening invitations to take a side on an issue illustrated for students that our individual perspectives can be so different. While discussing these two "would you rather" scenarios, students saw that argument is, indeed, a conversation and that sometimes our stance at the beginning can change based on the ideas other people contribute. As a teacher, this is what I hope my students will take away from the argue and persuade unit—all issues have conversations around them and, in order to make a thoughtful contribution to the conversation, all viewpoints should be considered.

From here, I opened a shared Google Doc that had a table in it for students to begin brainstorming and sharing their topic ideas. Students were asked to contribute at least one topic of interest found during their asynchronous work from Wednesday. The list of topics was varied (and, to be completely transparent, provided those students who had not done the asynchronous work with a list of topics shared by their peers).

Students then had the opportunity to share the articles they had found during asynchronous work and to select two meaningful quotes. These quotes served as evidence to support their thinking. Harris calls this "authorizing," "[w]hen you involve the expertise or status of another writer to support your thinking" (39). Put another way, this is when students can build their thinking by using quotes from the experts, adding credibility to the argument. It's important for students to understand that good written arguments are a combination of information found in other articles that is then connected with their own thinking about the topic.

FIGURE 6.4: Slide Outlining Initial Practice with Using the "They Say / I Say" Templates

On the reading side of your notebook . . .

The Source Says (evidence) (Write actual lines from the text below)	I Say (commentary) (Record your response and thinking to the text lines here.)
Example: 1. They're cheap, nutritious, some say delicious, and they're exceptionally sustainable, according to a new study from the University of Copenhagen. 2. Halloran and her team wanted to test claims that cricket farming could be a sustainable alternative to traditional livestock operations, which have been shown to negatively impact the environment.	1. This means that bugs are a good food source. The Western world should try them. 2. This matters because every effort should be made to save our fragile environment. *Think of how you can explain your source information by either explaining what it means or why it matters — or BOTH!

Then, as shown in Figure 6.4, I encouraged them to engage in some of the "moves" that Harris describes in his book while also introducing them to Graff and Birkenstein's "They Say/I Say" templates (2021).

Specifically, students elaborated on the quotes they selected to provide commentary on their thinking by using the "this means" and "this matters" prompts. This intentional scaffolding of the commentary helps to visually illustrate that what an article says is important; in other words, explaining what it means and why it matters helps bring one's thinking on a stance into clear focus for the reader. As a form of prewriting, these sentences would sometimes be useful for students in their actual essay yet were most often just used as a moment to articulate one's thinking while in conversation with classmates.

At this point, the students were ready to finalize their thinking and write a claim statement. This order of teaching argument may seem inverted—typically teachers start with a stance or claim followed by the search for evidence to support it. The C3WP program intentionally puts the claim writing later in the process and only after careful consideration of many viewpoints on the issue. Oftentimes, students come into a topic with one line of thinking but end up with a more sophisticated claim when asked to consider the issue from all sides. Sometimes, students start with one stance on a topic, but after surveying all sides, change their mind completely, resulting in a claim statement that would never happen had the order been the traditional claim first, then research.

We looked again at the idea that claims can be debated and defended, an important, yet often underlooked distinction when thinking about the ways we traditionally approached a thesis statement in a five-paragraph essay. A key component of the C3WP program is that claims must be "debatable," "defensible," "nuanced," and "compelling." These four adjectives drove our discussion of the kinds of claims that my students created. We discussed a few sample claims, engaging in a hearty discussion ourselves of whether these claims, drawn from C3WP materials, met all four criteria:

- Schools should increase recess time because it improves our health.
- Civilian drones should be banned in wildfire areas because they put firefighters in danger.
- We should care about space debris because if there is no way to safely remove it, then our planet is in danger.

Again, after having the chance to read an article on their own during the asynchronous lesson, students selected pieces of evidence from the article that either supported their thinking so far or was a good point in opposition. From there, students elaborated on the quotes they selected to provide commentary on their thinking. This intentional scaffolding of the commentary helps to visually illustrate that what an article says is important but explaining what it means and why it matters helps bring one's thinking on a stance into clear focus for the reader.

To move this further, I modeled how students could develop a "simple claim starter" to begin and then more sophisticated ones. For instance, the goal is to have students articulate a position that someone (whether an individual, a group, or an even larger organization or entity such as a country) should take, then following up with a statement of why that position should be taken, following the "because" statement, like this:

- ___ (person, people, or group) should ___ (action verb) because (rationale)
- ___ (person, people, or group) should not ___ (action verb) because (rationale).

An example, in the context of this unit, would be "The United States should consider bugs as a sustainable food source because they are safer for the environment and can taste good." This format, though brief, at least gets them started in the process of developing their claim and putting some stakes to that claim. Also, I encouraged students to change words around slightly if needed because sometimes the template doesn't fit everyone's topic or writing style.

Then we looked at ways to make a more complex claim. In each of these examples, students were able to see how they could bring in the voice of the naysayer to provide some nuance. With the first template, students thought about how their own position may have changed over time and, with the second, articulated the stance of someone else in order to open the dialogue:

- While at one time it may have been true that ___ (general description of another claim), I have learned that ___ (own claim backed with evidence).
- ___ (person, people, or group) makes sense when she/he/they argue ___ (restatement of the other claim), we must also consider ___ (author's own claim).

Whether they chose one of the simple or more complex claim templates, students tried to write a claim that reflected their thinking about eating bugs (as we had all been doing as a class) and then transfer this skill to their own topic. Like training wheels on a bike, using sentence starters for writing claims allows students to bump up their level of sophistication, and it also allows them to see that there are multiple ways an effective claim statement can be written. Students who struggle with writing, especially those with IEPs, English language learners, and students with 504 plans, are provided an equitable framework to begin.

Once students had practiced writing a claim statement in a couple of ways using the provided sentence starters, they moved to breakout rooms to share with their peers. By conferring with fellow students and—as much as I could by jumping from breakout room to breakout room—me as the teacher, I can say that every student in my class was able to get some feedback on this initial component of their own argument.

Notes from Troy

Moving back and forth between the whole-class example and their own writing—and by having claim templates that they could quite literally copy and paste from Jill's slides—students involved in this lesson were able to, as the BIT-ELA contends, engage in "equitable solutions that employ technology in culturally responsive ways, drawing on students' and teachers' existing funds of knowledge related to literacy, learning, and using digital devices/networks." As a reminder, Jill's district had worked to ensure that everyone who needed a laptop and/or mobile internet access were able to get it, so she could move through this lesson using accessible tools. By modeling the reading and writing process, then encouraging students to take their newfound skills and apply them to their own topic, Jill demonstrates a robust use of the tools, in real time, and with the goal of moving students to the next stage of peer response.

Lesson 4: Starting a Kernel Essay

At this point, the students were armed with all of the elements they needed to begin an argument. This is where we returned to Bernabei's ideas—and a resource developed for the C3WP—with a variety of organizational patterns for them to expand their initial claim into "kernels" based on popular structures (e.g., point/counterpoint; smallest idea to bigger idea to biggest idea). The slides, as shown in Figures 6.5 and 6.6, for helping students develop their kernel essays first invite them to work with the same topic of eating insects and show my model of a kernel essay with my claim statement highlighted. Because this lesson was done in small chunks, across multiple days,

FIGURE 6.5: Slide Showing Kernel Essay Templates

FIGURE 6.6: Slide Showing Sample Kernel Essay

students seemed to have a good idea of what they wanted to write and the evidence they wanted to use. They used their writer's notebooks throughout the process, drawing on the sentence stems that spoke to them. I found that it bolstered the confidence of writers at all ability levels: my reluctant writers, who sometimes struggle to include all the elements of a nuanced argument, composed a comprehensive piece of writing with a level of sophistication that would not be possible without the sentence stems scaffolding while my advanced writers learned how an argument can be written succinctly.

The instructions for the kernel essay gave students some insights for getting started with a variety of structures such as:

- First, I thought this, then I learned this, and now I think this

- Overview of the issue, one side thinks, the other side things, and I believe

- One aspect of the issue, another aspect of the issue, yet another aspect of the issue, and my claim

- My claim on the issue, in addition I will add, in addition I will also add, my refined claim

These kernel essay structures provide a way to write about a topic without having to think too deeply about the structure, as the prompts provide that for students. I encourage them to choose one of the kernel structures to begin, and to have them write from their existing notes and what they have discussed with classmates about their topics. At this point, they do not have to provide exact citations to their source material, yet the kernel prompts do begin to help them see that they will, eventually, need to cite their sources. I model one of the kernel essay structures for them—first I thought, then I learned, now I think this—sharing this brief example:

> When asked to think about the idea of eating bugs, my first thought was, "Gross!" The picture created in my mind came from the many seasons of *Survivor* I have watched on TV where the survivors have to eat really gross things in hopes of scoring a pizza or a peanut butter sandwich. There would be no crunch, slime, or disgusting taste for me—no way!
>
> Then I learned that bugs are a sustainable, environmentally friendly food source. According to a new study from the University of Copenhagen, bugs are inexpensive, nutritious, and they can taste good. Additionally, there are at least 1,900 species of edible insects on the planet. Entomophagy, the study of bugs, states that a stink bug tastes like apples, and a termite can be a lovely substitute for a carrot. This means that bugs could replace some of the food we eat while using fewer resources than traditional farming methods. All of this makes sense because our environment is fragile enough; I could do my part by trying bugs as a substitute for beef and other foods that are unnecessarily using our environmental resources.
>
> While it's true that most Americans would feel the same as I did about eating bugs, I have learned that bugs are a sustainable, environmentally friendly food source that should be considered. Our country needs to break away from the steak and potato meal plan and open our minds to bugs. Someday soon when asked what's for dinner, I hope to say, "Tonight we will be having tarantulas with a side of stink bugs and termites."

FIGURE 6.7: Angela's Essay

Although bugs may seem disgusting at first, it is believed that soon they could become a popular sustainable food source in our everyday lives. A new study at the University of Copenhagen has surfaced which claims and proves that bugs are inexpensive, nutritious, can taste good, and there are at least 1900 different species of edible bugs on the planet. This all seems like a strong argument, but the majority of the population wouldn't agree. Bugs have been popularized as disgusting things to eat, whether it be on game shows where contestants have to walk through bins of bugs, eat bugs, or play with them. While watching such shows you never go "oh those look like a good source of food". Since bugs have been seen as disgusting, although there is much scientific research going against it, it would be hard to get the majority of the population eating bugs. I believe that with time and convincing, bugs could be a sustainable food source, but for now that is not the case.

From these kernels, some strong essays emerged. For instance, above is Angela's writing (Figure 6.7). She has a 504 plan that offers her accommodations for reading and writing. She has anxiety issues and doubts herself often. While the vast majority of students wrote essays in favor of eating bugs, Angela took a different perspective on the issue. Rather than arguing for the sustainability of bugs as a food source, she contends that it will be difficult to get the Western world to buy into this idea because of popular TV shows and media portraying bugs as gross. Her point that scientific research cannot overcome popular culture is one that resonates not only for this instance of eating bugs, so this is an approach that might serve her well when developing arguments in the future.

A second example comes from Arnold (Figure 6.8), who takes the kernel structure and sentence stems as a foundation, and he adds his voice to this writing (I know that I won't think about exoskeletons and wings in quite the same way again!). He even references that he did "extra research" on this topic, which adds to his knowledge base and stance on the issue. While not all students like Arnold went the extra mile on our class topic, this essay shows that when students buy into the argument writing process by taking a stance through a debatable, defensible, nuanced claim, our students are thinking critically. It also opens the door for them to consider different viewpoints, encouraging them to engage with new ideas, all of which, we hope, will lead to a more just world.

My students really liked this assignment because it built their confidence as argument writers. Ellen, a student in my last class of the day, remarked,

> I didn't understand at first why you were making us do all of the short writings in our writer's notebook, but when it came time to put together my essay, I had all of the writing done. I just needed to decide which sentence stems to use and what kernel structure would work best for my claim.

Figure 6.8: Arnold's Essay

When I first learned about the concept of eating bugs, I immediately dismissed the idea, and didn't want to hear more about it. I associated bugs with the terms "slimy," "gross," and "disgusting." I didn't like the thought of hearing "fresh tarantula" on the menu at any restaurant, and certainly was not planning on cooking up fresh bugs as a snack. Benefits of eating bugs were non-existent in my mind when I compared them to a juicy, protein-filled piece of poultry. There was no way an exoskeleton along with a pair of wings was ever going to end up on my plate and in my stomach.

As I continued to think about this topic even more, and did extra research on it, I realized there *was* a whole list of advantages that came with eating bugs. Afton Halloran, lead author and entomophagy advocate, gathered some data on the environmental impact of bugs and the "study showed that cricket farming indeed earns its sustainable title." On top of the excellent sustainability of bugs, these types of diets are also very "efficient sources of iron and vitamin B12," and are very beneficial to your health because many bugs also have "all the essential amino acids." This means that having a diet with bugs paves the way for a more environmentally sustainable future, without having to sacrifice any key nutrients along the way. Individuals on Earth need to reduce their carbon footprint, and one way people can easily do this on their own is by cutting back on meat to transition to the nutritious and sustainable alternative of bugs.

There are many opinions on the inclusion of bugs in an individual's diet. Some say bugs are disgusting and should stay outdoors. Others argue that bugs are a nutritious, environmentally-friendly food source. I would say that bugs are a great alternative to regular meats, because not only are they tasty, they lead the future of sustainable cuisine. Individuals, particularly in the West, should research more on the topic of eating bugs. Just like me, I had a terrible mindset about eating bugs initially. However, as I was educated about all the benefits of this type of diet, I am now all for eating bugs, and I'm sure other individuals would be as well if they did some research. In the future, I hope that we no longer hear about how cows produce too much methane, and more about how to fine-tune our recipes for the perfect crickets.

Having already explored their own topics just a little bit, students returned to the sources that they had found from Gale's *Opposing Viewpoints in Context* and began to move through the same series of steps that we used with our shared topic of eating bugs. A simple or complex claim. A kernel essay structure. Opportunities for feedback. The next few lessons progressed in the same manner and did so over both synchronous and asynchronous work time. Our main tech tools—up to this point—were really nothing out of the ordinary: using our electronic library, Google Docs, and Zoom meetings. As we moved toward the final stage, a public service announcement, we then started to look at additional resources.

Before a deeper look at my students' final project, it is worth pausing for a moment to see how another educator, Ms. Smith, introduced to us by Detra Price-Dennis, engages students in argumentation of a different sort. Ms. Smith's students were immersed in a sustained, inquiry-driven process of creating short, persuasive films where they also work to bring awareness to gender equality concerns, both in terms of the content they are exploring and the collaborative groups in which they are working.

From the Classroom: "Integrating Technology to Support Text Production" by Detra Price-Dennis

Detra Price-Dennis is a professor of teaching and learning and the director of digital Education and Innovation in Teaching and Learning at The Ohio State University's College of Education and Human Ecology. Her award-winning scholarship draws on ethnographic and sociocultural lenses to examine the intersections of critical literacy education, technology, and equity-based curriculum development in K–8 classrooms.

"Wow," I said to Ms. Smith during our first meeting. "This certainly does not look like any fifth-grade classroom I have ever visited." I don't recall how the rest of the conversation went, but I do remember that feeling of hopeful curiosity I had as I talked with her about teaching and took a tour of the learning spaces she co-designed with her class.

Classroom design can influence how students imagine themselves as learners within a school space. In the best of scenarios, the spaces we create for our students in the classroom can reveal possibilities for engaging with content and learning in ways that are generative and vibrant. This vignette is an example of how space, pedagogy, and technology can converge in a language arts classroom to support imagination and social action.

For several years, I had the pleasure of working with an incredible fifth-grade classroom teacher, Ms. Smith, in Austin, Texas, to better understand how students consumed and produced multimodal texts with digital tools. I remember my first visit to her classroom. I entered the building assuming the space would look like any other fifth-grade classroom located in a building that was constructed during the 1960s. However, once I opened the door and walked inside, it was like entering a cozy, industrial tech startup with a maker-space vibe. As I scanned the room, I saw inspirational quotes displayed on the walls in large letters and in framed pictures; books displayed everywhere as well as tucked into cozy corners of the room; iPads, laptops, and desktop computers were in bins or clustered around seating areas for easy access; art supplies, sensory materials, and notebooks were visible and strategically placed around the room; and eclectic furniture styled at different heights and in different configurations. The space Ms. Smith created for herself to teach in and for students to learn in—and, for that matter, to teach one another—felt like an invitation for them to determine what they needed when working on projects and what type of space made most sense to get the work done. I realized very quickly that space itself was also positioned as a teaching tool to facilitate learning in very deliberate and meaningful ways.

For almost three years, I observed teaching and learning in this classroom. I documented the ways student inquiry about equity and social change was foundational to the curriculum. During a unit of study about gender and equity, I had the privilege to work with a small group of students who were serving as the production crew on the stop-motion animation film their team developed about gender inequality. To share some context, in the weeks before my work with this small group, the class decided to learn more about gender identity and create projects that would examine the cause of gender inequality. For this project, they decided to create a stop-motion animation film modeled after mentor texts they saw on BrainPOP.

To get started on the project, Ms. Smith helped the students create two teams. One team decided to shift focus and study creativity, while the other team continued work on gender inequality. Each team researched their topic using guided questions from their teacher. At the end of each work time, the class met as a whole group to share what they were learning, seek help on any issues they were having with finding reliable sources, and pose questions they still wanted to know about their topic.

For instance, I remember one day when the students were trying to decide how they should directly and indirectly address gender norms in the film. Their goal was to disrupt the binary they experienced when shopping at local big box retailers to reflect the shopping aesthetic in Swedish stores that did not separate toys or clothes by gender. The students were frustrated by the ways fast food companies and stores dictated options for them based on gender norms. They shared ideas such as using the set design, characters, clothing for the characters, and the script for the gender equality guides to make this issue visible. They wanted the film to show the audience how ridiculous and limiting gender norms were without directly telling the audience what to think.

After the teams felt comfortable with their research, they reconfigured themselves into smaller groups to begin working on their films. Each team had script writers, set designers, character and voice-over actors, tech crew (which included the director), and a production crew. The students supported each other across these roles and met at the end of each class period to check in about their timeline and make adjustments to any tasks that still needed to be completed.

During my time with the production crew, we brainstormed ideas for how to approach editing the film, adding voiceovers, the possibility of adding subtitles (in English and

Spanish), and transitions between scenes and closing credits. The students moved between printed copies of the script, a storyboard of the scenes, and notes they made about voice innovation and capturing the essence of a BrainPOP character, Moby, and his signature, robotic communication style.

As we neared the end of the project, students used iMovie to edit the film and GarageBand to add voiceover tracks. On several occasions while the crew replayed edited cuts of the film, we noticed the actors' voices lagged behind the film; on other occasions, the actors' voices were ahead of the scene. Regardless of the issue, the group discussed several ways they could address the problem and often decided to play the clip for the actors, ultimately leading them to request a rerecording of a voice track. This process involved multiple iterations and problem solving across different modalities.

Throughout the process students were positioned as consumers of multimedia as well as producers. As the NCTE *Beliefs for Integrating Technology into the English Language Arts Classroom* contends, students were producing "media productions by combining video clips, images, sound, music, voice-overs, and other media." They took on the responsibility of bringing their team's vision to the screen and as such they had to think about how to translate the script and unedited film clips into a film that also included voice and sound effects. In essence, as I stepped away from Ms. Smith's classroom for the final time, I knew they were designing, revising, editing, remixing, and producing as viewers and creators of text.

Notes from Troy

As Detra Price-Dennis describes Mrs. Smith's classroom and the work in which the students are engaged, I am reminded of a refrain that has been part of the ELA conversation for what seems like forever yet is rarely articulated so clearly: the process of reading and writing, speaking and listening, viewing and visually representing are integrated and interactive. In addition to illustrating many of the ideas from the BIT-ELA, she illustrates many of the elements that are evident in NCTE's *Definition of Literacy in a Digital Age*, including the ideas that students can, simultaneously, "engage critically, thoughtfully, and across a wide variety of inclusive texts and tools/modalities," "[e]xamine the rights, responsibilities, and ethical implications of the use and creation of information," and "[d]etermine how and to what extent texts and tools amplify one's own and others' narratives as well as counter unproductive narratives."

Indeed, none of these literacy practices are ones that can be separated out, like a single benchmark, to be met in isolation. Teachers who are engaged in a model of holistic, integrated ELA instruction must bring many skills together in these ways. Ms. Smith, in particular, honors the various abilities and interests of her students by inviting them to take on different roles in the process and feel an equal amount of investment in accomplishing the group's goals. Together, they were able to engage in the BIT-ELA's call for "critical literacy—paying attention to the construction of individual and cultural identities," as well as meeting the standards in their ELA curriculum.

Mastery Assessment: Public Service Announcement

As students moved through the topic of their essay and expanded their initial claim statement and kernel paragraphs, we began to think about how they could move their argument into another format: a public service announcement (PSA). And, while the PSA form can be considered a common way for students to move from the essay into a different form, when scaffolded in a thorough and thoughtful manner, the PSA can also become a tool for multimedia composing. Portions of the assignment for the PSA Campaign are shown below, with a link to the entire assignment as a Google Doc available on the book's companion page.

First, students were asked to identify whether they wanted to work alone or in a group and to consider the following related to the overall argument, as well as to the design of the PSA:

- With the argument:
  - Writing a nuanced claim statement using claim starters
  - Providing evidence to support your claim
  - Appealing to ethos, pathos, logos as a way to convince your audience
  - Considering and defining your audience
- With the visual design:
  - Selecting impactful images and imagery
  - Considering the impact of color choice
  - Using font(s) to create a coherent message across the PSA products being created

In the planning template, students then had to articulate a brief response to the following rhetorical elements:

- What is your topic or message? Use research sources to help you find a topic.
- Who is your target audience or demographic? Remember that the general public is not a target audience! Think carefully about who you are trying to reach.
- What is it that you want the audience to think, feel, believe, or behave? Examples could be to donate time or money, sign a petition, attend a rally, visit a website, talk to a doctor, volunteer, etc.

Finally, they had to choose two products from a list—or propose their own—such as an Instagram post, a poster or billboard, a TikTok video, a brochure, or a TV commercial. They were also given the option to create audio in the form of a radio spot, knowing that they would be doing at least one other visual product. As shown on the Google Doc for the assignment, students were then given many resources that they could use to investigate their topic, design their PSA, and find additional media resources.

A few items to note in the assignment include:

- Students had a choice in terms of working individually or as a group. Whether students chose to work alone or with partners, they created two media artifacts. On their own, students had complete creative freedom to make what they wished. As a duo or trio, they needed to work together to make a coordinated campaign.

- While students were required to make their products focus on the same topic and message, they were encouraged to "[c]onsider designing different products for different target audiences within your topic." This is both about aiming at audiences that might be in traditional demographic binaries (younger or older, men or women), and it is also about targeting within a demographic that might have varying perspectives (teens who are likely to vaccinate and need a nudge or teens who are unlikely to vaccinate due to personal concerns).

- Finally, the checklists that are provided were considered heuristic (that is, focused on open-ended problem solving) as compared to specific criteria for a rubric. This intentional choice to steer clear of elements that "must" be included gave students the flexibility to be creative and, to be entirely honest, teachers a bit of freedom from the minutiae of grading student work at the end of the year. Though we still provided them with feedback, we were not nearly as confined by levels of proficiency on a rubric.

As I reviewed these mastery projects with my colleagues, I was impressed by the PSA materials that my students produced. For instance, one student created an Instagram post and was able to make a radio commercial about the idea of "cancel culture," recorded as an MP3. In his commercial, he concludes that we must acknowledge how our greatness comes from our mistakes. Another student, in a campaign to save the Arctic and fight climate change, used Adobe Creative Cloud Express (at the time, named Adobe Spark) to create a billboard-style image showing a polar bear stranded on a piece of melting ice with a link to an online petition. She also created a few Instagram posts, too.

A third, AJ, created a radio commercial and several Instagram posts that outlined the benefits of all Americans getting vaccinated, designed to be posted as a series in Instagram's "story" format (Figure 6.9, with a link to all images on the book's companion site). AJ's approach to using an Instagram story both appeals to his audience in terms of format, and he also anticipated many of the objections that youth might have. For instance, in the third image, he notes the concerns that had been raised about deaths following administration of one of the vaccines to a small number of people, encouraging his viewers by stating: "Let's put things into perspective," then going on to provide even more context. He also appeals to pathos, encouraging his peers to get the vaccine in order to get back to the things they had been missing in their lives such

FIGURES 6.9: AJ's Instagram-Style Posts Created in the Spring of 2021

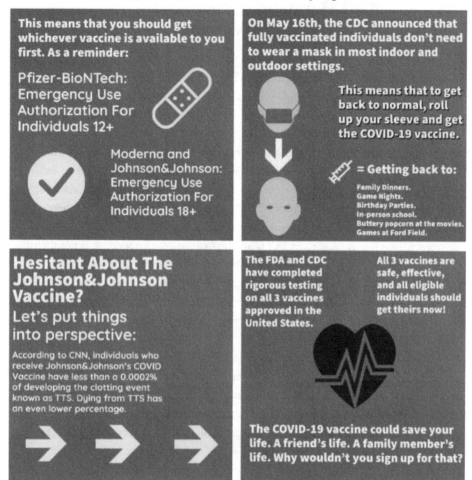

as family dinners, game nights, and even "buttery popcorn at the movies." In total, the nine images comprise a compelling story that presents his argument to an audience of his peers in a format they are likely to engage with. They were very successful offering strategies for other teens to recognize when a teen is in crisis and resources to get help. (Note: AJ produced this PSA in the spring of 2021, before the CDC updated guidance on masking as a result of the Delta and Omicron variants.)

Coming both to the end of this unit as well as the end of the school year, I was again reminded that students could share their ideas in compelling ways, moving their "simple claims" into more complex and nuanced essays that, in turn, became an incredible gallery of PSAs. Just as the BIT-ELA suggests, my students, too, were able to use digital technologies o access "new opportunities to read, write, listen, view, record, compose, and interact with both the texts themselves and with other people."

Final Thoughts from Troy and Jill: Arguing and Persuading with the BIT-ELA Principles in Mind

The goal of argument—as we have come to learn from our work with the C3WP and various scholars including Harris, Graff and Birkenstein, and others—is to open up dialogue, not simply to "win" based on one's own opinion. For our students (and, let's be honest, for adults, too), it is challenging to step outside of one's own perspective. By introducing different texts—both the ideas and evidence in those texts as well as multiple textual forms—to our students, we are able to help them see, hear, and experience these broader conversations. We are reminded of Diana Hess's idea that there are "open" and "closed" parts of different debates (Hess, 2009). While there are times where we need to help students see that certain aspects of a debate are not up for conversation (for instance, the fact that climate change is happening is not up for discussion), yet the ways to approach a solution are (for instance how do we best move forward to mitigate climate change?). Troy, with Kristen Turner, has also taken up the idea of argument with digital tools, considering how various forms of media affect the claims a writer might make, as well as the evidence and reasoning that a writer might employ (2016).

The BIT-ELA principles further these ideas, helping our students to both examine existing arguments across media forms and construct their own. For instance, in Belief 1, we are reminded to "encourage multimodal digital communication while modeling how to effectively compose images, presentations, graphics, or other media productions by combining video clips, images, sound, music, voice-overs, and other media." As Jill's students demonstrated, these critical and creative approaches to presenting their claims come both in the form of the academic essay as well as the other media noted above such as a radio commercial, social media posts, and billboards.

Helping students to see what parts of the topics they are most interested in and that we are still open to discussion—even in our contentious political climate—is an important part of the work we need to do when teaching argument writing.

To guide further discussion and exploration, we encourage teachers to think about the following:

- In what ways are you introducing topics to students so they can see the breadth and depth of conversation? What voices are being valued in your text sets? What kinds of media (articles, books, websites, podcasts, videos, and other media forms) are being valued in your text sets?

- When scaffolding them through the writing process, in what ways are the intentional moves from "simple claims" to "complex claims" and then into patterns for "kernel essays" potentially useful for your students?

- As students produce their own PSAs, what additional elements from the BIT-ELA statement related to digital and critical literacies can be intentionally taught in the process of developing multimodal texts?

Chapter Seven

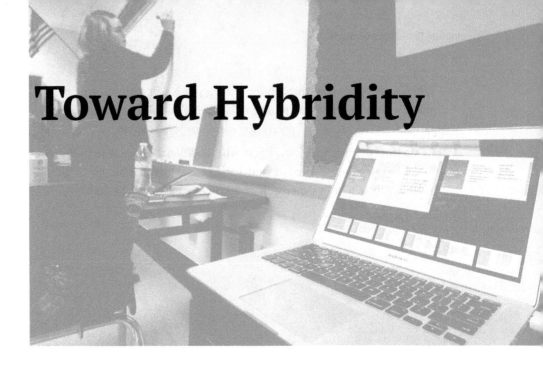

Toward Hybridity

*A*s we wrap up the bulk of our work on this manuscript—in the fall of 2021—it feels as though the shifts (to and from, back and forth, in school and out) have all put another level of complexity on education that wasn't anticipated when we returned to learn in person. With the emergence of yet another COVID-19 variant as we head into winter, we simply don't know what to expect. More importantly, we are reminded by scholars and activists that what we consider "normal" in our educational systems is not "normal" at all; instead, we need to remember that schooling happens in a system that has been designed, instituted, and reinscribed from classroom to classroom, from one school year to the next. As we consider what it means to teach now, having learned the opportunities and challenges of remote instruction, there are lessons learned that can remind us of what works, yes, yet what also needs to change.

We return to Jill's perspective here, as she offers reflections on the current moment.

"This will feel familiar, like riding a bike," I thought.

I was wrong about that.

The seeming comfort of going back to school, to be in person with my students, and teach in my classroom all had layers of complexity, both pedagogically and, to be honest, emotionally. Early in the fall of 2021, our district has already encountered three unscheduled school cancellations for what my superintendent has called students' and staff members' mental health and overall safety amongst rising rates of COVID transmission. I thought that stepping back into the classroom would be a relatively easy transition, yet it is not.

Put another way, students have been gone from school for the better part of two years, a reminder that I hear echoed by other educators, parents, and caregivers. This is not to say that they are developmentally delayed or that we are fretting about "learning loss," but it is to say that the norms of a given school day, week, and year have been disrupted. A recent report on our local NPR radio station brought in the voice of a teacher whose students were in the midst of an active group activity and then, as if a blanket had been thrown on the room, all of them stood in the classroom simply staring at one another, silent. The teacher described their lack of motivation and willingness to engage as eerie. This is just one example of how changes in classroom norms—let alone bigger productions like homecoming pep rallies and parades, school dances, and dress-up days— have all been disrupted.

All that said, our principal has led a rallying cry. The philosophy for the year, he continues to repeat, is that "we are not going back." We want to move forward with a more informed approach to mental health and well-being, a critical and creative mindset toward using technology, and an overall recommitment to mastery-based learning and providing students with choice.

Context and Connections to the BIT-ELA Statement: Three Snapshots from Jill of Learning from the Pre-Pandemic Classroom, during Remote Learning, and Now

To summarize some of these changes and look at the new stance I—and many of my colleagues—are taking, I capture my perspective on three key components of instruction and how my thinking has changed in 1) pre-pandemic times, 2) during remote learning, and 3) in the current moment and moving forward. To put some of these changes into context, I began listing just some of the ways that things look different in my classroom, specifically as it relates to our use of computers, the impact of socio-emotional learning (SEL), and my approach to grades and feedback. Here are some of the ways that things have evolved.

For a student who would have walked into my classroom in the early part of the 2019–2020 school year, they would have experienced:

- Computers on carts, where teachers used a reservation system and the carts moved around to classrooms based on need.

- A sense of SEL being present but not top of mind. I thought that building relationships with my students and having supportive procedures in the classroom would suffice.

- Complex grading procedures where students earned points for a myriad of tasks. The point values associated with each assignment was subjective and my decision. Students either passed or failed my class. Failing students would take the course again at another juncture in their high school career.

These ways of working (if, indeed, they had been working at all) underwent some major changes in the shift to emergency remote teaching in the spring of 2020 and—with my district keeping middle and high school students online nearly the entire time—during the 2020–2021 school year.

For a student in my remote classroom during the 2020–2021 school year, they would have experienced:

- Having technology became imperative—their own school-issued Chromebook, access to the Schoology LMS, and a strong internet connection (with cellular data/Wi-Fi hotspots issued to those in need)—as they were the only way to stay connected to course content.

- SEL became top of mind, with check-ins during Zoom chat and individual breakout rooms. Casual one-on-one conversations were not usually an option during regular class time, though individual conferences with students were possible, especially on our completely asynchronous Wednesdays.

- Grading and feedback embraced "process work," which was awarded one point per assignment along with any needed feedback. Mastery work was given a larger point value but was heavily based on student self-assessment of their level of mastery. Additionally, students could earn a traditional letter grade for the course, but the addition of NC (no credit) and C (credit) were offered in lieu of a failing grade.

As we continue in the 2021–2022 academic year, I am still making some changes, keeping a number of the ideas in place that seem to be working well and adapting them to our more consistent schedule offered by face-to-face instruction.

For a student in the current iteration of my classroom, they are experiencing:

- The benefit of still having their Chromebooks, where courses are designed and materials are delivered through Schoology, yet group work and whole class discussions are occurring during real-time, face-to-face sessions, much the way we remembered them to be.

- SEL is now intentionally supported through lesson design and content delivery. Relationship building and classroom procedures are back in place with the much-needed improvements outlined below.

- And, with grading, the 2020–2021 grading system is still in place with the addition of a building wide, year-long discussion of grading. The administration and teaching staff are all reading *Grading for Equity: What It Is, Why It Matters, and How It Can Transform Schools and Classrooms* by Joe Feldman (2018) to keep thinking about these issues.

Even with these new opportunities, we are caught in the paradox that is schooling, especially schooling for middle level students, caught between the tension of our principal's mantra of "not going back" and trying to reimagine the new normal. Of note, our school's administration opened the 2021–2022 school year with a message from Dr. Bettina Love—a professor at the University of Georgia who argues for "abolitionist teaching" (Love, 2019)—who has made the argument that schools "played their hand" by suddenly providing an immense amount of technology and technical support during the crisis (Byrd Farmer, 2021), and further argues that we can't go back, hence the rallying cry. So, with many of the same structures in place, we are still trying to find our balance as we get back on the metaphorical bike I mentioned at the start of this chapter.

Still, we will move through daily schedules of five 72-minute periods in a trimester, away from the longer segments of time we had with students in remote learning. Those asynchronous Wednesdays that we had last year for planning with colleagues and meeting with individual students are gone, back to a normal school day. Students are still figuring out how best to navigate multiple spaces and demands, and some are still entirely virtual, in asynchronous learning (of note, no teachers are expected to teach class in a "dual delivery" mode anymore, simultaneously on Zoom and to a classroom with students present).

This is not to say that we have completely "gone back," nor that we have "moved forward." It is a strange limbo, this new hybridity. There are ways in which we are trying to hack or adapt the intensely crazy schedule we used to maintain. These ideas will be explored in a bit more detail later in the chapter, though a quick list of strategies we have explored include 1) a focus on grading for equity, with single-point rubrics and continued opportunities for mastery learning, 2) refocusing our mid-week teaching and learning with "Workshop Wednesdays" for students to work independently and confer with us as teachers, and 3) organizing our lessons in Schoology in a consistent, coherent manner. With these general strategies in mind, we'll share a more detailed description of how we are enacting the BIT-ELA principles through these strategies in the sections below.

And, before we move into a final set of suggestions that might help our ELA colleagues move to hybridity, we hear from one more colleague, Alex Corbitt, who describes a unit that he taught in 2017. Even then, Corbitt was already making moves in his classroom that could support a hybrid approach to exploring literary analysis and narrative writing, specifically the epistolary genre which is built on the format of characters writing letters and moving the story forward. Given the range of independent and collaborative activities, as well as the technologies being employed, we can see ways that this vignette could be a model for teaching ELA in the spirit of the BIT-ELA document, whether fully face-to-face, fully online, or in a hybrid format.

From the Classroom: "Rethinking Narrative Writing with E-pistolary Stories" by Alex Corbitt

Alex Corbitt (@Alex_Corbitt) is a doctoral student at Boston College. He works with youth to understand how they use gaming and technologies for writing and composition. Before living in Boston, Alex taught seventh-grade English language arts in the Bronx, New York.

The first time I taught with "texting stories"—that is, digital "e-pistolary" narratives (Santini, 2019) that are composed in the form of text message conversations—was on Halloween in 2017. Our classroom was dark, and the students sat in a tense silence. My phone glowed at the front of the room as a document camera projected the phone screen onto the whiteboard. Slowly, I clicked through a story on an iOS app called Hooked. The narrative was a spooky story told entirely through a text message conversation between a boy and his father. We read along in suspense as the messages popped onto the screen. The boy explains how there is a mysterious figure in the yard that resembles the father. But to our horror, the father messages, "That's not me." And, then, "Get away from the window." The students' gasps were audible...

For weeks after Halloween, my students asked to read more Hooked stories. I put off their requests because the additional stories on the app were subscription-based, and we had other texts to read for class. Then, one day a student brought a new phone application to my attention: TextingStory. She showed me how the app was free and allowed users to craft texting stories. "We could write our own versions of Hooked!" she said. Until that point in my career, I had only taught narrative writing with Word and Google Docs. And while I was inspired by my student's enthusiasm for texting stories, I doubted the "rigor" of the new genre. Texting stories were entertaining, but were they a mode of robust storytelling?

I must admit that I love new technologies. However, I always try to be "technology agnostic" when considering the affordances of digital teaching tools. Like books and film, technologies are political and imbued with ideologies. I am wary of "edtech," "gamification," and other trends insofar as they can repackage traditional (and often oppressive) pedagogies in new, enticing digital formats. They are skill and drill exercises in a different form. To this end, I always ask two questions when I encounter new learning platforms: 1) How does this tool redefine my literacies pedagogies?, and 2) How does this tool reproduce my literacies pedagogies? Or as noted in the NCTE *Beliefs for Integrating Technology into the English Language Arts Classroom*, I work to ensure that "new technologies should be considered only when it is clear how they can enhance, expand, and/or deepen engaging and sound practices related to literacy instruction." This stance and these questions help me stay critical as I assess the instructional potential of new technologies.

So, I wondered: how could epistolary-style texting stories redefine my literacies pedagogies? First, I noticed that the genre centers youths' breadth of linguistic repertoires (including emojis); texting stories do not police students' grammar and usage like traditional schooling. Second, I considered how students could craft texting stories together as different characters within the narrative. This kind of collaboration could, potentially, scaffold and enrich the composing process. Finally, I noted the genre's limited capacity for exposition. Since texting stories are only told between messages, students would have to embed background information and setting details within their characters' discourse. Put another way, texting stories require students to be very aware of how dialog can propel and contextualize narratives.

But texting stories aren't without their ideological shortcomings. They also reinforce the dominance of letters and numbers (i.e., alphanumeric language). Whereas television and film center a breadth of visual and auditory modes of storytelling, texting stories primarily focus on the written word. Thus, texting stories do not necessarily reinvent literacies instruction as we know it. However, creative opportunities are available, and I will detail below an example of how a group of students added visual and auditory components to their collaborative texting story in ways that radically shifted my thinking about the genre.

After a few weeks of consideration, I finally gave students the option to compose texting stories. Some students used the TextingStory app, and others used the standard texting feature on their phones. Each group emailed me screen recordings of their narratives and we celebrated their projects and writerly choices around a "Craft Campfire." During the event, we arranged our chairs into a big circle around the whiteboard. A campfire was projected on the board as we ate marshmallows (because there are some parts of a campfire that you just can't reinvent virtually) and took turns premiering our texting stories to the class. After each viewing, we discussed the various craft moves the creators employed.

One group project, in particular, exemplified the potential of texting stories. This project unfolded in a group chat as four characters casually recount the events of their day. Slowly they all realize that they are being haunted by a spirit. In addition to texting, the characters exchange videos and audio recordings of paranormal phenomena in their apartments. This layering of writing, audio, and film highlighted the breadth of literacies practices that texting stories can employ. Beyond excitement and admiration, this project left our class in a state of awe.

At the risk of being misinterpreted, I do not intend to overemphasize the value of texting stories or the e-pistolary genre. Rather, I share this vignette to spotlight a moment in which digital tools, expansive youth literacies, and instructional reflexivity converged to redefine how I understand technology integration in the classroom. And, in the spirit of inquiry and professional community, I seek out similar "e-phiphany" stories from my colleagues as we share our learning, from text to tweet and beyond.

Notes from Troy

With this exploration of the e-pistolary genre, Corbitt is truly enacting the interconnected goal of "sponsoring students in digital writing and connected reading to collaboratively construct knowledge, participate in immersive learning experiences, and reach out to their own community and a global audience." In addition to teaching the traditional ELA skills related to literary analysis and narrative writing, his multifaceted approach to studying the affordances of the e-pistolary genre shows a unique technique that, to the delight of his students, was both intellectually and emotionally engaging. Being near Halloween, I'm sure, certainly helped his process of teaching the unit, though the skills with which he was able to navigate multiple technologies and teaching strategies are well worth noting here, too. Corbitt's approach could be adapted to remote teaching with the built-in connections to digital writing tools, allowing for even more opportunities for creative expression and collaboration.

Putting the BIT-ELA Principles into Practice: Three Suggestions for Moving toward Hybridity in Jill's Classroom

As we close our exploration of the BIT-ELA statement—as well as Jill's 2020–2021 school year—we are reflecting on our work and seeing how three main ideas have emerged from our inquiry. Like many books about teaching, these are not definitive statements about what *could* or *should* happen in anyone's classroom and teaching context, yet they do offer insights on three themes that Jill has seen in her own planning and preparation, real-time instruction, and follow-up with feedback for students (as well as additional collaboration with colleagues). We will explore each in turn:

1. Using the Computer More Intentionally

2. Encouraging Both Physical and Digital Notebooks

3. Reestablishing Daily and Weekly Routines

Notes from Troy

As we prepare to look more closely at the ways that Jill has brought hybridity to life in her classroom, extending the uses of technology and a recommitment to (SEL) and equitable grading, it is worth reiterating the four *Beliefs for Integrating Technology into the English Language Arts Classroom*, copied here directly from the statement:

Literacy means *literacies*. Literacy is more than reading, writing, speaking, listening, and viewing as traditionally defined. It is more useful to think of *literacies*, which are social practices that transcend individual modes of communication.

Consider literacies before technologies. New technologies should be considered only when it is clear how they can enhance, expand, and/or deepen engaging and sound practices related to literacies instruction.

Technologies provide new ways to consume and produce texts. What it means to consume and produce texts is changing as digital technologies offer new opportunities to read, write, listen, view, record, compose, and interact with both the texts themselves and with other people.

Technologies and their associated literacies are not neutral. While access to technology and the internet has the potential to lessen issues of inequity, they can also perpetuate and even accelerate discrimination based on gender, race, socioeconomic status, and other factors.

The ways in which we, as educators, enact these beliefs can vary, as Jill and our many vignette contributors have shown throughout this collection. We must use technologies in ways that both embrace students' existing literacy practices and challenge them to learn new practices as a way to be critical, creative, and civically engaged. The shifts that we have highlighted in this book—and summarize with ideas about moving toward hybridity below—are all still in motion and ones that we need to continue to interrogate as we teach our middle level learners in the months and years ahead.

Idea 1: Using the Computer More Intentionally

During our year of learning remotely, both teachers and students acquired new ways of utilizing devices to make connections with the lessons and each other. On the one hand, with our digital lives being what they are, you would have thought that this would be seamless, causing no problems at all in our communication patterns. On the other hand, this change happened quickly, forcing both teachers and students to develop new ways of thinking about our computers and strategies to use them, all in ways that made the curriculum and materials accessible.

One example of this new thinking manifested in the daily "lesson slides." In the past, lesson slides were used solely by me as the teacher and viewed by students on a screen at the front of the classroom. Students didn't have access to these slides; instead, most teachers required students to pay attention and take any necessary notes as the slides were presented. During remote learning, slides were presented during a lesson that mimicked the in-person class, but for my colleagues and me, new ways of intentionally using the slides along with one-to-one computers evolved. Even at the beginning of the 2020–2021 school year, many students did not review the lesson slides ahead of time or have them open on a separate tab during the lesson. What happened over the course of the school year was that we all learned that any student could benefit from two strategies: 1) listening and watching the teacher present the slides during a Zoom class and 2) having the lesson slides open on their computers in a separate tab from the Zoom class meeting. In other words, they could follow along with my presentation and take notes on their own copy of the Google Slides.

This was beneficial for them while all together in the main Zoom room and had an extra side effect; when doing group work in a breakout room, the instructions for what to do, questions to answer, and how long to work that were built into a slide in the lesson sequence could remain open on their own computer, even though the teacher was no longer sharing the screen. Additionally, teachers learned the importance of having lesson slide decks prepared and loaded into Schoology ahead of class so students could preview the lesson before class began. This intentional front-loading of lesson slides helped students begin to activate their knowledge of the day's lesson as well as formulate questions that needed to be answered before class ended. For whatever reason, these were not classroom practices that I ever used before 2020–2021. They evolved out of necessity during remote learning and continue now that we are back to in-person learning.

As I continue to think about what is important to retain from our remote learning year, two really important changes noted in my opening list of "shifts" have carried over from virtual learning: all students have a Chromebook, and Schoology is the district-supported LMS. On the surface, these two changes don't seem to be significant, but it didn't take very long to realize that these make a huge impact on how I think about teaching on a daily basis. As I began to plan lessons for the same ninth-grade units I taught remotely last year, my thoughts this fall were that this process would be smoother. Of course, I could implement the collaborative lessons I planned with my colleagues and used last year, as well as provide structured time for reading and writing during class sessions.

Yet finding balance remains a challenge. Computers, slides with links, and Schoology are ever-present; yet I am always asking myself—"What is the proper balance between what remains from online learning and the personal connection that an in-person classroom setting provides?" Our COVID reality found us in a situation where a student could be present one day and gone for the next ten school days due to contact tracing or testing positive. This is also a reality for teachers as well.

To illustrate this balancing act, on the one hand, hours can be spent thinking about a lesson delivered via Schoology: creating meaningful slides, screencast videos, and anticipating questions before they are asked. On the other hand, a lesson delivered in-person can veer off, in a "teachable moment" kind of way, to a place that I can't anticipate that feels really organic. And we still struggle with how to best serve a student who is home with robust instructional materials so they can work through lessons without being in class, and, at the same time, be prepared for the students in the room.

Even though I hear from other educators that they want students to take notes in a physical notebook or in their own word-processed document, it seems to me that having slides open on every student's computer could add to a student's learning, engagement, and understanding in ways I hadn't considered before. For example, if I ask students to take notes on vocabulary or a new skill we are learning, it is safe to say that there will be many students who finish this task before their classmates. Further, there are always one or two students who want to do a really good job but who work at a slower pace. Having the students each have the slides open on their computers provides us all with options:

1. I can move on in the lesson while the final people finish their notetaking, and I am comfortable knowing that the students still writing can look at the board and join the rest of the class without losing much content. If needed, a student can go back and review any slides that were missed and ask me for clarification. They can use the "commenting" tool or the notes space to capture their own thinking.

2. Students who drift away from the lesson can look at their computer screens and see that the slide on the computer doesn't match where I am, and they can try to regroup. Without the computer open and the slide deck open, who knows how long a student may daydream before they try to re-engage with the material!

3. The slides offer answers to questions students have. One advantage I have found with using the slides with all students is if questions arise, I can refer a student to a specific slide, or just tell them the answer to the question is in the slides and move on. Students can easily answer their own questions, which then frees me to conference with students or move on with a lesson.

Additional advantages to having the same robust slide decks this year as I did during our online year is something that we have always dealt with—and will, sadly continue to wrestle with as COVID settles into an endemic status—student absence. I have students gone for a variety of reasons: sports, appointments, illness, bereavement, family trips, and more. When we talk together about the upcoming absence, it works really well to point them to Schoology and the course materials. I tell students to review the slides for the lesson(s) missed, and then ask that they do their best to complete any work assigned. As mentioned earlier and shown throughout the book, the Ann Arbor Public Schools tech team created a slide template for lessons that most teachers employed last year, so this feels familiar to students, and they know their way around the lesson slide decks.

The balance then becomes maintaining as much of the preplanned, front-loaded organization and support for student learning using Schoology coupled with in-class lessons that can feel more organic, catering to the needs and interests of the students in any given section of the classes I teach. At times it feels like I am double planning; this is something that feels unsustainable, though perhaps it will become more natural, a practice that informs my planning and instruction and will evolve over time to be more manageable.

As the 2021–2022 school year is now underway, there are a few more ideas that are falling into place. First, my slide decks have shifted from a daily deck to a weekly deck that encompasses all of the lessons for the week. I place a slide with a bright blue background in between each lesson with the day of the week in huge, bold letters, as shown in Figure 7.1 below. This allows students to scroll through a slide deck and find the beginning and ending of a day's lesson easily. The students all know from last year that class will start with learning targets and a "Do Now" task that has targets out on the side including SEL, vocabulary, and content. Then we move to an Agenda that includes deliverables for the lesson as well as homework assigned.

From there, each day will be different. While I don't always get to it, the last slide recaps a lesson in the form of questions in a "During today's lesson, did you...?" This is followed by a series of bullet-point questions that ask students to process the activities of the lesson. This slide also includes a Homework or "Before Next Time" section that shows them what needs to be done before I see them again. Even though I don't always explicitly show this slide to my students during the class period, it serves two purposes. First, as the slide creator and lesson designer, making this slide helps me look back at a day's lesson and process the main points that students should take away from that day's learning. I also evaluate how the lesson fits in with the curriculum, offering a balance of activities and transitions. This simple exercise at the end of each slide deck forces me to analyze my lesson, making edits when needed. Second, this slide works well for students to self-assess their progress. They can use it as a tool to determine what needs to be done outside of class as homework by looking at this slide. Again, all of these can be seen in a thumbnail version in Figure 7.1 and more clearly in Figures 7.2 and 7.3.

The addition of what we call a "deliverable" manifested last year as a response to remote learning. What in the past was considered work to complete as part of the lesson now needed to be delineated and clarified for students as a deliverable—a task or small product, like taking notes in the writer's notebook. Having a list of deliverables allowed students to see what was required of them in the upcoming lesson. These daily deliverables provided the stepping stones or practice for assignment completion. While they had always existed in my planning and lessons, they were never labeled as such, and I didn't make the expectations explicit for students. My style of teaching also had lots of latitude for what we now call a deliverable to be done "on the fly"; that is,

FIGURE 7.1: Slidedeck Layout for a Week's Worth of Lessons

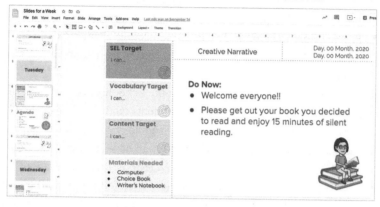

FIGURE 7.2: Agenda for a Daily Lesson

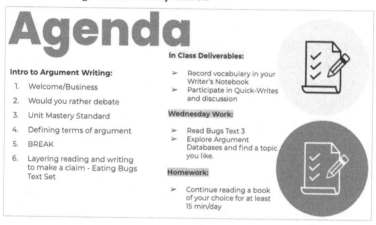

FIGURE 7.3: Last Slide in a Daily Lesson including "Did You? Review Questions . . ." and "Homework . . ."

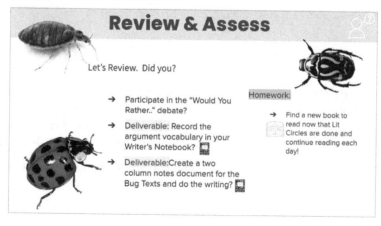

I might quickly assign a writing-to-learn task or a note check so I could tell that my students grasped the concept being taught. What my year of digital teaching taught me is that making these small stepping stones overt and calculated, in turn, helped students see what I expected from them during each lesson meeting. Planning them ahead of time has been an adjustment for me, but one I am getting used to and now including in each day's agenda (as shown in Figure 7.3).

Having my lessons on slides (and linked in the Schoology course materials) also allows the different layers of support some students require to be included in the day-to-day happenings in my class. Most of my Schoology courses include special-ed teachers, school social workers, and coteachers. They all have administrator rights to my classes, so they may look at the gradebook, preview lessons, create adaptations for the students they serve, and collaborate with me, when needed, to best serve our students. This allows them to see what is happening when it is convenient for them, reduces the amount of email exchanges, and can even prevent extra meetings that eat up our planning time.

The intentional use of computers during class time and Schoology for lesson design has made me a better lesson planner and teacher. While I had decades of experience teaching prior to 2020, I realize now the ways in which my planning fell short, at least compared to what I do now. My thinking goes beyond what was once a bullet-point list of items to cover in a lesson, just enough to make an agenda on the board for each day. The rest was just done by reading the room and relying on my tried-and-true methods of working with students: making connections, bringing my enthusiasm for the content I teach, and giving students choice in the ways that they are able to demonstrate their learning.

Now, I think about different points for planning. For instance, how much time should I be talking, when should students be talking to each other and the class? When do we use computers and for what reason? How can the computer be a tool for learning in ways that in-person classroom practices can't offer? How does our use of Schoology and the computer push students forward in their learning? These are changes that I feel have been helpful, and I am certainly not going back on any of those.

Notes from Troy

Jill's intentional use of computers in the classroom—coupled with Schoology as LMS and Google Slides as a consistent lesson-planning and delivery tool—provides numerous connections to the BIT-ELA, enacting a number of practices that support middle level learners. For instance, I see how she is engaged in the following practices, directly or indirectly, as she utilizes the technologies, time, and teaching strategies available to her:

- "promote digital citizenship by modeling and mentoring students' use of devices, tools, social media, and apps to create media and interact with others."   **>**

- "design assignments, activities, and assessments that encourage interdisciplinary thinking, community and civic engagement, and technological integration informed by theories relevant to ELA."

- "examine to what degree access to and support of digital tools/technologies and instruction in schools reflects and/or perpetuates inequality."

- "articulate how policies and financial support at various levels (local, state, and national) inform both the infrastructure and the capacities for intellectual freedom to engage with literacies in personally and socially transformative ways."

- "focus on inquiry that balances the novelty of digital tools with the overarching importance of teaching and learning for deep meaning-making, substantive conversation, and critical thinking."

- "advocate for equitable solutions that employ technology in culturally responsive ways, drawing on students' and teachers' existing funds of knowledge related to literacy, learning, and using digital devices/networks."

As teachers reflect on the strategies Jill has shared just in Idea 1, I wonder how they might look at the intersections of school policies, technology integration, and their own teaching style in similar, robust ways. What lessons can we learn from Jill's restructuring of her lesson planning, instructional time, and flexibility in working with students and colleagues?

Idea 2: Encouraging Both Physical and Digital Notebooks

As shown in Chapter 1, the writer's notebook is the lifeblood of my middle level classroom. Last year was the first time I considered a digital version because it was all I had. This year, I wanted to honor those students who love technology and like to use the computer (perhaps because they fear their own penmanship) as well as those who would prefer a traditional, analog notebook (perhaps because the old way of doing it made sense to them in their quest to be a better writer).

This leads me to ask questions about notebooks—in particular when it comes to building a robust notebook that represents a student's process of learning and practicing new skills: is a digital notebook or a paper notebook better? I found that offering a choice, as both have their own distinct advantages and disadvantages, is best for students. Paper notebooks are easy for me to endorse because they have been around since I started teaching. Digital notebooks intrigued me but never seemed to be as successful because I used a digital notebook template that someone else made.

There is, of course, an ongoing debate about the role of handwriting in our classrooms, with some educators and researchers decrying the state of students' penmanship, others worried about their lack of touch-typing skills, and those who feel that there simply isn't enough writing of any kind at all. The science on this issue of handwriting as a literacy learning tool—one that encourages a deeper level of thought and information processing, as compared to touch typing—continues to develop, with at least one recent research article making the case that the motor functions of handwriting does help the brain solidify the learning of a new language, more so than using typing (Wiley and Rapp, 2021). No matter what format my students take with their initial notebook writing, we are often moving back and forth from paper to digital, so I do encourage them to use both sets of motor skills.

Still, it all comes back to a simple mantra: we need to read and write every day. I don't want to make any strong claims about *exactly* how much time I used to give students for reading and writing, on average, in a given day. I know I did, but I know I did a lot of talking. To be honest, I would guess that the total amount of time I used to offer my middle level students to engage in reading and writing, during class time, was probably about 10 percent of the precious minutes we had each day. What I can say now is that we spend about 40 percent of our time during any given week—especially during our Wednesday work time—reading a choice book as well as composing in our writer's notebook, and these pieces of writing can be anything from a freewrite to writing in a style or form of a mentor text or responding to a prompt.

Sometimes, about one to two times a week, our fifteen minutes of choice book reading that opens class is followed by time to write. This is usually a ten-minute timed writing in which students are offered a variety of things to write about. What I have learned over my years of teaching is that some students do very well and prefer to write about their own ideas, sometimes continuing their writing from the previous free writing time, whereas some students will stare at a blank screen or page, struggling for an idea to explore, unless they are given writing prompts to consider. Therefore, I offer both when writing time is given. Students are presented with a slide with three or four writing prompts with the last one being "write about a topic of your own choice."

During our year of remote learning, I struggled in providing a way to do digital notebooks that offered students a place to do short notetaking, write to process information in a write-pair-share exercise, and to write next to mentor texts that could become much longer writing pieces. A quick search for sites like SlidesGo or SlidesMania will yield many notebook templates, which can be found and adapted, though I still find them to be a bit cluttered. Many of the Google Docs and Slides templates I found had all kinds of unnecessary stuff in them, and students found them confusing.

This year, rather than using one of those templates, I used a simplified model developed by a colleague. The notebook was offered as a running series of slides in Google Slides. The entry spaces are simple, adaptable, and reproducible. There is a place for a date and title of the entry. Under that is a space for the writing. As many of my students continue to use digital notebooks, some of the positive things I have heard this year are the following:

- Students always know where their notebook can be found.

- The format adapts to their writing needs.

- It can be organized in sections or read like a blog, in reverse chronological order.

- It is searchable, making it easy to find past material.

- Slides can easily incorporate video and pictures, allowing students to incorporate more digital components to their writing.

While the physical and digital notebook both remain a choice in my classroom, there may come a time where a consistent modality may be necessary. When both are offered within the same class, it can present some challenges that are still manageable, but it currently feels like time is wasted for the following things:

- Students using a digital notebook can waste time transitioning to a notebook activity if their computer is still stowed in a backpack.

- While all students seem to have their computers in class, there are times when the computer needs charging. This can either waste time getting pluggedin or makes the computer unusable because the battery dies.

- Despite the aforementioned advantage of a student always knowing where to find a digital notebook, there are about ten to fifteen percent of students who waste time finding their digital notebooks because their Google Drive space is so unorganized.

- Digital notebooks are another monitoring step for the teacher. Just because a student has a computer open, eyes on the screen, and fingers typing does not necessarily mean that writing is happening. Let's face it, even with district filters, there are many distractions offered by the computer and internet that can allow students to look like they are engaged in digital writing.

As previously stated, paper notebooks are something I know well, but when used in the same context as a digital notebook, there are some ways that they, too, can interfere with the flow of a lesson. For example, when I ask students to add new vocabulary presented on the lesson slides to their writer's notebook, the paper notebook students take much longer because the students using the digital version can copy and paste into their notebooks from the lesson slides. Handwriting takes much longer. What results is that students who opted for a digital notebook sit waiting for the paper notebook classmates to accomplish the same task. Additionally, at risk of stating the obvious, a paper notebook can also be more time consuming to add pictures to and is incapable of having music or video linked from it. Sometimes, I want my students engaged in multiomodal notetaking so they have these materials to refer to later on.

Notebooks will always be an important part of my class, but this year will be a time of observation and reflection, considering when and whether giving students a choice is more important than the inconsistencies that result from two notebook modalities existing in my classroom. Furthermore, there may be strategies I haven't thought of yet to manage this disconnect that will come with using them both this year, and I will continue to learn and adapt. Eventually, I may even go to a "dual" mode, where students are often given the option to use either format, yet sometimes I demand that they use one over the other for particular tasks.

Notes from Troy

As we consider the role of digital and physical notebooks, there are a few elements of the BIT-ELA worth reiterating, noting that Jill is still figuring out these new norms for writing in her classroom. Still, it is clear that she is thinking about how students can "harness online platforms for collaborative writing," as evidenced by the ways that they can share documents and help one another in collaborative protocols like "think, pair, share." Also, even in the lesson overview slides, she is encouraging them to "read, annotate, and discuss both alphabetic and visual texts" with the affordances of commenting tools and, for the slides, the notes space on each one. While these changes may seem minor or modest, they also reiterate the ways in which Jill is making shifts in her teaching that, cumulatively, will help her enact the vision described in the BIT-ELA statement.

Ideas 3: Reestablishing Daily and Weekly Routines

As we bring our work on this manuscript to a close in the fall of 2021, it has been compelling to talk with our colleagues in Jill's district and beyond about what stays the same in face-to-face learning and what changes need to be made. Unfortunately, despite district expectations, many have abandoned their LMS; at the same time, others have continued to up their game, bringing Schoology, Google Suite and other tools into their daily teaching practice. What, then, does a daily and weekly routine look like, and how are technologies being intentionally integrated into the process?

Elements of our daily routine, as noted above, include:

- Consistent use of slides to frame the lesson and learning targets.
- A daily "do now," tied to learning targets, at the beginning of the lesson.
- Writer's notebooks utilized digitally as a Google Slides deck that can later be embedded into a student portfolio of work.
- Schoology is at the center of our digital ecosystem, allowing teachers to post course materials, assignments, announcements, and grades.
- Teachers add to their Schoology courses as administrators but also serve as students themselves in the Schoology LMS, completing deliverables for weekly meetings and online PD courses for local- and state-required training.
- A daily wrapup and review at the end of each class with a closing slide in the lesson slide deck that asks students questions to assess their learning as well as a recap of deliverables, assignments, and what to complete before the next class meeting.

Elements of our weekly routine include:

- The entire slide deck laid out for the week, as shown above.

- Additional, self-paced work in Schoology that students can complete at home or during our Wednesday work time, as outlined below and illustrated in Figure 7.4.

- A weekly "exit ticket" as a Google Form, also described below.

- Students and teachers can do grade checks throughout the week or at the end of instructional units as Schoology syncs progress with PowerSchool. This allows students to advocate for themselves and account for when the work was submitted.

- Weekly Schoology folders that display a snapshot of the lessons for the week as well as assignments given. See below for more information.

Framing Weekly Tasks in Schoology

Using Schoology as the LMS for our coursework allows students to see each week at a glance because there is a running list of folders, much like a blog that is in reverse chronological order, one for each week.

In my class, students are able to look at the running list of weeks and see not only what curricular concepts were covered, but the assignments associated with the week. I created a folder for assignments, separate from the weekly materials, allowing students to see a numbered list of assignments and links to complete them. The pink digital assignments folder sits at the top of the course materials feed. Each weekly folder, therefore, references the pink assignments folder that is associated with that week. While there is no mandated uniformity in the way this is presented among teachers at Skyline High School, we each have a version of the weekly folder that allows students to look back at coursework and easily find the information needed. This allows teachers and students to go completely paperless; all work is completed in the digital platforms assigned

FIGURE 7.4: View of Schoology course materials folders, arranged by week

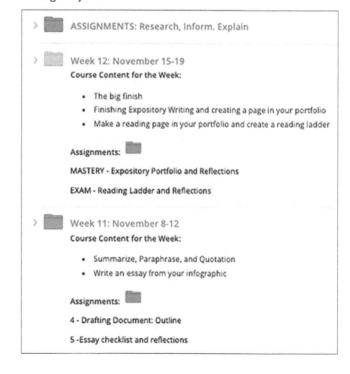

and funnels through Schoology, ultimately syncing to PowerSchool, the official record for student transcripts.

Maintaining an In-Person Version of Asynchronous Wednesdays

During the remote 2020–2021 school year, AAPS students worked through asynchronous lessons on Wednesdays that offered extensions of the previous lessons, more time to complete an assignment from an earlier synchronous lesson, as well as extra time to complete any missing assignments. Both students and teachers looked forward to Wednesdays as not only a wellness break from the many hours of screen time required for remote learning, but also a chance midweek to take a cleansing curricular breath. As the 2021–2022 school year began and we were back in person five days a week, I started to hear, "I miss asynchronous Wednesdays" from students. As I paused to think about this, I realized that I missed them too. After conferring with many Skyline High School English teachers, we all agreed that the asynchronous Wednesdays needed to stay, but we had to adapt them to our current in person status. Thus, the version of hybrid asynchronous Wednesday was born. Some teachers call it "Wellness Wednesday" while others, me included, call it "Workshop Wednesday."

This more humane approach to teaching and learning doesn't reduce the rigor. Instead, Workshop Wednesdays provide struggling students with the extra time needed to conference with teachers and catch up on work not turned in, while students needing a challenge use the time to dive deeper into supplemental activities and extensions. Students in my classes have the predictable routine of coming to class on Wednesdays while also knowing that no new content will be covered. They have time to read, conference with their teacher, get in-person feedback from their peers or teacher, visit the Skyline Writing Center to get feedback from a peer tutor, and make up any missing work with support in the room. Those who are caught up have time to go to the library for new books to read as well as a weekly invitation to check out reading and writing sites like Jason Reynolds' "Write, Rite, Right" (link on the book's companion site) or blogs with journal ideas.

What we all learned from working remotely last year was that the pace at which students and teachers do their work is frenzied and, at times, inhumane. Workshop Wednesday builds in the teacher-student connection points that were so difficult to maintain in an online class. This intentionally-placed day to continue our work together in a way that feels relaxed and supportive has turned out to be one of the best hybrid moves to come out of the early days of the 2021–2022 school year.

Completion Folders Offer Skills Work

Another move toward a hybridity is Schoology's completion folder. This technology feature within Schoology allows teachers to create pathways to learning that students complete on their own, when time permits. These completion folders work much like a Hyperdoc, in the sense that students are completing their work, with some choices, in an organized fashion; also, there is an added benefit of automation in terms of grading. Students can earn credit for completing the tasks, in order, as well as earning a score on a quiz. All of this is automated to the school's online grading system.

For teachers, the work of creating the folders is time-consuming and has to be front-loaded, cutting down on some of the impromptu opportunities that I relied on in the past to teach discrete skills. Therefore, deciding to teaching a mini-lesson or to add a quiz or a video on the fly doesn't work. The thought and intention of the skills being taught and how to get students to master it has to be done ahead of time. For example, one of the ways in which I hope to utilize completion folders this year is for grammar and punctuation mini-units. A weekly grammar skill or punctuation rule can be presented as a whole class mini-lesson early in the week. This is followed by a completion folder in Schoology. To complete the digital folder, a teacher can embed the tasks, like watching supplemental videos, completing skill practice, and taking an automated graded assessment. The completion folder feature in Schoology can be assigned to individual students as well as to the whole class. This matters because students who already know the skill can be spared the extra work while the students who need it can be assigned the folder individually. This allows students to work on their own to demonstrate mastery of the week's mini-lesson.

Weekly Exit Tickets for Reflection and Accountability

As an accountability measure, I used to ask students to fill out a paper exit slip and write down what was accomplished during class. If students complete the daily deliverables, it is unlikely that they will fall behind in the progression and due dates of the assignments and projects given in class. Still, for the exit ticket, I now use a Google Form at the end of each week. Students complete the form and, then in my Google Spreadsheet, I can see a chronological glimpse of what, specifically, kids are articulating each week about their progress. I do not read all of them or require it as an assignment for points; instead, I provide this as an opportunity for students to be metacognitive about their progress. In turn, this supplies me with data about what students are choosing to do when latitude is offered.

This exit slip, while not an assignment, is another kind of deliverable, a pathway to mastery in the form of a tangible task or measurable progress. The weekly exit ticket allows me a one-stop glimpse of an entire class, via the spreadsheet feature of the Google Form. I also use it as a check-in tool with students. I may say, "I notice you haven't filled out the weekly exit ticket in a couple of weeks. What can I do to support your progress?" The low-stakes exit ticket opens a door to a conversation with students that puts the ball back in their court. They are then tasked with articulating their struggle and, together, we can find a solution.

This weekly exit ticket strategy also allows me to offer a nudge to students who can push past mastery. Again, it provides an opportunity for conversation—I can say, "I notice this unit seems to come easily to you. What else would you like to explore?" At this point we can talk about a passion project, supplemental reading, or a more rigorous mastery assignment. The digital snapshot offered through exit tickets in Google Forms offers lots of good information to inform my instruction as well as individualizing materials to meet the needs of my students.

Notes from Troy

As we consider the ways that Jill is restructuring her time—for planning, for teaching, and for feedback—I feel there is an oversight in the BIT-ELA that (as has often been the case for many other insights that we can only see in hindsight if I can push the "sight" metaphor that far!), became clear during remote instruction. It is the simple acknowledgement that teachers have always—and will continue to—balance a number of competing interests and stressors in their service to students. There are many instructional decisions to make in each class session. On top of that, recent battles over the role of race in our classrooms, curricula, and communities as well as discussions of health and safety protocols in our schools are just two of the challenges that seem to be top of mind today. As one of the co-leaders of the BIT-ELA revision, I will admit that we overlooked the important role of mental health and well-being, especially as it relates to living and learning in our technology-saturated world. There is always room to grow, and we will need to think more about these issues in the months and years ahead.

As we come to a close, we offer one last vignette from Joseph Pizzo, who builds on many of the ideas that Jill has shared above, especially related to empathy in an era where COVID is still present—and inequities are, too.

From the Classroom: "Using Technology to Foster Acceptance" by Joseph S. Pizzo

A middle-school English teacher of 48 years in Chester, NJ, Joseph Pizzo has been the Educator of the Year for AMLE, NJCTE, NJAMLE, and NJ S.H.I.N.E. This NCTE Historian and former president and current Executive Board member of NJCTE and NJAMLE has taught at Union County College, Centenary University, and College of St. Elizabeth. An NJ Schools to Watch Leadership Team member, Pizzo's podcasts include A Writer's Journey *and* A Spot of Poetry. *Elected to WWOR-TV Ch. 9's A+ for Teachers Hall of Fame, this Barron's Educational Series author provides scripting and narration for HTV Media Productions.*

We as educators recognize that students learn best when given the opportunity to explore, collaborate, create, edit, and finalize their projects by using technology. It has been argued that "Technology helps to create a more interactive and engaging space in a classroom" (Lee, 2020, p. 8), though this demands a purposeful approach. When it is used as a vehicle rather than a destination, technology allows students to incorporate a familiar tool to enhance their creativity. Documents can become living collaborations. Summarization can be taught when essays are distilled into slide presentations. Position statements of gratitude can become video tributes to heroes of the COVID-19 pandemic.

Technology, in this sense, can be used as a tool for teaching empathy and fostering acceptance. When training future social workers, Segal and Wagaman observe that "Social empathy is well suited to teaching social justice because of the attention given to developing interpersonal empathy skills, teaching about historical patterns of discrimination and oppression, and helping people to learn about their sense of who they are in the context of the larger world" (Segal and Wagaman, 2017, p. 204). During February of 2021, my preservice teacher Devon Villacampa from Drew University and I therefore built many learning engagements in our classroom upon a foundation of social-emotional learning (SEL). This approach allowed our students to add meaning and relevance to the data they compiled, the arguments they wanted to make. By giving our students the opportunity to be active learners rather than passive compilers, we increased the probability that learning becomes meaningful, rather than rote and routine. Moreover, we concur with NCTE that "'Writing' refers to the act of creating composed knowledge. Composition takes place across a range of contexts and for a variety of purposes" (NCTE, 2018). Finally, our activities celebrate "the joy of teaching" as we are identifying "the multimodal elements that make (our) lesson available to the diverse needs of (our) learners" (Kunz and Lapp, 2020, p. 14).

With this reasoning as a foundation, our students worked to create an award to honor a hero of their choosing. This activity supports those being done both for Black History Month as well as for learning engagements experienced throughout the year. We have paid tribute to heroes deserving recognition for their selfless service during the COVID-19 pandemic. These were presented in multiple ways. Some were Flipgrid videos. Using Google Slides, we have paid homage to people, pets, and aspects of life that provide support and positivity to our daily lives. We wrote original letters to poet Amanda Gorman to honor her genius demonstrated during U.S. President Biden's January 2021 inauguration. Peer and teacher/student reviews were conducted by the students via Google Docs. In fact, we designed activities that blended writing with technology to create a synergistic relationship between the material we aimed to teach (the skills and processes of writing) and its subsequent delivery (through the technologies noted above).

Next, our students each identified a hero to celebrate during Black History Month. They conducted research online to compile information about their heroes. Tribute was paid to the heroes as each student included three quotes underscoring the strength of their heroes' character traits. Our students were given the challenge to create an award for their hero from any reasonable segment of society. The qualifier: the heroic actions being noted must serve as model behaviors for others to emulate.

Furthermore, the award must have criteria. These criteria could include positive attributes including strength of conviction, courage in the face of adversity, and a positive impact upon society.

For example, one student chose Congresswoman Shirley Chisholm as her hero. We learned that the congresswoman had first become a teacher and then held positions in childcare and child welfare until she became the first Black congresswoman. During her seven terms in office, Chisholm served on the Veteran's Affairs, Education, and Labor Committees. She was also responsible for creating the Congressional Black Caucus (History.com, 2020). These positions clearly fit the criteria mentioned earlier and became the basis of this student's video presentation.

Our students presented their awards either in Screencastify or Flipgrid videos since these options are the most popular among our students. Giving voice to their tributes provides our students with the opportunity to engage their audiences authentically. The passion of their words comes through clearly in their videos. One student paid tribute to Rosa Parks "for ending segregation between the black and white communities" while another student cited the NFL's Russell Wilson "for donating one million meals to (the organizations) Feeding America and Food Lifeline to help those affected by the COVID-19 pandemic." These programs for recording audio and video allow listeners to experience the passion felt by each of our student presenters and, as the NCTE *Beliefs for Integrating Technology into the English Language Arts Classroom* argue, "investigate their stance on social issues through the multimodal inquiry methods."

To gain respect for our various cultures and to foster acceptance, we must first understand that we are a nation of different backgrounds. These backgrounds require an acceptance of our differences, as well as our similarities. By celebrating events such as Black History Month, we all gain an opportunity to increase our knowledge and expand our horizons as we begin to understand our similarities and celebrate our differences.

Final Thoughts from Troy and Jill on the Move toward Hybridity with the BIT-ELA Principles in Mind

When the BIT-ELA statement was revised and published between 2016 and 2018, there was really no way to imagine the ways that a global pandemic would have suddenly affected the role of English language arts instruction and the middle level. We will steer clear of hyperbole here, noting that the changes in the spring of 2020 were often centered around providing "enrichment" for students and a way to bring closure to a school year cut short, whereas 2020–2021 was more focused on making remote learning work. Now, as we write these closing words in the fall of 2021, we are still trying to figure out the ways that dedicated middle level ELA educators like Jill, the contributors to this book, and those who are reading it are all committing to a shared effort at rethinking what it means to teach students who need our support, encouragement, and insights as they navigate their classrooms, communities, and civic life.

We hope that some of the stories and strategies shared here offer our readers innovative ways to continue moving forward as, to return to the BIT-ELA statement one final time, we too have attempted "to be responsive to such changes in meaningful ways without abandoning the kinds of practices and principles that we as English educators have come to value and know to work." Even though these principles were composed in pre-pandemic times, our hope is that the many ideas shared in this chapter—and throughout the book—provide ELA teachers with possibilities for reimagining their instruction. By putting literacies *before* technologies, we are encouraged to see so many educators doing just that, opening up new opportunities for their students as readers, writers, thinkers, and doers in a digital world.

To guide further discussion and exploration, we encourage teachers to think about the following:

- What are the practices and policies that have remained consistent for you and your students, whether in-person, remote, or in hybrid/blended forms of instruction? What are the routines that you have started anew?

- In what ways are you providing time and space for socio-emotional learning? How does SEL learning connect to the broader goals of ELA instruction including literary analysis and academic writing?

- How are students encouraged to use the vast number of digital tools available to them as a way to maintain focus and improve their productivity? What are the "hacks" that you are offering them to make better use of common tools like Google Docs and email?

- Taking it to another level, how might you be able to use more advanced features in the tools that you are already using (like the "completion folder" in Schoology) as a way to manage your students' workflow and your own grading practices?

- How have your grading practices changed? Do you see a "grade" representing something different than it did before? When and how do you provide feedback to students?

Voices from the Middle Reprint: The Next Decade of Digital Writing

The Next Decade of Digital Writing

TROY **HICKS**

Digital writing—both as a concept in K–12 schools and in terms of particular hardware, software, and networked opportunities—has come a long way in the past ten years.

For decades, of course, teachers and teacher educators had been thinking about and using technology in English classrooms, including innovations such as film, radio, and computers. By the early 2000s, there were books, articles, conference sessions, and workshops that encouraged us to use emerging technologies such as blogs, wikis, and podcasts. These were important steps, each one bringing a broader concept of digital writing to the front of our minds and into our classrooms.

With the publication of my book, *The Digital Writing Workshop* (2009), I blended two great ideas—digital writing (Writing in Digital Environments (WIDE) Research Center Collective, 2005) and writing workshop (Atwell, 1998; Calkins, 1994; Graves, 1983)—together. In the words of Ken Martin, Director of the Maine Writing Project, my book was able to keep the focus on the writing and the technology in ways that other texts had not done before, noting, "The result is parallel sequences, one of which substantiates our understanding of writing workshop while the other advances our understanding of technology. Together, these sequences converge to define writing in a digital context" (2010).

It is this combination of "parallel sequences" that I have maintained throughout my career and in my work with hundreds of teachers. In order to bring

> *In order to bring substantive change to our classrooms, we must keep the focus first on best practices in teaching writing and then, in a very close second, on thoughtful use of technology.*

substantive change to our classrooms, we must keep the focus first on best practices in teaching writing and then, in a very close second, on thoughtful use of technology. In conversations with countless teachers over the past decade, I hope that we have all brought "digital writing" into our English/language arts lexicon.

I am honored to be invited by Sara Kajder and Shelbie Witte to open this issue of *Voices from the Middle*, and I want to take a few paragraphs to reflect on where we have come with digital writing. Then, in the remainder of the article, I will argue that the path for the potential of digital writing doesn't end here. Digital writing still has a long way to go, and my hope is that the examples of colleagues cited in this article will rekindle your interest, inspiring you to examine new modes, media, audiences, and purposes for digital writing with your students.

Digital Writing: From Then to Now

Just over twenty years ago, at the same time I was finishing my preservice teacher education program and preparing for my first job at a middle school, I had been introduced to the NCTE/IRA Standards for the English Language Arts (1996). Like many English majors, my love for the printed word—both creating and consuming it—led me to my chosen career. Yet, it was with this standards document that I had first discovered new ideas that valued and elevated "print and non-print texts" as well as "a variety of technological and information resources." While I had tinkered with a Commodore 64 as a teen and was just starting to understand how email and a personal web space on the university's server could be useful, these new phrases describing what it meant to be literate were unanticipated and liberating.

Additionally, the Michigan Department of Education had just released the *Michigan Curriculum Framework* in which they described the English language arts as a content area that "encompass[es] process and content—**how** people communicate as well as **what** they communicate" (1996, emphasis in original). The standards went on: "All students are literate and can engage successfully in reading, discovering, creating, and analyzing spoken, written, electronic, and visual texts which reflect multiple perspectives and diverse communities."

> *With digital writing, we need to think with words, of course; yet we also need to begin thinking like artists, web designers, recording engineers, photographers, and filmmakers.*

Both the NCTE/IRA and MDE definitions gave me pause. I began to rethink everything I'd just learned about being an English teacher. Having been flooded with ideas about competing modes of literary criticism, approaching writing from a rhetorical perspective, and thinking carefully about a variety of multicultural perspectives to canonical literature, the idea that we could both study and create "non-print," "electronic," and "visual" texts was quite astounding.

How could we have known, just over twenty years ago, that these processes of "reading, discovering, creating, and analyzing" various kinds of texts could still require the same fundamental skills crucial to the English classroom, and yet how our world—enabled by networked technology—would have changed so incredibly much? As I made the shift from middle school teacher to graduate student and then to teacher educator, I witnessed the change . . . then I became part of it.

What it means to teach the English language arts with websites, apps, and social media continues to evolve quickly, both in terms of the tools as well as in terms of the practices. We need to approach the task carefully, critically, and creatively. In 2013, in *Crafting Digital Writing*, I argued,

> With digital writing, we need to think with words, of course; yet we also need to begin thinking like artists, web designers, recording engineers, photographers, and filmmakers. In other words, intentional choices about craft can lead to creative work in a variety of writing media. (pp. 18–19)

Certainly, *Voices from the Middle* has been a space for considering these types of decisions. In a themed issue on "Remix," Toby Emert (2014) shared ideas about creating a teaching and learning lab for students to create digital narratives and, in that same issue, Crystal Shelby-Caffey and her family described how "it is possible for educators to remix instruction in ways that use technology to bridge achievement gaps and to develop a sense of social responsibility in students while empowering them." (p. 52). Also, within NCTE we are fortunate to count among our colleagues a number of incredible middle level teachers like Kevin Hodgson (@dogtrax on Twitter), Tony Keefer (@TonyKeefer), and Katharine Hale (@KatharinehHale), among many others. On the whole, we are doing well.

Still, we are not doing enough.

Realistically, how many of the digital projects we ask our students to do are pushing them to create their own knowledge and contribute thoughtfully to ongoing academic and civic conversations? Or, are they simply replicating the types of traditional academic literacies required to succeed in a formulaic essay, presentation, book report, or other perfunctory task? Are they truly engaged in the process of digital writing? If we are being entirely honest, I don't know that we are doing enough. And, as Kristen Hawley Turner and I have argued, these skills are no longer a luxury; innovative approaches to teaching digital literacy, indeed, can't wait (Hicks & Turner, 2013).

Thus, my goal here is to introduce a number of interesting and innovative teacher-researchers and teacher educators who are pushing us to think more carefully about when, how, and why we might integrate digital writing into our classrooms. What I want to suggest now is that we begin moving even deeper, more intentionally into multimodal composing practices. Let's take a look at the future that's happening right now.

Digital Writing: From Now to Next

Yes, it is amazing that so many of us are willing and able to bring digital writing tools and processes into our English classrooms. From students blogging and creating websites to the production of podcasts and digital video, there are many middle level educators who are engaging students through digital writing processes. There are also ways that we can invite students to use social media for productive purposes, including examples such as KQED's #DoNow initiative (https://ww2.kqed.org/education/collections/do-now/) and to have our students share their reading lives with #booksnaps and #shelfies. These are important literacy practices, and ones that live in parallel with more academic notions of what it means to write in school settings.

As we move into the second decade of fully exploring and enacting digital writing practices in our classrooms, my hope is that we can invite students to be knowledge creators, not just consumers and remixers. Of course, at some level, students must consume and remix materials in order to become creators. Nothing is created in a vacuum. At the same time I would agree with JuliAnna Ávila and Jessica Zacher Pandya, who argue,

> Critical literacies educators would do well to integrate the digital dimension into their work to build upon the practices and engagement that our learners already utilize as they participate in digital literacies, where they are positioned as creators and authors. (2012, p. 4)

In order to accomplish these goals, we need to provide intellectual and emotional space for students to explore new ideas, gather their own evidence, and present academic arguments through media other than just the printed word. We will need to trust our students to take the lead in guiding one another to the process of composing images, audio, maps, and other data sets. In the segments that follow, I briefly introduce five different educators with ideas for expanding digital writing practices.

Creating Space for Critical Digital Literacies: Detra Price-Dennis

The role of the English language arts teacher has always been and will continue to be—in addition to simply teaching the "skills" of reading, writing, listening, speaking, viewing, and visually representing—someone who introduces students to critical literacy practices. Among the many teachers and teacher educators who are reinvigorating this approach across digital spaces, Detra Price-Dennis offers us one unique perspective by focusing her work on the lives of Black girls.

In her article "Developing Curriculum to Support Black Girls' Literacies in Digital Spaces," Price-Dennis argues that her students must be engaged deeply in a variety of literacy practices, engaging various tools with

We need to provide intellectual and emotional space for students to explore new ideas, gather their own evidence, and present academic arguments through media other than just the printed word.

a variety of critical perspectives. She notes:

> Again, these experiences provided multiple opportunities for Black girls in the class to explore social issues across modalities and raise questions about audience, privilege, power, voice, and equity. The questions they raised in discussions and the work they produced drew on multiple literacies that were tied to their identities as Black girls. (2016, p. 357)

It is through this work that the girls are able to develop perspective-taking and empathy, along with specific digital literacy skills. By creating physical spaces in which students, in this case Black girls, could convene and collaborate outside of typical school settings, Price-Dennis and her colleagues allowed students the intellectual and emotional freedom that they needed in order to fully participate in digital literacies.

To the extent that we have a "curriculum" that we must "cover" in school, I can understand how teachers may struggle to integrate these kinds of literacy practices into digital writing instruction. Yet, if we do not, Price-Denis's example reminds us that the tasks we typically ask students to do, such as creating a digital poster or recording themselves reading an essay will not have the same type of purpose, nor give students as authors the agency that they require in order to be fully engaged in the process. Digital writing requires time, space, and attention, as well as an inquiry stance.

Crafting Audio as Ethnography: Jon Wargo and Cassie Brownell

In an era when civic discourse and basic listening behaviors are being taught with increased interest, helping students become attentive to their own environments, the people around them, and the world we shape together has become incredibly important. At a time when we have so many opportunities by plugging in our earbuds and simply listening to the music or voices from our own echo chambers, we need to teach students how to engage in literacy practices that help us hear both what is being said, as well as how it is being said.

In their "#hearmyhome" project (http://hearmyhome. matrix.msu.edu/), Jon Wargo, Cassie Brownell, and many preservice teachers have documented the everyday sounds in their communities, especially urban communities. In doing so, they have created a number of "soundscapes" where preservice teachers themselves and their own students are able to create rich, ethnographic portraits of their homes, neighborhoods, schools, stores, and other spaces.

Each week, Wargo and Brownell framed a prompt for a different "sonic event," such as the one in which they explored "the politics of sound."

> Rhythms of recent riots, pulses of contemporary protest marches, and the acoustics of American sit-ins serve as a starting point to explore the sonic intensities and politics of sound. In recent weeks, individuals have taken to the streets to demonstrate alliance with and affinity for making their collective voices heard. (Wargo & Brownell, 2016)

By inviting students to focus mainly on the sounds—and not worry necessarily with image or video—Wargo and Brownell build on a rich tradition in oral history, storytelling, audio engineering, and rhetoric/composition to help preservice teachers make distinct connections with their students and also to recognize areas of difference. Digital writing requires that we explore all forms of media as text worthy of analysis, including what could otherwise be dismissed as just ambient noise.

Crafting Snaps as Self-Identity: Jonathan Bartels

For anyone teaching at the middle level right now, it is clear that Snapchat is the social media of choice. In addition to the countless selfies posted, Pew Research reported in 2016 that "Snapchat won over a number of big news names this year for its group of Discover publishers" including CNN, NBC, and *The New York Times* (Shearer & Gottfried, 2017).

Even with venerable news outlets and other media producers moving toward Snapchat as a viable space for publication, we also need to consider the literacy practices that are evident and inherent in Snapchat, as based on users' experiences. In his recent *English Journal* article, "Snapchat and the Sophistication of Multimodal Composition," Jonathan Bartels discusses the way that his former and current students use the tool.

> At first glance, Snapchat may not seem much different from other image sharing or instant messaging applications. However, on closer examination, it becomes clear that the ephemerality built into the software, the exclusivity assured by restricting access to mobile devices, and the relationship of visual and textual elements in

> Snapchat have the potential to require sophisticated composition strategies. (2017, p. 91)

Put another way, there are a whole lot of design decisions that go into creating a single "snap"—much more than simply taking the photo.

Even in talking with my own daughter, currently a high school sophomore, she described to me a number of decisions that she makes including the intended receiver (whether the person is a close friend, acquaintance, boyfriend, or adult; the likelihood that the receiver will save or share the snap with others), the time (time of day, day of the week, month, during the school year or during vacation), the location (inside/outside, at home/ elsewhere), the lighting, the font size and color, use of emojis or other "stickers," duration of the conversation (and whether it is part of a "Snap Streak" of multiple days), and whether or not to use time and location tags provided by Snapchat. Again, digital writing requires that we explore all forms of media as text worthy of analysis, especially when students are actively composing texts with numerous options such as these.

Engaging in Computational Thinking: Tom Liam Lynch

Back in the heady days of the early 2000s, when we were being introduced to a variety of nifty Web 2.0 services such as talking avatars, zooming slideshows, and funky photo editors, we were quick to integrate these tools into our teaching practices. One of those tools, word clouds, has evolved quite a bit since then. At the time, yes, it was kind of cool that students could create a word cloud—from their own writing or the writing of others—and then use that as a tool for visualization. However, that was just about where the story ended. While we might have seen some essays enhanced based on the relative frequency of words copied/pasted into a word cloud generator, my strong suspicion is that most teachers did not push this kind of thinking too much further. Instead, word clouds were ultimately used as decorative features.

Over the past few years, however, these types of tools have become more sophisticated, and one voice that has emerged to help us think critically, carefully, and creatively about the role of computational thinking in English language arts has been Tom Liam Lynch. In his "Soft(a)ware" column in *English Journal*, he has introduced a variety of ideas for how we might bring different perspectives on literature—both the content as well as the analysis—into a sharper perspective, pushing us to think about how, when, and why computers work to present texts in the way that they do.

In one of his 2015 columns, "Counting Characters: Quantitative Approaches to Literary Study," Lynch describes the ways that he uses Voyant Tools (https://voyant-tools.org/)—described as "a web-based reading and analysis environment for digital texts"—to analyze text in a variety of ways including word clouds as well as a number of other methods. Lynch argues, "We can treat as evidence not only language from the texts but also numerical data and visualizations that result from inviting software to read and respond with us" (2015, p. 73).

Digital writing requires us to rethink interdisciplinarity and the ways that students can integrate numerous tools in their effort to create dynamic, multimedia texts.

For instance, when exploring canonical literature that is available in the public domain through websites such as Project Gutenberg, students could take a small selection, a chapter, or the entire book and, quite literally, copy and paste the text into Voyant. Then, students could use the evidence from the text—in the form of a chart for word frequency—to make an argument about particular themes, characters, metaphors, or other types of literary analysis. Digital writing requires us to rethink our approach to text, textual analysis, and the ways in which we build our arguments from evidence that was, heretofore, invisible.

Mapping Literacy: Lincoln A. Mullen

When I was learning to drive, we still had to use an atlas, a folding map, or even handwritten directions, along with the basic skills of figuring out a map. In our modern age, where GPS now lives in our pocket and is embedded in our vehicles, and when self-driving cars are on the verge of mass-market breakthrough, our need to read and interpret maps has become even more essential. Historian Lincoln A. Mullen reminds us of the cultural, historical, and political significance of learning how to read maps for a variety of purposes:

> How does one read a map? This can mean quite literally introducing students to the basic conventions of maps. But more importantly it means learning how to read maps the past as primary sources, and how to read maps from scholars as secondary sources, and how to read texts with an eye to their spatial contexts. (Mullen, n.d.)

At one level, we as English language arts teachers could look at mapping literacy as a task best left for social studies teachers. However, to do so, we ignore existing resources available on sites like Google Lit Trips (http://www.googlelittrips.org/) or photo/storytelling sites

such as History Pin (https://www.historypin.org/en/) that can significantly enhance our language arts curriculum. More importantly, there are a number of ways in which we can build maps and mapping literacy into the narrative, informational, and argument pieces that our students are developing. For instance, the Pulitzer prize-winning *New York Times* multimedia feature, "Snow Fall: The Avalanche at Tunnel Creek" (Branch, 2012) is an excellent example of how interactive mapping can eliminate the story being told. Digital writing requires us to rethink interdisciplinarity and the ways that students can integrate numerous tools in their effort to create dynamic, multimedia texts.

The Next Decade of Digital Writing

In closing this conversation, thinking about what else we need to do in order to rethink digital writing, I strongly encourage readers to explore the 2016 revision of the *ISTE Standards for Students* (http://www.iste.org/standards/for-students), all of which have implications for literacy instruction in the next decade. In addition to the work of the teachers and teacher educators noted here, if there was one other source that I would encourage readers to review for inspiration, it would be the Educator Innovator site, powered by the National Writing Project, which includes webinars, blog posts, and a variety of other resources for teaching writing in a digital age: https://educatorinnovator.org/

Finally, the KnightLab at Northwestern University (http://knightlab.com/) offers a variety of interactive storytelling tools, for free, that are in use by professional journalists around the world. They include tools such as StoryMap JS (which allows users to connect places on Google Maps with text, images, and video), Juxtapose (which allows users to make framed comparisons of similar images), Souncite (which allows users to insert "inline audio" into web-based text), and Timeline (which allows users to connect text, images, and video into a seamless timeline). These tools may take a bit of time to master, but the results will demand higher-order thinking, effective writing, and applications of visual literacy.

Digital writing has come a long way in the past decade, but let's be sure to integrate it into our classrooms and our students' writing lives even more strategically and creatively in the years ahead. If there were ever a time to get all of our colleagues, and I mean *all* of our colleagues—even the most reticent, device-averse, "shoe organizer hanging in the back of the classroom to collect cell phones as kids walk in the door" type of colleague—to recognize that literacy and technology are intricately interwoven and a part of our students' lived lives, that digital writing does, indeed, matter, the time is now. Let's begin our next decade with a generative sense of purpose, creativity, and renewal. Please join me—and the other contributors to this issue—and continue the conversation.

REFERENCES

Atwell, N. (1998). *In the middle: New understandings about writing, reading, and learning* (2nd ed.). Portsmouth, NH: Boynton/ Cook.

Ávila, J., & Pandya, J. Z. (Eds.). (2012). *Critical digital literacies as social praxis: Intersections and challenges.* New York, NY: Peter Lang Publishing.

Bartels, J. (2017). Snapchat and the sophistication of multimodal composition. *English Journal, 106*(5), 90–92.

Branch, J. (2012). Snow fall: The avalanche at Tunnel Creek. Retrieved February 11, 2014, from http://www.nytimes.com/ projects/2012/snow-fall/

Calkins, L. (1994). *The art of teaching writing* (2nd ed.). Portsmouth, NH: Heinemann.

Emert, T. (2014). "Hear a story, tell a story, teach a story": Digital narratives and refugee middle schoolers. *Voices from the Middle, 21*(4), 33–39.

Graves, D. H. (1983). *Writing: Teachers and children at work.* Exeter, NH: Heinemann Educational.

Hicks, T. (2009). *The digital writing workshop* (1st ed.). Portsmouth, NH: Heinemann.

Hicks, T. (2013). *Crafting digital writing: Composing texts across media and genres.* Portsmouth, NH: Heinemann.

Hicks, T., & Turner, K. H. (2013). No longer a luxury: Digital literacy can't wait. *English Journal, 102*(6), 58–65.

Lynch, T. L. (2015). Counting characters: Quantitative approach to literary study. *English Journal, 104*(6), 71–74.

Martin, K. (2010, February 11). Book review: *The digital writing workshop.* Retrieved December 30, 2010, from http:// www.nwp.org/cs/public/print/resource/3066

Michigan Department of Education. (1996). *Michigan curriculum framework.* Lansing, MI. Retrieved from http://mmc.edzone.net/documents/micurriculumdocs/ MichiganCurriculumFramework_8172_7.pdf

Mullen, L. (n.d.). Map literacy. Retrieved November 27, 2017, from http://lincolnmullen.com/projects/spatial-workshop/ literacy.html

National Council of Teachers of English & International Reading Association. (1996). *NCTE / IRA Standards for the English Language Arts.* Retrieved April 4, 2011, from http:// www.ncte.org/standards

Price-Dennis, D. (2016). Developing curriculum to support black girls' literacies in digital spaces. *English Education, 48*(4), 337–361.

Shearer, E., & Gottfried, J. (2017, September 7). News use across social media platforms 2017. Retrieved December 1, 2017, from http://www.journalism.org/2017/09/07/ news-use-across-social-media-platforms-2017/

Shelby-Caffey, C. V., Caffey, R., Caffey, C. A., & Caffey, K. A. (2014). The promise of remix: An open message to educators. *Voices from the Middle, 21*(4), 47–53.

Wargo, J., & Brownell, C. (2016). #hearmyhome. Retrieved November 27, 2017, from http://hearmyhome.matrix.msu.edu/

Writing in Digital Environments (WIDE) Research Center Collective. (2005). Why teach digital writing? Retrieved from http:// english.ttu.edu/kairos/10.1/binder2.html?coverweb/wide/ index.html

Annotated Bibliography

TROY HICKS

Any effort to make an annotated bibliography will, by its very nature, require us to draw some lines around the scope of the project. In an effort to provide up-to-date resources related to teaching middle level English language arts with technology, this particular annotated bibliography came from an effort to limit the search to items produced in the past few years and to introduce as wide a variety of authors as possible. Many of the authors mentioned in this bibliography have work that stretches back much further than 2018, worthy of exploration, and I have inherently needed to leave some foundational articles, chapters, books, and related projects prior to this out, not to mention many additional scholars and citations worthy of note. I appreciate the efforts of all educational researchers and classroom teachers who are integrating digital literacies into middle level classrooms, even if I did not have space to include everyone's work here.

Beach, R. W., & Smith, B. E. (2020). Using digital tools for studying about and addressing climate change. *Handbook of Research on Integrating Digital Technology with Literacy Pedagogies;* IGI Global. 346-370. https://doi.org/10.4018/978-1-7998-0246-4.ch015

Connecting the authentic challenge of climate change with the goal of developing digital literacy skills, Richard Beach and Blaine Smith outline the ways in which common technology tools can be repurposed for critical conversations and engagement. For instance, they note the example of the long-standing digital annotation tool Diigo being repurposed by students "to respond to one another's perceptions of measurements of emissions at the Mauna Loa observatory in Hawaii" (348). Also, they describe a number of climate visualization tools such as Climate Interactive (www.climateinteractive.org) and digital story

telling spaces such as the Climate Stories Project (www.climatestoriesproject.org) that can be used as prompts for reflective writing or rhetorical analysis. They even offer resources on augmented reality (AR) and virtual reality (VR) activities to support climate-focused inquiry. With many examples throughout, Beach and Smith briefly describe a project in which middle school students "calculated the effects of their carbon footprint, observed visual representations of greenhouse gas effects, conducted experiments on greenhouse gases, and studied how differences in population size influences greenhouse gas production" (351), and offer a number of youth-focused climate action organizations through which students and teachers can become civically engaged.

Boardman, A. G., Garcia, A., Dalton, B., & Polman, J. L. (2021). *Compose our world: Project-based learning in secondary English language arts.* Teachers College Press.

With the goal that "teachers envision students as valued civic actors who are composers, creators, and designers at the same time as they are critical consumers of text, from canonical literature to media messages and social and political rhetoric" (3), the authors of this collection pose an overarching question to other educators and their students: "How is our world composed for us and how can we compose our world?" (3). Building on the long-standing idea that composition can take numerous forms and integrating a number of other educational principles such as project-based learning, Universal Design for Learning, socio-emotional learning, and authentic making/maker spaces, the collection offers glimpses into a number of classrooms, describing ways in which educators provide students with choices for reading and writing, while still grappling with substantive inquiry questions. In one vignette, a

Michigan educator, Carrie Mattern, illustrates PBL and ELA principles "in ways that serve each other, rather than sacrificing one for the other" (110). With numerous examples of student work, this collection provides ELA educators with pathways into the kinds of ideas outlined in the BIT-ELA principles.

Breakstone, J., McGrew, S., Smith, M., Ortega, T., & Wineburg, S. (2018). Why we need a new approach to teaching digital literacy. *The Phi Delta Kappan*, *99*(6), 27–32.

In this brief article designed for a general audience of educators, this team from the Stanford History Education Group provides a rationale for what they described as "reading laterally," where fact checkers are not trying to determine the credibility of a website based on the site itself, yet instead are "opening up new browser tabs and searching across the web to see what they could find about the trustworthiness of the source of information" (28). They describe the process that corporate PR firms will use to pose as a grassroots initiative, "a practice commonly known as astroturfing" (30) and offer two versions of a website analysis: first with a typical approach using the ubiquitous CRAAP test, and then offering an alternative approach through lateral reading and fact checking. They conclude that checklist thinking alone will not solve issues surrounding mis- and disinformation, and that "teachers must be provided professional development about how to evaluate online information" and "need instruction in how to integrate these new digital strategies into their classrooms" (31). As a summary of their lateral reading approach, the article is both concise and accessible for a wide audience.

Buchholz, B. A., DeHart, J., & Moorman, G. (2020). Digital citizenship during a global pandemic: Moving beyond digital literacy. *Journal of Adolescent & Adult Literacy*, *64*(1), 11–17. https://doi.org/10.1002/jaal.1076

Published in the summer of 2020 as a commentary in the *Journal of Adolescent & Adult Literacy*, the authors "make an argument that critical digital literacy and citizenship must be viewed as participatory" (11) and that the abrupt move to remote teaching and learning may, perhaps, have the potential to strengthen digital literacy practices of teachers and students if approached critically, creatively, and carefully. Buchholz, DeHart, and Moorman contend that "[b]eing a digitally literate citizen encompasses the ability to read, write, and interact on/across screens to engage with diverse online communities, with an orientation for social justice" (12) and to move beyond "[l]ists of technical proficiencies and simplistic rules for safely engaging online [that] have dominated the curricula for digital citizenship" (12). Providing a number of "classroom invitations," the authors offer examples that include responses to the global pandemic, civic online discourse, and climate change, among others, concluding with the idea that "[e]ducators must be prepared to play a central role in helping nurture digital citizens who can engage ethically to (re-)create a more equitable world" (16).

Cassidy, J., Ortlieb, E., & Grote-Garcia, S. (2021). What's hot in literacy: New topics and new frontiers are abuzz. *Literacy Research and Instruction*, *60*(1), 1–12. https://doi.org/10.1080/19388071.2020.1800202

Linking back to their 2014 report and arguing that "[t]he preponderance of online and digital literacies has not only increased access to innumerable literacy resources for youth but has also created challenging environments to navigate as students seek to procure, synthesize, and create meaning between and within texts" (7), Cassidy, Ortleib, and Grote-Smith begin this annual report with the science of reading debate, dyslexia, and social justice and equity are the hottest of the topics in the survey, they contend that digital and multimodal literacies remain equally as important and "are no longer optional within optimal frameworks that promote literacy success" (7). They conclude with the idea that educators and their communities will need to create "a better integrated system of hybrid pedagogies, using traditional and digital environments in unison to provide optimal literacy experiences for all learners" (9), and encourage their readers to "collaborate with community partners and families to empower literacy learners" (10).

Ellison, T. L., & Solomon, M. (2019). Counter-storytelling vs. deficit thinking around African American children and families, digital literacies, race, and the digital divide. *Research in the Teaching of English, 53*(3), 223–244.

Beginning with the idea that African-American families have often been overlooked in conversations about digital literacy and out-of-school learning, Ellison and Solomon propose that "counter-storytelling" can push ELA teachers and researchers to "(re)consider the ways African American families' lives and stories are perceived in the digital world, and [how we[must approach issues of race and digital literacies in ways that honor these narratives rather than marginalizing them" (224). Building on the techniques of counter-storytelling as a way to "examine other ways of knowing and understanding" (224), the authors provide an extensive literature review and also document the history and insidious effects of the digital divide in terms of hardware and connectivity as well as skills and contexts. With an explicit focus on two cases (Ellison's on an African American family, two children and one parent who was highly skilled in digital literacies herself; Solomon's on a group of African American first graders from an elementary school, including two girls, Penny and Jordan), the authors analyze these cases and suggest that educators should be mindful of five elements of access (material, transformative, critical, experiential, and functional, all drawn from Adam J. Banks's 2006 book, *Race, Rhetoric, and Technology: Searching for Higher Ground*). They conclude with the argument that "English teachers should also be aware of their own assumptions about the digital divide and access, ones that may manifest as deficit thinking, thus skewing pedagogical decisions and outcomes," (239), emphasizing the ways that complex challenges of the digital divide can begin to be addressed in our approaches to teaching digital literacy.

Garcia, M., Marlatt, R., McDermott, M., & O'Byrne, W. I. (2021). Today is the tomorrow we should have prepared for yesterday: Rebuilding our classrooms to facilitate student-centered, teacher-sustaining, tech-supported education. *Voices from the Middle, 28*(4), 21–25.

Beginning with the argument that "brick-and-mortar" teaching has always been a multimodal enterprise," in which "[t]eachers call on complex processes of multimodal instruction and assessment" (21) as they present new ideas, check for understanding, encourage students to engage with content in critical and creative ways, Merideth Garcia, Rick Marlatt, Maureen McDermott, and W. Ian O'Byrne contend that these approaches have taken on new forms—and urgency—in spaces like Google Classroom and Zoom. They offer for guidelines for teaching across modalities, including the idea that we should "be even more critical about how and in what ways we engage our students, the privacy and security of the platforms through which we interact, and our navigation of human connections within digital spaces" (22) and that "we must make intentional instructional decisions that empower students to encode and decode meaning through the roles of producer and recipient" (23). The authors recognize that this is no easy task, especially in an era of remote teaching and learning, and yet conclude that "understanding how best to leverage these digital and web literacies in our work is central to our collective future" (24), thus making a constant reexamination of our priorities and our pedagogies a habit of mind for effective ELA teaching.

Haddix, M. M. (2018). What's radical about youth writing?: Seeing and honoring youth writers and their literacies. *Voices from the Middle, 25*(3), 8–12.

Through her extensive work in developing and leading the Writing Our Lives after-school project, Marcelle Haddix provides insights on the "radical' youth literacies" (8) that she has seen young people employ in a variety of spaces including performances of plays, engaging in music production and promotion, maintaining blogs, and writing novels. Across these projects, she notes the ways that youth have become "critical ethnographers of their own writing lives" (9), and how "[w]riting is one way that students can give voice to their experiences and think critically about how their personal perspectives are part of a broader dialogue" (10). Arguing that the definition of writing must move beyond the simple one employed in school and that "[t]eachers must honor and respect youth-led and youth-centered writing practices" (11), Haddix provides a glimpse into the many ways that educators and youth can work together to enact these radical literacies. She points to additional work that has been done since she began the project in 2009, all the while encouraging youth by "raising their voices, their hands, their pens, and their smartphones" (11) to push back against prevailing deficit-focused narratives of their schools and communities.

Hobbs, R. (2017). *Create to learn: Introduction to digital literacy*. Wiley-Blackwell.

Though designed for high school students or college undergraduates, Renee Hobbs brings her sensibility and experience related to media literacy into the world of composition and it can be valuable for middle grades learners. Arguing that "the concept of literacy is expanding as a result of changes in media, technology and the nature of knowledge" (5), Hobbs argues that when "we create media, we internalize knowledge deeply–we own it" (7). Thus, the mindset of "creating to learn" is imperative as students begin to use "images, language, sound, music, multimedia, and interactivity with the goal of deepening your learning experience and contributing to the learning of others" (9). Throughout the book and on her companion website (createtolearn.online), Hobbs presents numerous examples of student projects that demonstrate the create-to-learn principles in action. She also offers a suggestion from her work with communications where writers, designers, and media producers will develop a "creative brief," or "a kind of mind map that serves as the framework or foundation for your work" (27). This concept of the creative brief can cross assignment boundaries and encourage students to think critically and carefully about the mode, media, audience, and purpose for their work. In sum, Hobbs captures the spirit of critical media literacy analysis and flips it around, helping students envision the media creation process in a new way.

Jang, B. G., & Henretty, D. (2019). Understanding multiple profiles of reading attitudes among adolescents. *Middle School Journal, 50*(3), 26–35. https://doi.org/10.1080/00940771.2019.1603803

With the goal "to provide educators and classroom teachers with practical ways to apply the findings from our larger study" (27), Bong Gee Jang and Dawnelle Henretty outline "four attitudinal profiles of adolescent readers include 1) recreational digital only readers, 2) engaged digital readers, 3) engaged print readers, and 4) digital preferred readers" (29). By examining these profiles and encouraging conversation amongst students, Jang and Henretty offer ELA educators a number of suggested reading and writing activities that could appeal to a wide variety of students. In particular, they conclude with the suggestion that "[i]ncorporating a variety of digital texts into the reading curriculum, as well as print texts like graphic novels and comics that include images, may encourage reluctant readers to develop overall positive attitudes toward reading" (33). By inviting students to take agency in their own reading and writing, the authors are hopeful that educator can identify the multiple adolescents' reading profiles and help solve the problem of aliteracy, where capable readers actively choose activities other than reading.

Karam, F. J. (2018). Language and identity construction: The case of a refugee digital bricoleur. *Journal of Adolescent & Adult Literacy, 61*(5), 511–521. https://doi.org/10.1002/jaal.719

Pointing toward the varying multilingual and multicultural literacy practices that a 14-year-old Iraqi English language learner, Zein, brought to the experience of both in-school and out-of-school learning, Karam describes the way in which identity construction is mediated through writing, and especially how "[w]ithin the context of traditional school-based literacy practices in class, Zein had limited opportunities to use language—in its multimodal and multilingual dimensions—as a means to project an identity as a coder" (512). As Zein resisted the types of literacy practices that were present in the classroom because he found the readings disconnected from his life and was also concerned about participating due to his accent, one of the primary reasons for disengagement was the lack of the social support network with friends. However, when classroom tasks were reformulated, "Zein's resistance turned into engagement when classroom tasks were of a digital nature" (515), including opportunities to chat online and demonstrate a video game he had produced. Karam acknowledges that "it is impossible to expect teachers to attend to the myriad interests of all students" (520) yet encourages ELA educators to consider additional opportunities for all students, and especially refugee ELLs, to express themselves in multimodal ways.

Kim, D., Yatsu, D. K., & Li, Y. (2021). A multimodal model for analyzing middle school English language learners' digital stories. *International Journal of Educational Research Open*, 2–2, 100067. https://doi.org/10.1016/j.ijedro.2021.100067

Assessing multimodal projects has long been a challenge for educators, especially when working to balance the needs of more traditional reading and writing assignments. Noting that "that many educators lack training and expertise in multimodal composition" (2), and proposing a model for analyzing multimodal, digital stories, Deoksoon Kim, Drina Kei Yatsu, and Yan Li provide a deep analysis of two digital stories created by English language learners at the middle school level. With four dimensions—representational, interpersonal, compositional, and sociocultural—the authors were able to ask questions about the story itself, the authors' relationships with their audiences, the particular authorial choices within the story, and the broader "social, cultural, and political positionality" (4) in which the students were situated. After providing substantive analysis of the two artifacts, Kim, Yatsu, and Li argue that their framework "can help educators and analysts to interpret the complex reflection and identity development that are both implicitly and explicitly accomplished in digital stories" (8).

Kohnen, A. M., Mertens, G. E., Dawson, K., Hampton, J., & Fu, D. (2021). A study of middle school students' online credibility assessments: Challenges and possibilities. *Research in the Teaching of English*, *56*(1), 33–59.

Beginning with the idea that "the nature of many ELA classrooms makes teaching critical information literacy complicated" as educators work "to celebrate students' unique voices, to entertain multiple perspectives, to eschew single right answers and rigid hierarchies of authority," Kohnen et al. cite the BIT-ELA statement and note the many challenges of teaching online reading comprehension. In their study, 25 eighth-grade students engaged in an adaptation of Wineburg and McGrew's protocol (2019, cited in this text as part of the work of the Stanford History Education Group), inviting them to engage in think alouds as they search for information and evaluated existing websites. Their stark assessment: "Based on the scoring rubrics, participants were unsuccessful at the tasks" (43), even though "students used 431 strategies to evaluate the credibility of presented websites, with over 2/3 appearing to have an instructional origin" (43). Basic reading comprehension strategies for use of the CRAAP test were insufficient for determining website credibility, and very few students used any background knowledge related to their topics or understanding about the ways in which search engines prioritize information. And, while "encouragingly, participants in this study seemed to draw upon previous instruction in their efforts to assess credibility" (51), the authors conclude that ELA educators must make significant curricular and instructional changes in order to fully engage their students in online source evaluation.

Lynch, T. L. (2019). Electrical evocations: Computer science, the teaching of literature, and the future of English education. *English Education*, *52*(1), 15–37. https://library.ncte.org/journals/ee/issues/v52-1/30312

In this highly personal essay about his own youth, a tenuous relationship with his mother, and rationale for integrating computer science and the study of literature, Tom Liam Lynch describes how his initial fascination with "how even the simplest line graphs of word frequencies had the potential to spark new kinds of conversations in the literature classroom" (18). From there, he documents the development of a graph in which he analyzes the characters Clarissa, Peter, and Septimus from Virginia Woolf's *Mrs. Dalloway*, and sees, quite literally in the graph, that "Septimus was a counterpoint to Clarissa and Peter" and that "[t]heir love only prevails because Septimus dies. It's quantitatively undeniable, computationally cold" (19). Lynch goes on to describe the way that he adopted Rosenblatt's efferent and aesthetic reading stances to develop a new form of "computational reading" in which referential associations such as word counts, sentence length, and sentiment scores can provide new insight on texts, especially longer texts like novels. He offers a number of suggestions for ELA educators and concludes with the idea that "[t]he future of teaching English must be one that melds quantities with qualities, numbers with letters, queries with inquiries, algorithms with attitudes, the efferent with the aesthetic, and computationality with humanity" (34). To learn more about this work and to use the tools he has developed, visit his website, Plotting Plots (plottingplots.com).

Mirra, N. (2018). *Educating for empathy: Literacy learning and civic engagement*. Teachers College Press.

With the premise that, "[e]ven if not named explicitly, empathy has long held a place in U.S. public schools," Nicole Mirra frames here argument that "empathy becomes the foundation for a democratic society," and the work of ELA educators should place empathy at the core. Throughout the book, she documents many of the challenges present in our current society and schooling practices yet develops a theory of "critical civic empathy" that employs three defining principles about understanding power and privilege, embracing the balance of personal experience in civic life, and fostering "democratic dialogue and civic action committed to equity and justice" (7). With numerous examples of digital literacy in the context of civic action and engagement that include experiences in high school classrooms, Mirra demonstrates ways that ELA educators can encourage their students to take informed action while simultaneously embracing the spirit of empathy, all with examples that can be adapted for middle grades.

Olan, E. L., & Pantano, J. A. (2020). An "epiphania": Exploring students' identities through multimodal literacies. *English Journal, 109*(4), 78–86. https://library.ncte.org/journals/ej/issues/v109-4/30558

Beginning with a vignette describing how Julie Pantano interacted with a highly reluctant seventh grader—in which the student shared how she felt valued during the sharing time of writing workshop—Elsie Olan and Pantano go on to describe their work "examining multimodal literacies in diverse learning communities," specifically the ways in which they "use literacy contracts and quadrants to help students to examine their identities via writing and the creative arts" (78). They go on to contend that "[m]ultimodal literacies cultivate not only different but also collaborative and mutual ways of knowing, caring, and understanding about who our students are and who they wish to become" (80), documenting a variety of projects including spoken word poetry, rap music, illustrations, and mixed media artwork. Concluding with the idea that "[m]ultimodal learning representations are the touch-stones of students' worlds and words, which allow teachers to be part of their students' identities, cultural knowledge, and academic journeys" (85), Olan and Pantano encourage ELA educators to look at texts that offer a variety of ways to begin exploring significant themes and invite students to respond to them in multimodal ways.

Palmeri, J., & McCorkle, B. (2021). *100 years of new media pedagogy*. University of Michigan Press. https://www.digitalrhetoriccollaborative.org/100-years-of-new-media-pedagogy/

Beginning with their preview video in which they argue that [in a world full of boring, dusty English pedagogy, there lies a hidden history of technological innovation and multimodal production . . . you just have to know how to look for it,] Jason Palmeri and

Ben McCorkle dispel the idea that English teachers are slow to adopt to technological changes and, instead, that they have been doing so for decades. Throughout this born-digital book, Palmeri and McCorkle demonstrate a nuanced approach to understanding what the teaching of English actually is, providing insights on radio, film, television, computers, and more across 100 years' worth of articles in the pages of NCTE flagship publication, *English Journal*. In their "Coda," the authors outline a very web-friendly list of seven key take aways, including the idea that we should "[l]earn with students," "[h]ack the tech," and "fight for access and justice for all." Taken together, their compelling writing and quirky videos give us a glimpse into the future that was and provide ELA educators with additional ideas for moving our work forward.

Price-Dennis, D., & Sealey-Ruiz, Y. (2021). *Advancing racial literacies in teacher education: Activism for equity in digital spaces*. Teachers College Press.

Building on their core arguments that racism is taught and learned and that Whiteness permeates all of what we do in society, and especially in the classroom, Price-Dennis and Sealey-Ruiz offer a number of examples where digital literacies can be imbued with a sense of racial justice. Cutting right to the core of contemporary debates around racial literacies in schools, the authors focus mostly on the ways that teacher educators can address issues such as White Nationalism, racial trauma, and enslavement by using their "Racial Literacy for Activism," or #RL4A framework to explore curriculum, assessments, and institutional contexts. With many examples of student projects and their conclusion that this work "can shift the ways we talk about racism and begin to lay the groundwork for advocacy for racial justice and abolition of racist practices" (104), Price-Dennis and Sealey-Ruiz provide teachers and teacher educators with specific ways to accomplish these goals, many of which rely on critical digital literacies.

Rainey, E. C., & Storm, S. (2017). Teaching digital literary literacies in secondary English language arts.

Journal of Adolescent & Adult Literacy, 61(2), 203–207. https://doi.org/10.1002/jaal.677

Beginning with the question "[h]ow might digital and disciplinary literacy teaching be productively combined in secondary English language arts classrooms for the benefit of young people?" (203), Emily C. Rainey (a literacy researcher) and Scott Storm (an English teacher) describe a variety of ways in which literacy can be imagined as participation. For instance, in his "#LitAnalysis4Life" project, Storm's students bring everything from music videos to text messages, and then "collectively examine the focal artifact and generate a series of questions about what they notice or find surprising about it" (204). Using a variety of literary lenses, they also offer a number of archives and tools that can be used to engage in a kind of mixed literary analysis. Storm also encourages students to "add to the on-going scholarly conversation by articulating unique interpretive claims" (206), so they, too, can become experts and develop "their digital literacies, disciplinary literacies, and, indeed, their critical literacies" (207).

Turchi, L. B., Bondar, N. A., & Aguilar, L. L. (2020). What really changed? Environments, instruction, and 21st century tools in emergency online English language arts teaching in United States schools during the first pandemic response. *Frontiers in Education, 5*, 235. https://doi.org/10.3389/feduc.2020.583963

Beginning with the idea that a great deal had changed for ELA educators in the shift to the emergency room of teaching in the spring of 2020, the three authors—Turchi a teacher educator, and Bondar and Aguilar both high school teachers— began to explore a fundamental question: "What really changed?" In so doing, they engaged in ongoing narrative inquiry that help them articulate three elements: changed environment, newly focused purposes, and twenty-first century learning. With examples of the kinds of activities and technologies that each of the three authors used to support students in their context, their discussion of the three themes demonstrates a number of challenges. For instance, "[w]ith a constant flow of new administrative decisions, the teacher-researchers found that their teaching needed to adapt as quickly as they would have in a physical classroom," and each also "used digital tools and the online learning platforms for one-on-one conferences and consultations with students." Still, benefits included: a (re)new(ed) focus on learning goals, explicit instructions, a combination of both independent and collaborative work, and developing relationships. And, in light of twenty-first learning, the authors reported that their students missed some aspects of typical school days and routines, yet "[s]tudents wanted and valued autonomy, preferring virtual discussions that were open-ended and student driven." As ELA educators move into a new era of blended and online learning, some of these ideas can inform a more intentional, focused form of teaching and learning for our middle grades students.

Turner, K. H., Hicks, T., & Zucker, L. (2020). Connected reading: A framework for understanding how adolescents encounter, evaluate, and engage with texts in the digital age. *Reading Research Quarterly*, *55*(2), 291–309. https://doi.org/10.1002/rrq.271

In collaboration with Kristen Hawley Turner and Lauren Zucker, Troy has worked to articulate a framework for describing how readers work to encounter, engage, and evaluate texts across networked spaces. Encountering, or the way in which a reader first experiences a text, can come in many forms from a web search, to scrolling social media, to receiving a text message or email. The second element, engaging, refers to the broad variety of activities that a reader can do with a text, just before reading begins, during the reading process, or once done with reading. Finally, the act of evaluating a text requires connected readers to place a value upon it, normally in the form of whether that text will be curated or shared more widely. In sum, they contend that "[U]nderstanding the recursive, ongoing nature of being a reader, finding new texts, documenting what one has learned from existing texts (both print and digital), and actively connecting other associated readers to texts they might appreciate should be a primary goal of reading instruction" (307).

Tynes, B. M., Stewart, A., Hamilton, M., & Willis, H. A. (2021). From Google searches to Russian disinformation: Adolescent critical race digital literacy needs and skills. *International Journal of Multicultural Education*, *23*(1), 110–130.

Building on the idea of a Critical Race Digital Literacy (CRDL) framework that is informed by Crenshaw et al.'s work on Critical Race Theory as well as online civic reasoning drawn from the Stanford History Education Group, Brendesha M. Tynes, Ashley Stewart, Matthew Hamilton, and Henry A. Willis argue that students need the "knowledge, skill, and awareness required to access, identify, organize, integrate, evaluate, synthesize, critique, create, counter, and cope with race-related media and technologies" (112). From there, the authors describe a number of ways in which race-related incidents occur online through social media debates, disinformation campaigns, and other more insidious forms of white supremacy that are embedded in online spaces. Their CRDL framework was developed through surveys of 302 diverse youth, including African Americans and Latinxs/Hispanics aged 11–19 (115). In this survey, participants were asked basic demographic data and prompted to critically evaluate examples of online information including search for civil rights on Google, a tweet from Kanye West, a video from Prager University, and the "Blacktivist Facebook Group." Using the criteria developed from the Stanford History Education Group, researchers analyzed participants' responses, concluding that "[w]here they appeared to have the most challenge was pairing a sophisticated analysis of racism with an understanding of how to / recognize propaganda, disinformation campaigns, and misinformation" (123–124) and make a call for the redesign of digital media and literacy curricula.

Vu, V., Warschauer, M., & Yim, S. (2019). Digital storytelling: A district initiative for academic literacy improvement. *Journal of Adolescent & Adult Literacy*, *63*(3), 257–267. https://doi.org/10.1002/jaal.962

Describing digital storytelling (DST) as "a critical form of multimodal composition, which integrates multiple semiotic modes, such as text, speech, visuals, and sound, into both writing processes and products" (258), the authors describe a program in which a local school district and nonprofit organization were able to implement DST for youth enrichment and teacher professional development. Noting the lack of research on "the impact of DST integration in culturally and linguistically diverse settings and whether it presents unique affordances for supporting bilingual immigrants" (258), the authors engaged in a number of interviews, observations, and surveys to determine the effectiveness of DST practices, concluding that "DST assignments strengthening overall engagement and depth of learning and writing assignments being critical to developing writing ability" (262). They provide examples and analysis of students' digital stories, concluding with the idea that "[t]he digital stories created in these classrooms showcased tremendous student creativity and talent and demonstrated the potential for this instructional practice to help students develop the skills, knowledge, and competencies associated with 21st-century learning and English language arts" (265).

Wargo, J. M. (2021). "Seeing" difference differently: Inquiry-based learning as a site/sight of intersectional justice in English language arts. *Language Arts, 98*(3), 135–148. https://library.ncte.org/journals/la/issues/v98-3/31029

Though originally designed as the unit for an eighth grade civics course, and instead describing the ways in which he worked with first grade students and their teachers, Wargo's work here to explore the intersection of inquiry-based learning, critical literacy, and the use of digital tools to document learning in an urban community provides insights for middle level educators. In particular, he "locate[s] the inquiry-based unit at the intersection of three problem spaces: intersectionality, critical geography, and critical literacies studies" (137), connecting them by looking at a project, "Civic MakEY," in which youth participate in "civic action and engagement

through making and makerspace technologies" (139). With examples of their work and dialogue between teachers and students to illustrate these practices in action, Wargo contends that students were able to develop "an emergent awareness of how space was used to oppress, exploit, and dominate particular groups and communities" (145) and use "story and metaphor to showcase personal mobility while interrogating the many routes and rhythms of community" (146). Through this iterative process students engage deeply in critical and digital literacies with the intent to take civic action and "reframe community" (146).

Ziemke, K., & Muhtaris, K. (2019). *Read the world: Rethinking literacy for empathy and action in a digital age.* Heinemann.

Though aimed at an audience of elementary educators, middle grades ELA teachers can glean many useful ideas from Kristin Ziemke and Katie Muhtaris's book that—while certainly infused with elements of technology and digital literacy—also demonstrates that "with the help of technology, we can look beyond the walls of our classroom / to give students [literacy] opportunities that are authentic, significant, and relevant to the world beyond school" (15–16). They carry this premise forward through dozens of lesson ideas that range from comprehending and engaging with print and digital texts to composing videos, podcasts, and infographics. Throughout the text, they provide samples of their own anchor charts, resources to share with students, and "helpful language" callout boxes that include ways for talking about digital texts with students (e.g., "When we reread videos, we listen for new information and wonders. We also listen for answers to questions we had during the first viewing." p. 67). QR codes embedded in the text link to additional audio recordings of Ziemke and Muhtaris describing their teaching practices in even more detail, inviting the reader to join the ongoing conversation.

References

Anderson, L. H. (1999). *Speak* (Reprint edition). Square Fish.

Association of College and Research Libraries. (2015). *Framework for information literacy for higher education*. http://www.ala.org/acrl/standards/ilframework

Bali, M. (2020, June 22). About that webcam obsession you're having…. *Reflecting Allowed*. https://blog.mahabali.me/educational-technology-2/about-that-webcam-obsession-youre-having/

Beers, K., & Probst, R. E. (2012). *Notice & note: Strategies for close reading*. Heinemann.

Beete, P. (2021, September 23). Hispanic Heritage Month spotlight: Elizabeth Acevedo. *National Endowment for the Arts Blog*. https://www.arts.gov/stories/blog/2021/hispanic-heritage-month-spotlight-elizabeth-acevedo

Bernabei, G. (2005). *Reviving the essay: How to teach structure without formula*. Discover Writing Company.

Bible, A. (2016, March 11). Podcasts pairings for the secondary ELA classroom: Podcasts to use in English class. *Building Book Love*. https://buildingbooklove.com/podcasts-to-use-in-classroom/

Bishop, R. S. (1990). Mirrors, windows, and sliding glass doors. *Perspectives: Choosing and Using Books for the Classroom*, 6(3).

Borsheim-Black, C., & Sarigianides, S. T. (2019). *Letting go of literary whiteness: Antiracist literature instruction for white students*. Teachers College Press.

Brightman, H. J., & Gutmore, D. (2002). The educational-industrial complex. *The Educational Forum*, 66(4), 302–308. https://doi.org/10.1080/00131720208984848

Brockman, E. (2020). Reframing writing prompts to foster nuanced arguments: To what extent? *English Journal*, 109(6), 37–44.

Burke, K. (1974). *The philosophy of literary form* (3rd edition). University of California Press.

Byrd Farmer, C. (2021, April 26). They played their hand, and we have to say, "we're not going back." *Alliance for Self-Directed Education*. https://www.self-directed.org/tp/we-are-not-going-back/

Campbell, K. H., & Latimer, K. (2012). *Beyond the five-paragraph essay*. Stenhouse Publishers.

Caulfield, M. (2019, May 12). Introducing SIFT, a four moves acronym. *Hapgood*. https://hapgood.us/2019/05/12/sift-and-a-check-please-preview/

Choney, S. (2018, June 18). Microsoft and Flipgrid unite to bring social learning to students around the world. *The Official Microsoft Blog*. https://blogs.microsoft.com/blog/2018/06/18/microsoft-and-flipgrid-unite-to-bring-social-learning-to-students-around-the-world/

Coiro, J., & Hobbs, R. (2021). *Digital learning anytime and real time: Elementary school*. W. W. Norton & Company.

Council of Writing Program Administrators, National Council of Teachers of English, & National Writing Project. (2011, January). *Framework for success in postsecondary writing*. http://wpacouncil.org/framework/

Crash Course. (n.d.). About Us. *Crash Course*. https://thecrashcourse.com/about

Dinwiddie, M. (2020, July 8). How to spruce up your Zoom chat game. *Creative Sandbox Solutions*. https://creativesandbox.solutions/how-to-spruce-up-your-zoom-chat-game/

Ebarvia, T. (2021, January 2). January 2021 statement. *Disrupt Texts*. https://disrupttexts.org/2021/01/02/january-2021-statement/

Ebarvia, T., Germán, L., Parker, K., & Torres, J. (2018, May 13). What is #Disrupt Texts? *Disrupt Texts*. https://disrupttexts.org/lets-get-to-work/

English Language Arts Teacher Educators Commission on Digital Literacy in Teacher Education. (2018). *Beliefs for integrating technology into the English language arts classroom.* National Council of Teachers of English. http://www2.ncte.org/statement/beliefs-technology-preparation-english-teachers/

Equity Unbound, & OneHE. (n.d.). Community building activities. https://onehe.org/equity-unbound/

Feldman, J. (2018). *Grading for equity: What it is, why it matters, and how it can transform schools and classrooms.* Corwin.

Fleischer, C., & Andrew-Vaughan, S. (2009). *Writing outside your comfort zone: Helping students navigate unfamiliar genres.* Heinemann.

Gallagher, K. (2009). *Readicide: How schools are killing reading and what you can do about it.* Stenhouse Publishers.

Gallagher, K. (2011). *Write like this: Teaching real-world writing through modeling and mentor texts.* Stenhouse Publishers.

Gallagher, K., & Kittle, P. (2018). *180 days: Two teachers and the quest to engage and empower adolescents.* Heinemann.

Gardner, T. (2011). *Designing writing assignments.* National Council of Teachers of English. https://wac.colostate.edu/books/gardner/

Goldstein, D. (2020, May 9). The class divide: Remote learning at 2 schools, private and public. *The New York Times.* https://www.nytimes.com/2020/05/09/us/coronavirus-public-private-school.html

Gonchar, M. (2017, March 1). 401 prompts for argumentative writing. *The New York Times.* https://www.nytimes.com/2017/03/01/learning/lesson-plans/401-prompts-for-argumentative-writing.html

Graff, G., & Birkenstein, C. (2021). *"They say / I say": The moves that matter in academic writing* (Fifth Edition). W. W. Norton & Company.

Green, J. (2019, January 15). Transcript | The facts about fact checking: Crash course navigating digital information #2. *Nerdfighteria Wiki.* https://nerdfighteria.info//v/EZsaA0w_0z0/

Guskey, T. R. (2010, October 1). Lessons of mastery learning. ASCD. https://www.ascd.org/el/articles/lessons-of-mastery-learning

Hammond, Z. L. (2014). *Culturally responsive teaching and the brain: Promoting authentic engagement and rigor among culturally and linguistically diverse students.* Corwin.

Harris, J. (2006). *Rewriting: How to do things with texts.* Utah State University Press.

Harris, J. (2017). *Rewriting: How to do things with texts* (Second edition). Utah State University Press.

Harris, T. (2019). *The right tools: A guide to selecting, evaluating, and implementing classroom resources and practices.* Heinemann.

Harvard Project Zero. (n.d.). Thinking routines toolbox. http://www.pz.harvard.edu/thinking-routines

Harvey, S., & Goudvis, A. (2017). *Strategies that work, 3rd edition: Teaching comprehension for engagement, understanding, and building knowledge, grades K-8* (Third edition). Stenhouse Publishers.

Hess, D. E. (2009). *Controversy in the classroom: The democratic power of discussion.* Routledge.

Hicks, T. (2013). *Crafting digital writing: Composing texts across media and genres.* Heinemann.

Hicks, T., Hyler, J., & Pangle, W. (2020). *Ask, explore, write! : An inquiry-driven approach to science and literacy learning.* Routledge / Eye of Education.

Hicks, T., & Schoenborn, A. (2020). *Creating confident writers: For high school, college, and life.* W. W. Norton & Company.

Highfill, L., Hilton, K., & Landis, S. (2016). *The hyperdoc handbook: Digital lesson design using Google apps.* EdTechTeam.

Hinton, S. E. (1967). *The outsiders.* Viking Press.

History.com. (2020). Shirley Chisholm. https://www.history.com/topics/us-politics/shirley-chisholm.

Hobbs, R. (2010). *Copyright clarity: How fair use supports digital learning.* Corwin Press.

Hodges, C. B., Moore, S., Trust, T., & Bond, M. A. (2020, March 27). The difference between emergency remote teaching and online learning. *Educause Review.* https://er.educause.edu/articles/2020/3/the-difference-between-emergency-remote-teaching-and-online-learning

Howard, T. C., & Banks, J. A. (2020). *Why race and culture matter in schools: Closing the achievement gap in America's classrooms* (2nd edition). Teachers College Press.

Hyler, J., & Hicks, T. (2014). *Create, compose, connect! Reading, writing, and learning with digital tools.* Routledge / Eye on Education.

Irwin, V., Zhang, J., Wang, X., Hein, S., Wang, K., Roberts, A., York, C., Barmer, A., Mann, F. B., Dilig, R., Parker, S., Nachazel, T., Barnett, M., & Purcell, S. (2021). *Report on the condition of education 2021.* U.S. Department of Education National Center for Education Statistics. https://nces.ed.gov/pubsearch/pubsinfo.asp?pubid=2021144

Keene, E. O., & Zimmermann, S. (2007). *Mosaic of thought: The power of comprehension strategy instruction, second edition* (2nd edition). Heinemann.

Kittle, P. (2013). *Book love: Developing depth, stamina, and passion in adolescent readers.* Heinemann.

KQED Education. (n.d.a.). *Above the noise.* https://www.kqed.org/education/collection/above-the-noise

KQED Education. (n.d.b.). *The lowdown lesson plans.* https://www.kqed.org/lowdown

Kunz, K., & Lapp, D. (2020). Focus on Comprehension: Supporting learners in becoming more fluent comprehenders in a virtual classroom. *Literacy Today, 38*(2), 12-14.

Lane, B. (2003). *51 wacky we-search reports: Face the facts with fun.* Discover Writing Press.

Lee, A. (2020). Technology in the classroom. *Leadership Magazine, 49*(5),8.

Lee, H. (1960). *To kill a mockingbird.* J. B. Lippincott & Co.

Lehman, C., & Roberts, K. (2013). *Falling in love with close reading: Lessons for analyzing texts—and life (Annotated edition).* Heinemann.

Levine, G. C. (1997). *Ella enchanted (Reissue edition).* HarperCollins.

Longley, R. (2020, October 14). What is astroturfing in politics? Definition and examples. *ThoughtCo.* https://www.thoughtco.com/what-is-astroturfing-definition-and-examples-5082082

Lynch, T. L. (2021, August 9). An English teacher's guide to plotting plots. *Plotting Plots.* https://plottingplots.com/an-english-teachers-guide-to-plotting-plots/

Marchetti, A., & O'Dell, R. (2015). *Writing with mentors: How to reach every writer in the room using current, engaging mentor texts.* Heinemann.

Marsh, K. (2018). *Nowhere boy.* Roaring Brook Press.

Martin, T. M. (2016, August 23). #BookSnaps—Snapping for learning. *Tara M Martin.* https://www.tarammartin.com/booksnaps-snapping-for-learning/

Marzano, R. J. (2009, September 1). Six steps to better vocabulary instruction. The art and science of teaching. *Educational Leadership.* https://www.ascd.org/el/articles/six-steps-to-better-vocabulary-instruction

McGrew, S., Breakstone, J., Ortega, T., Smith, M., & Wineburg, S. (2019). How students evaluate digital news sources. In W. Journell (Ed.), *Unpacking fake news: An educator's guide to navigating the media with students* (pp. 60–73). Teachers College Press.

Minor, C. (2018). *We got this: Equity, access, and the quest to be who our students need us to be.* Heinemann.

Mirra, N., Garcia, A., & Morrell, E. (2015). *Doing youth participatory action research.* Routledge.

National Association for Media Literacy Education, Student Television Network, Media Commission of the National Council of Teachers of English, Action Coalition for Media Education, & Visual Communication Division of the International Communication Association. (2018). *Code of best practices in fair use for media literacy education.* https://ncte.org/statement/fairusemedialiteracy/

National Council of Teachers of English. (2018). *Understanding and teaching writing: Guiding principles.* https://ncte.org/statement/teachingcomposition

National Council of Teachers of English. (2019a, November 7). *Definition of literacy in a digital age.* https://ncte.org/statement/nctes-definition-literacy-digital-age/

National Council of Teachers of English. (2019b, December 5). *The act of reading: Instructional foundations and policy guidelines.* NCTE. https://ncte.org/statement/the-act-of-reading/

National School Reform Faculty. (2018, May 31). What are protocols. https://nsrfharmony.org/whatareprotocols/

National Writing Project. (n.d.a.). College, career, and community writers program. https://sites.google.com/nwp.org/c3wp/home

National Writing Project. (n.d.b.). Joining a conversation in progress. https://sites.google.com/nwp.org/c3wp/instructional-resources/joining-a-conversation-in-progress

National Writing Project. (n.d.c.). Practicing writing recursive claims. https://sites.google.com/nwp.org/c3wp/instructional-resources/practicing-writing-recursive-claims

National Writing Project. (n.d.d.). What is C3WP? https://sites.google.com/nwp.org/c3wp/home/what-is-c3wp

Ng, C. (2015). *Everything I never told you (Reprint edition).* Penguin Books.

Noah, T. (2016). *Born a crime: Stories from a South African childhood.* One World.

Ochoa, J. (2020). *Already readers and writers: Honoring students' rights to read and write in the middle grade classroom.* National Council of Teachers of English.

Palmeri, J., & McCorkle, B. (2021). *100 years of new media pedagogy.* University of Michigan Press. https://www.digitalrhetoriccollaborative.org/100-years-of-new-media-pedagogy/

Picciano, A. G., & Spring, J. (2012). The great American education-industrial complex: Ideology, technology, and profit. Routledge.

Poetry Foundation. (n.d.). New Criticism | Glossary of poetic terms. https://www.poetryfoundation.org/learn/glossary-terms/new-criticism

Potash, B. (2020, September 11). Hexagonal thinking: A colorful tool for discussion. *Cult of Pedagogy.* https://www.cultofpedagogy.com/hexagonal-thinking/

Reed, D., & Hicks, T. (2015). *Research writing rewired: Lessons that ground students' digital learning.* Corwin.

Ribay, R. (2020). *Patron saints of nothing (Reprint edition).* Penguin Books.

Rosenblatt, L. M. (1978). *The reader, the text, the poem: The transactional theory of the literary work.* Southern Illinois University Press.

Ross Smith, B. (2017, June 12). Hyphen-nation. *The New York Times.* https://www.nytimes.com/interactive/projects/storywall/hyphen-nation

Ross Smith, B. (n.d.). Bayeté Ross Smith. http://www.bayeterosssmith.com

Rush-Levine, C. (n.d.). Reader response as an entry to conferring. *Choice Literacy.* https://choiceliteracy.com/article/reader-response-as-an-entry-to-conferring/

Sachar, L. (1998). *Holes.* Yearling.

Sáenz, B. A. (2014). *Aristotle and Dante discover the secrets of the universe (Reprint edition).* Simon & Schuster Books for Young Readers.

Santini, L. (2019). The short form reshaped: Email, blog, SMS, and MSN in twenty-first century e-pistolary novels. *Iperstoria,* 14.

School Reform Initiative adapted from Spencer Kagan. (2017, March 30). Jigsaw description. https://www.schoolreforminitiative.org/download/jigsaw-description/

Schroeder, B. (2019, August 14). Disrupting education. The rise of K-12 online and the entrepreneurial opportunities. *Forbes*. https://www.forbes.com/sites/bernhardschroeder/2019/08/14/disrupting-education-the-rise-of-k-12-online-and-the-entrepreneurial-opportunities/?sh=f26339c48a2f

Segal, E. A., & Wagaman, A. M. (2017) Social empathy as a framework for teaching social justice. *Journal of Social Work Education*, *53*(2), 201-11

Shannon, P. (2013). *Closer readings of the Common Core: Asking big questions about the English/language arts standards*. Heinemann.

Shusterman, N. (2009). *Unwind (Reprint edition)*. Simon & Schuster Books for Young Readers.

Smith, B. E., & Shen, J. (2017). Scaffolding digital literacies for disciplinary learning: Adolescents collaboratively composing multimodal science fictions. *Journal of Adolescent & Adult Literacy*, *61*(1), 85–90. https://doi.org/10.1002/jaal.660

Society of Professional Journalists. (2014, September 6). SPJ Code of Ethics. https://www.spj.org/ethicscode.asp

Southern Poverty Law Center. (n.d.a.). Extremist files groups: American College of Pediatricians. https://www.splcenter.org/fighting-hate/extremist-files/group/american-college-pediatricians

Southern Poverty Law Center. (n.d.b.). Extremist files. https://www.splcenter.org/fighting-hate/extremist-files

Stanford History Education Group. (2020, January 16). Sort fact from fiction online with lateral reading. https://youtu.be/SHNprb2hgzU

Stanford History Education Group. (n.d.a.). Civic online reasoning. https://cor.stanford.edu/

Stanford History Education Group. (n.d.b.). Teaching lateral reading. https://cor.stanford.edu/curriculum/collections/teaching-lateral-reading/

Styslinger, M. E. (2017). *Workshopping the canon*. National Council of Teachers of English.

Swenson, J., Rozema, R., Young, C. A., McGrail, E., & Whitin, P. (2005). Beliefs about technology and the preparation of English Teachers: Beginning the conversation. *Contemporary Issues in Technology and Teacher Education*. Available: https://citejournal.org/wp-content/uploads/2016/04/v5i3languagearts1.pdf

Thielman, S. (2018, June 21). One conservative group's successful infiltration of the media. *Columbia Journalism Review*. https://www.cjr.org/analysis/77-referendum-astroturf-tipping.php

Tovani, C. (2000). *I read it, but I don't get it: Comprehension strategies for adolescent readers*. Stenhouse.

Turner, K. H., & Hicks, T. (2015). *Connected reading: Teaching adolescent readers in a digital world*. National Council of Teachers of English.

Turner, K. H., & Hicks, T. (2016). *Argument in the real world: Teaching adolescents to read and write digital texts*. Heinemann.

United Nations Educational, Scientific and Cultural Organization. (2020, March 24). 1.37 billion students now home as COVID-19 school closures expand, ministers scale up multimedia approaches to ensure learning continuity. https://en.unesco.org/news/137-billion-students-now-home-covid-19-school-closures-expand-ministers-scale-multimedia

Walls, J. (2006). *The glass castle: A memoir*. Scribner Book Company.

Wikipedia Contributors. (2021). American College of Pediatricians. Wikipedia. https://en.wikipedia.org/wiki/American_College_of_Pediatricians

Wilkey Oh, E. (2020, May 7). 19 great learning podcasts for the classroom. *Common Sense Education*. https://www.commonsense.org/education/articles/19-great-learning-podcasts-for-the-classroom

Zucker, L., & Hicks, T. (2019). 23 months x 22 scholars: Collaboration, negotiation, and the revision of a position statement on technology in English language arts. *Contemporary Issues in Technology and Teacher Education, 19*(3). https://www.citejournal.org/volume-19/ issue-3-19/english-language-arts/23-months-x-22-scholars-collaboration-negotiation-and-the-revision-of-a-position-statement-on-technology-in-english-language-arts

Index

acceptance, using technology to foster, 154–156

accountability, exit tickets for, 153–154

The Act of Reading: Instructional Foundations and Policy Guidelines (NCTE), 36–37

Advancing racial literacies in teacher education: Activism for equity in digital spaces (Price-Dennis & Sealey-Ruiz), 173

Aguilar, L. L., 173–174

annotation, 42–44, 43f

Argue and Persuade (unit)
    C3WP (NWP) resources, 108–111
    context and connections to the BIT-ELA statement, 108–109
    eating bugs, 107–109
    the five-paragraph essay, 111–112
    mastery assessment, PSA, 129–132
    vignette, 107–108

Argue and Persuade (unit) lessons
    additional resources, 116–117
    digging deeper with asynchronous work, 115–117
    exploring the idea in real time, 112–115
    starting a kernel essay, 121–125
    summarizing with the BIT-ELA principles, 132
    from "Would You Rather?" to a first-draft claim, 118–121

asynchronous Wednesdays, 152

audio as ethnography, 162–163

audiobooks, 38–40

Ávila, Juli Anna, 162

Bali, Maha, 88–89

Bartels, Jonathan, 163

Beach, R. W., 167

Beliefs for Integrating Technology into the English Language Arts Classroom (BIT-ELA). *See also specific Beliefs*
    the Beliefs, xii–xx, 16

ideas informing, 15–16

Preamble, xi, 24

revision committee, 7–8

routines, establishing with the principles in mind, 33

Summary, xx

timeline, 17

unpacking, 24

Beliefs for Integrating Technology into the English Language Arts Classroom (BIT-ELA), connecting to
    digital writers' notebooks, 21–30

bias, resources on, 93

Black girls' literacies, 162

Black History Month, 93–94, 155–156

Boardman, A. G., et al., 167–168

Bomer, Randy, 35–36

Bondar, N. A., 173–174

book clubs, 9–12, 48–50

breakout rooms
    assigning, 46, 47f
    literature circles, 81–83, 86–88

Breakstone, J., et al., 168

Brockman, Elizabeth, 110

Brownell, Cassie, 162–163

Buchholz, B. A., 168

bugs, eating, 107–109

Burke, Kenneth, 110

Cassidy, J., 168

Caulfield, Mike, 56

Civic Online Reasoning (COR) curriculum (SHEG), 56, 61–62

Clancy, Patricia, 30–32

classroom design, 126–129

close reading
    context and connections to the BIT-ELA statement, 35–38

controversy, 35–36
defined, 36–37
jigsaw strategy, 42–43
principles into practice, 41
remote instruction lesson example, 45–48
summarizing with the BIT-ELA principles, 51–53
vignette, 34–35
College, Career, and Community Writers Program
        (C3WP) (National Writing Project), 108–111
Common Core Standards, close reading controversy,
        35–36
community, building
    book clubs for, 9–12
    student names, learning, 20–21
    writer's notebook for, 21, 26–30
completion folders, 152–153
*Compose our world: Project-based learning in secondary
        English language arts* (Boardman, et al.),
        167–168
computational thinking, 163–164
computer, intentional use of the, 141–146
"Connected reading: A framework for understanding
        how adolescents encounter, evaluate, and
        engage with texts in the digital age" (Turner,
        Hicks, & Zucker), 174
Consider literacies before technologies (Belief 2)
    close reading, 52
    definition of text, 25
    Research, Inform, Explain (unit), 78
    text of, xiv–xv
copyright and fair use, 29–30, 41–42
Corbitt, Alex, 138–140
Coronavirus Aid, Relief, and Economic Security
        (CARES) Act, 26
"Counterstorytelling vs. deficit thinking around African
        American children and families, digital
        literacies, race, and the digital divide" (Ellison
        & Solomon), 169
COVID-19 pandemic. *See also* hybridity model, move to
    move to hybridity, 137
    the new normal, 137
    pandemic remote classrooms, 136
    post-pandemic experience, 134–135, 136–137
    pre-pandemic classrooms, 135–136
    technology and, 18–19

"Crafting Audio as Ethnography" (Wargo & Brownell),
        162–163
"Crafting Snaps as Self-Identity" (Bartels), 163
Crash Course, 61
Create to learn: Introduction to digital literacy (Hobbs, R.),
        170
"Creating Space for Critical Digital Literacies" (Price-
        Dennis), 162

Definition of Literacy in a Digital Age (NCTE), 12, 16
DeHart, J., 168
deliverables, 144, 146
"Digital citizenship during a global pandemic: Moving
        beyond digital literacy" (Buchholz, DeHart, &
        Moorman), 168
digital literacies, creating space for, 162
"Digital storytelling: A district initiative for academic
        literacy improvement" (Vu, Warschauer, &
        Yim), 174–175
"Digital Writer's Notebooks" (Clancy), 30–32
digital writing, next decade of, 160–165

Ebarvia, Tricia, 103
EdPuzzle for lateral reading, 62–69
*Educating for empathy: Literacy learning and civic
        engagement* (Mirra), 172
educators, 5
"Electrical evocations: Computer science, the teaching
        of literature, and the future of English
        education" (Lynch, T. L), 171–172
Elementary and Secondary School Emergency Relief
        (ESSER) funds, 26
Ellison, T. L., 169
Emert, Toby, 161
engagement, video length and, 64
"Engaging in Computational Thinking" (Lynch),
        163–164
English department, Skyline High School, 4–5
"An "epiphania": Exploring students' identities through
        multimodal literacies" (Olan & Pantano), 172
e-pistolary stories, 138–140
equity gaps, digital, 25–26
ethnography, audio as, 162–163
exit tickets for reflection and accountability, 153–154

fact checking, 56–61

fake news, 8

Feliks, Alaina, 69–70

five-paragraph essay, 111–112

Fleischer, Cathy, 1–2

Flipgrid, 20–21

"Framework for Information Literacy for Higher Education" (Association of College and Research Libraries), 56

Gallagher, K., 21, 69, 79

Garcia, M., et al., 169

Germán, Lorena, 103

"From Google searches to Russian disinformation: Adolescent critical race digital literacy needs and skills" (Tynes, et al.), 174

Google Slides, 24–25, 99–105, 141–145

Green, Hank, 61

Green, John, 59, 61–65, 68, 79, 93

Grote-Garcia, S, 168

Haddix, M. M., 169–170

Hammond, Zaretta, 50

Handbook of Research on Integrating Digital Technology with Literacy Pedagogies (IGI Global), 167

Harris, Joseph, 110

Harris, Towanda, 48–50

#DisruptTexts movement, 103

Henretty, D., 170

Hess, Diana, 132

hexagonal thinking, 99–105

Hicks, T., 22, 174

Hobbs, R., 170

Hobbs, Renee, 30

Hodges, C. B., 6–7

honor a hero (activity), 155–156

hybridity model, move to
    asynchronous Wednesdays, 152
    completion folders, 152–153
    deliverables in the, 144, 146
    encouraging both physical and digital notebooks, 147–150
    exit tickets for reflection and accountability, 153–154
    finding balance, 142, 144
    lesson slides, 141–145
    reestablishing daily and weekly routines, 150–154
    strategies for, 137
    summarizing with the BIT-ELA principles, 156–157
    using the computer more intentionally, 141–146

"Hyphen-Nation" (Ross Smith), 91–93

identity, exploring, 14

inclusion
    Black girls' literacies, 162
    digital, 25–26

infographic, composing an, 69–75

"Integrating Technology to Support Text Production" (Price-Dennis), 126–129

internet veracity, validating. *See* Research, Inform, Explain (unit)

"Inviting Audio Books into the ELA Classroom" (Kowalski), 38–40

Jang, B. G., 170

jigsaw strategy, 42–43

Kami, 42–44, 43*f*

Karam, F. J., 170–171

kernel essays, 121–125

Kim, D., 171

Kittle, P., 21

Kohnen, A. M., et al., 171

Lane, Barry, 79

"Language and identity construction: The case of a refugee digital bricoleur" (Karam, F. J.), 170–171

lateral reading
    background, 56
    composing an infographic, 69–75
    EdPuzzle to prompt, 62–69

learning
    one-way process, 49, 51
    two-way process, 50

"Learning Ways: A Path to Student Connection" (Harris), 48–50

Lehman, Chris, 36

lesson slides, 141–145

Li, Y., 171

Literacy means *literacies* (Belief 1)

close reading, 51
Reading Literary Texts in Substantive Ways (literary
     analysis) (unit), 90
Research, Inform, Explain (unit), 55–59, 61
text of, xii–xiv
literary analysis. *See* Reading Literary Texts in
     Substantive Ways (unit)
literature circles, 81–83, 93–96, 99–105
Love, Bettina, 137
Lynch, T. L., 171–172
Lynch, Tom Liam, 163–164

"Mapping Literacy" (Mullen), 164
Marchetti, A., 23
mastery portfolio, 83–84
McCorkle, B., 172–173
mentor texts, 23, 41
Mirra, N., 172
Moorman, G, 168
Muhtaris, K., 175
Mullen, Lincoln A., 164
"A multimodal model for analyzing middle school
     English language learners' digital stories"
     (Kim, Yatsu, & Li), 171

narrative writing, 138–140
Nearpod, 49, 51
New Criticism, 36
"The Next Decade of Digital Writing (Hicks), 160–165

O'Dell, R., 23
Olan, E. L., 172
100 years of new media pedagogy (Palmeri & McCorkle),
     172–173
online/remote instruction
   Ann Arbor Public Schools schedule, 5
   collaborative, 4–5
   community in, 9–12, 19–20
   costs of, 7
   emergency, 6–7
   reading conferences, 96–99
   requirements and inequities, 18
   statistics, 18
   stereotype, 9–12
   text access, 85

Opposing Viewpoints in Context Database, 116
Ortlieb, E., 168

Palmeri, J., 172–173
Pandya, Jessica Zacher, 162
Pantano, J. A., 172
Parker, Kimberly N., 103
"In-Person/Virtual Collaborative Book Clubs"
     (Sanford), 9–11
Piktochart, 71–72
Pizzo, Joseph S., 154–156
Potash, Betsy, 99
Price-Dennis, D., 173
Price-Dennis, Detra, 126–129, 162
"Project Imagine the Future" (Smith), 76–78
protocols, defined, 48
public service announcement (PSA), 129–132

Rainey, E. C., 173
reading conferences, online, 96–99
Reading Literary Texts in Substantive Ways (unit)
   beginning the unit, 89
   big ideas, using, 86, 90–91
   breakout rooms, 81–83, 86–88, 90–92
   celebrating African American authors during Black
        History Month, 93–94
   context and connections to the BIT-ELA statement,
        83–84
   final project activities, 103–105
   habits of mind examined, 84
   literature circles, 81–83, 85, 93–96
   mastery standards, 90, 91*f*
   monitoring student discussions, 87–88
   principles into practice, 85–88
   recording, 88–89
   student participation, 88–89
   summarizing with the BIT-ELA principles, 105–106
   text access, 85
*Read the world: Rethinking literacy for empathy and action
     in a digital age* (Ziemke, K., & Muhtaris, K.),
     175
reflection, exit tickets for, 153–154
remote instruction. *See* online-slash;remote instruction
Research, Inform, Explain (unit)
   additional resources, 79

context and connections to the BIT-ELA statement, 55–59
    fact checking resources, 56
    goal, 59
    infographics, composing from lateral reading, 69–75
    lateral reading with EdPuzzle, 62–69
    principles into practice, 59–62
    sample lesson, 56–59
    summarizing with the BIT-ELA principles, 78–80
    vignette, 54–55
"Rethinking Narrative Writing with E-pistolary Stories" (Corbitt), 138–140
rewriting, 110–111
Riley, Kathleen, 20–21
rituals, relationships, and restrictions, 14
Roberts, Kate, 36
Rosenblatt, L. M., 36
Ross Smith, Bayeté, 91–92
routines, reestablishing daily and weekly, 150–154

Sanford, Jenny, 9–11
Schoenborn, A., 22
Sealey-Ruiz, Y., 173
""Seeing" difference differently: Inquiry-based learning as a site/sight of intersectional justice in English language arts" (Wargo, J. M.), 175
Segal, E. A., 155
self-identity, crafting snaps as, 163
Shannon, Patrick, 35
Shelby-Caffey, Crystal, 161
Shen, Ji, 76
SIFT model, 56
Skyline High School, 3–5
Smith, B. E., 167
Smith, Blaine, 76–78
Snapchat, 163
Solomon, M., 169
soundscapes, 162–163
"The Space Between: Engaging in Online Reading Conferences" (Stygles), 96–98
Stanford History Education Group (SHEG), 56, 61–62
Storm, S, 173
student names, learning, 20–21
"A study of middle school students' online credibility assessments: Challenges and possibilities" (Kohnen et al.), 171

Stygles, Justin, 96–98

Task Force on Critical Media Literacy (NCTE) recommendations, 56
teacher learning networks (TLNs), 4
"Teaching digital literary literacies in secondary English language arts" (Rainey & Storm), 173
Technologies and their associated literacies are not neutral (Belief 4)
    close reading, 52
    equity considerations, 25–26
    Reading Literary Texts in Substantive Ways (unit), 89, 92–93
    Research, Inform, Explain (unit), 61, 69
    text of, xviii–xx
Technologies provide new ways to consume and produce texts (Belief 3)
    close reading, 52
    teacher's role, 35
    text of, xvi–xviii
    unpacking, 24, 25
technology, COVID-19 pandemic and, 18–19
tech tools, additional resources, 2
text, meaning of, 25
texting stories, 138–140
textual forms, variety in, 38–40
thinking, computational, 163–164
"Today is the tomorrow we should have prepared for yesterday: Rebuilding our classrooms to facilitate student-centered, teacher-sustaining, techsupported education" (Garcia et al.), 169
Torres, Julia E., 103
transactional reader response theory, 36
Turchi, L. B., 173–174
Turner, K. H., 174
Turner, Kristen, 132, 161
Tynes, B. M., et al., 174

"Understanding multiple profiles of reading attitudes among adolescents" (Jang & Henretty), 170
"Using digital tools for studying about and addressing climate change" (Beach & Smith), 167
"Using Technology to Foster Acceptance" (Pizzo), 154–156

video length, engagement and, 64

Voyant Tools, 164
Vu, V., 174–175

Wagaman, A. M., 155
Wargo, J. M., 175
Wargo, Jon, 162–163
Warschauer, M., 174–175
website evaluation. *See* Research, Inform, Explain (unit)
"Welcoming Voices by Honoring Names with Flipgrid"
        (Riley), 20–21
"What really changed? Environments, instruction,
        and 21st century tools in emergency online
        English language arts teaching in United
        States schools during the first pandemic
        response" (Turchi, Bondar & Aguilar),
        173–174
"What's hot in literacy: New topics and new frontiers
        are abuzz" (Cassidy, Ortlieb, & Grote-Garcia,
        S), 168
"What's radical about youth writing?: Seeing and
        honoring youth writers and their literacies"
        (Haddix, M. M), 169–170

"Why we need a new approach to teaching digital
        literacy" (Breakstone et al.), 168
word clouds, 163
writers, creating, 31–32
writer's notebooks, digital
        copyright and fair use, 29–30
        "Digital Writer's Notebooks" (Clancy), 30–32
        and physical, using both, 147–150
writers' notebooks, digital
        conceptualizing, 21–26
        enacting, 26–30
writing, meaning of, 25

Yatsu, D. K., 171
Yim, S., 174–175

Ziemke, K., 175
Zucker, L., 174

Authors

Troy Hicks, PhD, is a professor of English and education at Central Michigan University, where he collaborates with K–12 colleagues to explore how they implement newer literacies in their classrooms. He directs the Chippewa River Writing Project, a site of the National Writing Project, and teaches master's and doctoral courses in educational technology. He is the recipient of a Teaching with Primary Sources grant through the National Council of Teachers of English and the Library of Congress, and former coeditor of the *Michigan Reading Journal.* A former middle school teacher, Hicks has earned numerous accolades, including recent awards from the Michigan Reading Association (Teacher Educator Award, 2018), Central Michigan University (Excellence in Teaching Award, 2020), and the Initiative for 21st Century Literacies Research (Divergent Award for Excellence, 2020). He consults regularly with schools, companies, and nonprofit organizations. He is a regular presenter at meetings of NCTE, the International Literacy Association (ILA), and the International Society for Technology in Education (ISTE). Hicks has authored dozens of books, articles, chapters, blog posts, and other resources broadly related to the teaching of literacy in our digital age.

Jill Runstrom, MEd, teaches English at Skyline High School in Ann Arbor, Michigan. When asked her reasons for teaching, she says they are simple: she connects with teenagers, she loves to learn, and she likes helping people. Jill credits her work with the Chippewa River Writing Project, a local site of the National Writing Project, for the many professional opportunities that have enriched her career. Of note, Jill served on the steering committee for the 4T Conference on Digital Writing, was awarded a fellowship at the Olga Lengyel Institute for Holocaust Studies and Human Rights in New York City, served on the teacher advisory board at the Holocaust Memorial Center in Farmington Hills, Michigan, and has presented numerous times at the NCTE Annual Convention. On home football Saturdays in the fall, you can find Jill wearing a sweater she knit herself at a Michigan tailgate party with her husband, Eric. They also have two adult children, Charlie and Katie, who are pretty fantastic.

This book was typeset in Adobe Caslon Pro and PT Serif by
Barbara Frazier.

Typefaces used on the cover include Chronicle Display, Avenir
Next Medium, Avenir LT Com 65 Medium, and Avenir Book.

The book was printed on 50-lb. white offset paper.